Table of Contents

Acknowledgements

I would like to extend a word of gratitude to the following individuals who played a significant role in allowing this book to arrive at the point that it is today.

Thanks To:

Above all, I am grateful to God who gave me the inspiration, words and Gospel, upon which this devotional is founded

Gary & Cheryl Darr, My Amazing Parents, as well as all my family and friends who have supported and encouraged me in every way possible over the course of my entire life.

Dr. David Wheeler, Professor of Evangelism and Student Ministries, Liberty University, for the incredible feedback and guidance that he has provided over the course of this writing journey.

Pastor David Nasser, President of Spiritual Development, Liberty University, for taking the time to provide valuable feedback and encouragement regarding this book, its content, and its mission to reach college students with the Gospel.

Maurice Victor II, Owner, MV2 Edits, for the incredible work that he provided on the design of the cover of this book.

*All passages taken from the King James Translation of the Gospel.

Dedicated to the loving memory of:

Vanessa "Aunt Nessa" Underwood

Cletus "Paw Paw" Darr

Eula "Grandma" Darr

Letter from the Author

Dear Reader,

I want to begin this letter by assuring you that, regardless of whether you are a college student in your first year, senior year, or have been out of school for five years, whatever it is that God has placed in your path leading up to this point, whatever trials, whatever struggles, whatever victories He has given you, are all for a purpose. Speaking specifically to those of you that are currently enjoying the late, coffee-fueled, sleep-deprived nights that come with the life of a college student, this will get better.

You may be in the early stages of your college career, and you are struggling to survive, wondering if you should pursue that major in Biology, or Computer Science, or Nursing. However, I would like to offer you a word of encouragement from someone who has been there. You will survive, and you will come out on the other side of this with a greater understanding of yourself, academia, and the world and the way it works after this episode in the series of life.

Now, before I close, I would like to make a request to those of you who will read this. I pray that you allow this book to become a catalyst to your studies of God's Word, creating a new, deeper curiosity about it, rather than allowing it to become a substitute. To conclude, I pray that you will continue to find success in your college career and far beyond and that you will pursue God and the mission that He has for your life, regardless of where it may take you in the world and in your life's journey. I pray that you continue to live life pursuing His will and that you will find joy in doing so.

Finally, in the way of thanksgiving, I would like to thank the people and organizations that helped this book to become reality. I would like to thank my parents, Gary and Cheryl Darr, for the life that they have given me, the trials that they have battled right along-side me, and for the way that they have pushed me closer to Christ in the way that they have raised me and handled whatever came our way. I would like to thank the faculty and staff at Liberty University for their support over the course of this book's construction. Lastly, a big thank you to my Liberty friends for their encouragement and feedback.

Sincerely,

Samuel C. Darr

Joy in the Face of Persecution

Blessed *are* they which are persecuted for righteousness' sake: for theirs is the kingdom of heaven

Matthew 5:10 KJV

In a time when it seems that everyone is pulling away from God and refusing to follow His plan for their lives, those who choose to follow Him and dedicate their lives to Him, are beginning to become fewer and fewer. For this reason, Christians are coming under an increasing amount of persecution for their choice to follow the one true God. To many, this would seem like a cause for remorse and concern. However, I would challenge you to lay aside that mindset for a moment and consider the idea that there is, within these times of persecution, a reason to find joy.

This was once a circumstance that I was faced with during my two years at community college. While I was not often directly confronted about my beliefs, as there were about a hundred other students in my classes, it was often the case that my friendly, warm professors would stand in front of the class during the lecture period and begin to, in the case of biology, speak of the theory of Evolution as if it were fact, or in the case of art, force students to look at pieces that depicted the Crucifixion, or other significant events in church history, in ways that took away all dignity from the event that God had planned for a specific purpose.

Now, if you are reading this and are like me, you have left the liberal college system and have found yourself in a slightly less persecutory college that aligns more with your beliefs. If this is not your situation, then this devotion will still have applications to you and how you can emerge from what may be an extremely liberal environment with your faith remaining intact.

I will begin by speaking to the first crowd that I mentioned, which is the crowd that is now residing in a private, most likely Christian institution. To you, I will say this; don't let your guard down on your faith, because that is when Satan likes to strike most.

In my case, when I finished my Associate of Arts degree at my community college, I emerged with the desire to attend Liberty University in Lynchburg, Virginia. It is no secret that this school has found its way into the headlines over the years because of their stances on various issues.

However, the issues that have brought them into the headlines are issues that are clearly spelled out in the Gospel.

When thinking of everything that has become a hot topic of discussion today, from ideas about abortion to other concepts such as what marriage and family should look like, these issues are repeatedly spelled out in the Gospel and therefore, give Christians a clear view of where God stands on them. However, this is not the only set of issues that Christians often face persecution about. There are also issues such as the idea of where all this life that we see today came from and other concepts that have slowly become the foundation for political campaigns and social movements. The Gospel clearly gives mounds of advice on many of these topics. Unfortunately, society does not tend to follow the advice set forth by the Gospel on these issues, so this is where Christians often encounter a hefty wall that must be overcome before they are able to reach these people for Christ.

The first thing that must be understood by the person that is trying to reach these people for Christ is something that is tossed around in media circles but may need some clarification. To reach these people for Christ, Christians must show them the love of Christ. What needs to be clarified is what it means to love someone. It does not mean that we as Christians walk around and tell everybody that what they're doing is okay. This is tolerance, not love. Christians show love to nonbelievers through showing them kindness in the shape of unsolicited acts of service or paying the person a kind word. While this may not immediately bring the person to Christ, you will begin to slowly chip away at any bad experiences that person may have had with other Christians who may have treated them poorly.

Something else that Christians can do to reach these people is to simply sit and talk with them. Many times, you will find that when you talk to an unbeliever, somewhere in their story is a reason that they either turned away from Christ or have never given their lives to Him in the first place. However, without speaking to the person, it is impossible to figure out how to best reach them with the Gospel.

Additionally, the ultimate measure that we, as Christ-followers can take when we are attempting to reach others for the Gospel is to simply yet comprehensively, share it with them. This means that we start that conversation and we make it a conversation centered on Christ, the Great Commission, and the Gospel. This means that we take the power of the Gospel and the power that it has to heal and to change lives, and we inject that into the minds and hearts of those who may have never heard the Gospel or seen it in action in the lives of those around them. However, we must resolve to not get so caught up in all those steps and forget to lay the pure, unfiltered Word of God in front of them and allow that element to do the work in that individual's life that it needs to do.

There is also another crowd of Christians that are probably more likely to encounter massive persecution for their beliefs, and that is the group of Christians who are pursuing a career at a liberal college. These Christians are the ones that often have access to the biggest mission field when it comes to reaching others for Christ. In this case, if you are one of these students, you likely will encounter everything from an atheist to a Muslim. While the message remains relatively unchanged, Christians at a liberal college are usually surrounded by many atheistic students and professors who may have a much broader knowledge of the Bible than they do. In this case, the first thing that must be done is to show them the love of Christ, which will likely spark curiosity as to where the love that you are showing comes from. In addition to this, it would also be a wise idea to come into the discussion with evidence for what you believe. While Christ does not require us to have evidence for His existence before we come to Him, often, this is what is required to start a discussion with someone who may have been hurt by what they may deem to be something that was caused or allowed by God. If you are reading this and are a Christian, as Christians, we know that God does not cause the evil that occurs in the world. This is all a result of the free will that we are given as followers of Christ. However, it all passes through God's hands. Therefore, if it occurs in your life, you can rest assured that God has a greater purpose for that event that you will see further down the road.

Message:

Persecution is a part of the Christian walk and this will always be the case until Christ returns and conquers sin forever. However, in the midst of persecution, search out opportunities to show the love of Christ to those around you, even if it means showing kindness to those who are persecuting you. Through doing this, those who persecute you could see Christ for the first time or in a brand-new way.

Share It!

Using these questions, reach out to your friends on social media and get the conversation started!

1. What are some challenges that you have been facing in reaching others for Christ?
2. How have you tried to overcome those challenges?
3. Who have you employed in the situation to help you deal with these challenges?

Seek Him FIRST

But seek ye first the kingdom of God, and his righteousness; and all these things shall be added unto you.

Matthew 6:33 KJV

Often, when we hear this verse, we probably start humming the hymn in our head, just as I did before I started writing this. However, do we ever really stop to think about what this verse is asking of us? What is being demanded in this verse and in these words spoken by Christ Himself, is that we abandon everything that is ours and rely completely on God's judgment before turning to our own often flawed judgment for every single issue that we face in life. This also applies to those college years.

Many times, it seems that we are so afraid to ask someone for help with something that we do not understand because we feel that there has to be something that we haven't tried yet that will be the magic key to the problem. It seems that, especially in college, students feel that this is a sign of weakness. It seems that asking questions or asking for assistance is an indication that someone is not as intelligent or as logically-minded as another student. However, this is not the case. Seeking help with a problem in life, whether it be academics or an issue in one's Christian walk, is one of the best things to do when one encounters an issue in one of these areas because it shows that the individual is willing to humble themselves for the sake of getting the task done correctly, or avoiding the path of self-destruction that can often come with choosing to do something our own way. However, this verse asks something even more courageous of believers. This verse, these words from the mouth of Christ, demand that we ask for God's intervention from the starting line of whatever we may be facing at the time.

Imagine walking into a lecture hall, and hearing that sound of bubble sheets hitting each seat and realizing that there is a test in the class that you had not even realized was scheduled. Also, imagine sitting down at your seat and calmly raising your hand as the test begins, and asking the professor to provide you some assistance with this unexpected exam that had been placed in front of you. Depending on the school and the professor, you may receive anything from an 'I can't. Just do your best' to a laugh and a turned back.

Fortunately, unlike a college professor, if we ask the God of this universe to help us with an obstacle that has been placed before us, and we give Him all of our resources and time to work with and listen attentively for the answer that He will eventually provide, you can rest assured that God will most definitely not turn His back or laugh in our face, because He wants to help us in our times of struggle and He wants us to come running to Him. This doesn't mean that we try everything that we know to do on our own and when that fails, we consult the internet, and when that fails, we go before God. The verse says to seek Him FIRST. It does not tell us to 'seek ye, when all else fails and you don't know what else to try, the kingdom of God'. That word first seems to imply that God might kind of know what He is doing, and since He ordained these events in our lives in the first place, the chances are pretty good that He has a plan for how He would bring us through them. Therefore, as Christians, we must strive to seek His will for everything that we come across in our lifetime to ensure that we are pursuing the most beneficial course of action for getting through the circumstances set before us.

Message:

It is commonly said that life is very unpredictable and that it tends to throw some unexpected curveballs. However, for every curveball that is thrown in our direction, there is a God in Heaven who knows exactly where that ball, or circumstance is going to end up and how it will impact us. He is always ready for that because He knew about that specific circumstance before you even existed. Therefore, while we would like to pop out our smartphone and search for similar situations and their outcomes, we must also realize that the God that we serve has a set of abilities and knowledge that is beyond anything that we could possibly even begin to comprehend. Therefore, in those moments when you don't know where to turn, rather than searching for an option that puts our efforts first, commit to seeking Him first.

Share It!

Using these questions, reach out to your friends on social media and get the conversation started!

1. What things, what pieces of your life are you seeking before God and the plans that He has for you?
2. What kinds of "blinders" do you have in your life right now that might be tuning out the will of God and the path that He has laid before you?
3. Name one person in your life that helps you tune back into the will and voice of God.

1.

Priorities: Where is Christ in Yours?

[24]Then said Jesus unto his disciples, If any *man* will come after me, let him deny himself, and take up his cross, and follow me. [25]For whosoever will save his life shall lose it: and whosoever will lose his life for my sake shall find it. [26]For what is a man profited, if he shall gain the whole world, and lose his own soul? or what shall a man give in exchange for his soul?

Matthew 16:24-26 KJV

Imagine that someone shows up at your front door with a check for $2 billion dollars, and says, "This check can be yours if you do this one thing for me. You can have this check if you will leave your house, your family, everything you own and follow me around the world to tell others how they too can have a check like this one". We would like to believe that we would accept this offer in a heartbeat, but when you consider that this would mean never seeing your family and friends again, giving up all your life savings, and leaving behind those beautiful cars that you worked so hard to call your own, the scope of this decision suddenly comes into perspective.

Now, imagine that someone comes to you in the grocery store parking lot and says that they can show you the one and only solution that would allow you to gain eternal life and the promise that one day, you could be in a place with no more sickness, death, violence, or any of the other things that plague the world today. What would you say? Many would, out of instinct say 'Of course! I'm in!'. However, this person continues to tell you that one condition of this gift is that you will have to be willing to give up all that you have, from your finances to many of your relationships, and you must be willing to leave your family if you are called to do so. With this addition, the gift becomes a little bit more intimidating and may require some reflection and thought about what value this gift holds in your mind. On one hand, you would have the guarantee that you would one day live in a completely pain-free, sinless state. On the other hand, you would have to face the reality that you may have to leave behind some of your most precious belongings and relationships. However, all these things are in the world and even though the relationships may be worth a lot to you, if you are not willing to sacrifice those relationships for a relationship with the one true God, it may be time for you to reevaluate your priorities and how they rank in your daily life.

When Christ went to die for every single person who has ever existed, currently exists, or will ever exist, there was no question as to where His priorities were. When Christ was hung upon that tree, He was not hanging there wishing that He had stayed with His disciples or that He had continued working as a carpenter. He hung upon that tree because He knew why He was there. He hung on that tree because He knew that, due to His suffering that He had endured from the beginning of His ministry to the very end as He was hanging on Calvary, millions and millions of people would go so far as to be persecuted by their own government, or kicked out of their home, just to follow Him and to dedicate their lives to Him. Now, the question becomes, are we willing to do that? Whether you are attending a Christian or a liberal college, once you emerge with that degree in your hand, you have a lot of decisions to make. You have to decide where you will work, where you want to live. You will have to decide what kind of lifestyle you want to live. However, the greatest, most important decision that you must make every day of your life, is whether you are willing to give all that up for the sake of following Christ. You must decide whether you are willing to set aside the fact that you spent four or more years of your life pursuing your dream major, and if you are prepared to wholeheartedly follow the plan that Christ has set before you as you leave all of that work behind. You will have a decision to make, and it will not be an easy one. Now, the question is, what are you going to do?

Message:

There has never been a worthier cause to follow than the cause of Christ. In countries around the world, people have been imprisoned by their government or even killed by their own families because they chose to follow Christ. With this in mind, there are two things that must be considered before you decide to follow Christ. The first is whether you are willing to face the possibility of imprisonment or even death for this cause. The second thing that must be considered is whether you would be willing to travel to those countries, if you were prompted by the Holy Spirit to do so, to spread the message of the Gospel to those people around the world who would consider the Gospel message something worth dying for.

Share It!

Using these questions, reach out to your friends on social media and get the conversation started!

1. What is one thing in your life that you would not be willing to give up for the sake of pursuing the mission that Christ has set before you? Why?
2. What are three things that are holding you back from pursuing the call that God has placed on your life?
3. What would it take for you to abandon that fear that is holding you back?

Making Christ the Standard

²¹Then came Peter to him, and said, Lord, how oft shall my brother sin against me, and I forgive him? till seven times? ²²Jesus saith unto him, I say not unto thee, Until seven times: but, Until seventy times seven.

Matthew 18:21-22 KJV

Forgiving someone who has hurt you. It's so much fun, right? Wrong. We've all been there at one point or another, whether it be in the context of our family, a relationship that we may be in, our friendships, or even someone outside of our everyday circles that has harmed you in one way or another. Eventually, there comes a day, whether it be soon after the wrongdoing or years down the road when we are convicted to the point that we must go before the person or people to whom we caused harm, and ask for their forgiveness concerning the actions we performed towards them. This is one of the hardest things in the world because, somewhere deep inside our heart, we know that we do not deserve the forgiveness that they are giving to us. However, on that same token, this fact makes the receipt of that forgiveness that much sweeter. This forgiveness brings us back to a place where nothing stands between ourselves and that person. It brings us a clean slate. This is great for the relationship, but for the person who may be doing the forgiving, often this decision is not an easy one and it can require some prayer and thought on their part because they often do not feel that the forgiveness is deserved by the person requesting it. However, because we have all found ourselves on both sides of the situation, it is worth remembering that Christ, the perfect, sinless, Son of God died for all the past, present, and future sins of the world as an act of forgiveness for sins that we haven't even committed yet.

When we think about this idea of forgiving those who have wronged us, we must be careful to remember that, in all situations, when we find ourselves asking what we should do, or in this case, whether we should do it, we must make Christ the standard. When we look at the sacrifice that Christ made on the cross, we always learn in church about the fact that He died for our sins, but we often fail to realize what this means. Christ's death on the cross was an atonement for the sins that we hadn't even committed yet. Regardless of what sin may be in your past, Christ died for that and has forgiven that. We hear this in Sunday school and in the church pews every week. It's common knowledge to anyone who has been anywhere near a church during their lifetime. This is one of the key principles of the Christian walk. However, when we think about this fact that Christ died for the sins of the world, including ours, thousands of years before we were born, we also need to realize something about this. Not only does Christ's death on the cross free us from bondage to our own sin, but it also presents somewhat of a responsibility to us as His followers. As followers of Christ, we have a responsibility to not only ask forgiveness from Him for the sins that we have committed in our lifetime, but there is also this responsibility on our part to grant forgiveness to those around us who may have caused pain in our lives at one point or another.

Today, we live in a time when forgiveness has gotten somewhat deformed. Forgiveness has come to mean that one side says that they forgive the other, when, in reality, no actual forgiveness has been granted at all. Whether it be in the context of an incident within one's immediate family or even within the church, this idea of granting forgiveness without boundaries, without constraints, without any limiting factors, is often hard to come by in this day in time. This is likely one of the reasons that this verse is often so difficult for people to understand, much less adopt. Today, forgiveness usually has terms and conditions attached that usually end up doing very little to resolve the issue. This is not the forgiveness that is being defined here.

When we look at these two verses, we find that Christ is setting a standard for us that often seems unrealistic in today's culture. We struggle to forgive someone once for hitting our car. Imagine having to go through this process as many as (for the sake of argument) seventy-seven times. Often, we tend to laugh at this number and we pose the question concerning the seventy-eighth time. However, when we take an objective look at this idea of forgiving someone, basically, as many times as we need to, that can be a hefty challenge for most people. To some, this may seem impossible because they will lose their mind before the fifth time. Therefore, the standard that is being set here is one that can often be difficult to live up to. One of the difficult parts about living up to this standard is the fact that Christ does not give us parameters for what this standard of forgiveness applies to. When reading this passage, we don't find a list of IF {this circumstance}, THEN {forgive this many times}. We don't find a list of exclusions where this standard doesn't apply. What we do find here is a no-questions-needed standard for how we can ensure that those relationships that mean the most to us will last for many years to come and that they will not be ruined because one person chose to hold onto some petty issue rather than forgiving it for the sake of making the relationship thrive.

Now, as we think about this idea of granting forgiveness to those who have wronged us, we often assume that this only applies to those people who ask for our forgiveness. However, imagine that you have wronged someone, and when you go before them to ask for their forgiveness, they tell you that they forgave you a long time ago. This is also what Christ is asking of us in this passage. When someone wrongs you, forgiving them will not always be easy. It will often seem impossible and you will be tempted to find as many philosophical quotes as you can that seem to permit holding onto someone's trespass against you. However, doing so not only inhibits our relationship with Christ and those closest to us, but it also goes against this standard that has been set for us by Christ Himself in His own words. Therefore, to find excuses that would allow us to avoid giving to others the forgiveness that has been afforded to us is to diminish the value and importance of the forgiveness that we have been given for all the trespasses that we have committed against the one who set the standard for true, unconditional forgiveness.

Message:

Is there something in your life, some trespass that was done by a friend or family member, that you continue to hold onto and have allowed to become a wedge between yourself and that person? If this is the case, challenge yourself to examine the situation through a biblical lens and attempt to understand why you may be holding onto that specific thing. If you begin to do this and continue to hold Christ as the standard, you will probably begin to find that your recollection of the trespass itself has decreased substantially. You will likely find that this trespass that once seemed so significant has become so minimal, that it is simply a speck in your eye that simply must be plucked out and tossed away. However, it is up to you to first decide to prepare yourself to forgive this trespass, whatever it may be, with the understanding that Christ gave His life to forgive everything you have done, are doing, and will ever do to Him. With this perspective, it will become extremely difficult for anyone to hold onto any trespass when they consider the magnitude of Christ's forgiveness and its coverage of all trespasses, past, present, and future.

Share It!

Using these questions, reach out to your friends on social media and get the conversation started!

1. What is that 78th trespass that you have been holding on to? Reach out to that person right now and tell them how they hurt you and offer the forgiveness that they may have never known that they needed.
2. Set up a coffee date with someone that you may not be on the best terms with. Take the opportunity to sit down and show the love of Christ to this person through the simple yet massive act of offering forgiveness without request.
3. Think back to a time when you did wrong to someone in your life and go to that person and ask their forgiveness. Give others the opportunity to forgive you for things you may have almost forgotten.

The Unexpected Appointment

[48]But and if that evil servant shall say in his heart, My lord delayeth his coming; [49] and shall begin to smite *his* fellowservants, and to eat and drink with the drunken; [50]The lord of that servant shall come in the day when he looketh not for him, and in an hour that he is not aware of

Matthew 24:48-51 KJV

It would probably be reasonable to say that, today, with smartphones in our hands and every part of our day being planned out two weeks in advance, between assignments that are due, and projects that are coming up, not to mention periodic get-togethers with friends and family, we usually have to know what we're doing and when we're doing it on a regular basis. With all these appointments and occasions that the average college student must remember, calendars and planning are a crucial tool that students must have at their disposal. However, no matter how much research and planning a person does, there is one thing that no one can plan for, and that is the return of Christ in the very near future.

Imagine that you are working in your office for a future (or current) employer, and in the entire time that you have worked there, the only view that you have had of the CEO has been at company-wide events. However, on this particular day, you hear that hair-raising voice at your cubicle that can silence any room. The CEO of your entire company is standing at your doorway and says that he was 'just wanting to check in and see what was happening out on the floor'. Luckily, when he comes to your office, you are working on a report that had just been given to you by your supervisor. However, had this man walked into your office just fifteen minutes earlier, he would have caught a glimpse of your news feed on one of your many social media accounts. The chances are pretty good that no employee who wants a paycheck in the near future would be caught by their superior doing this. However, does this mean that no one ever does it? Nope. You want your boss to catch you reading that book he told everyone to read. He never said that you would be tested on it, but it still looks good if he catches you reading it. Ultimately, while we may not spend our entire day doing "work", we want our superiors to believe that we do.

Now, imagine that you are sitting in your house watching a not so G-rated movie with your family, and suddenly, the house begins to shake, and the sky begins to turn blood-red, and before you know it, you are witnessing the rapture right before your very eyes. What will Christ, the man who died to save your life, say about what you were doing at the time of His return? This is something that should be on the mind of every Christian, as well as every non-believer, as both should be thinking about the results of how they are leading their lives and how that is viewed in the eyes of Christ. For the believer, what are you watching on TV? What kind of extracurricular activities are you involved in? What kind of language are you using during your daily conversations? All these things are something to keep in mind. For the Christian, this should be of a concern because when Christ returns to bring you with Him, He will likely have some questions for you at the Judgement Seat. For the nonbeliever, the concern should be even greater because the price will be much greater at the time of Judgement. This verse puts an even greater emphasis on the importance of coming to know Christ as one's Savior as soon as possible, because, as humans here on Earth, it is impossible to know at what time Christ will come back for His people. Therefore, to say, 'I'll do it tomorrow', is to risk the possibility that Christ will return in the dark of night, and tomorrow will suddenly be too late. Therefore, it is critical that everyone always be prepared, because, before anyone realizes what has happened, it will be too late to do anything about it.

It is also important that those who follow Christ ensure that they are living their lives for Christ every second of the day, because the moment that you let your guard down and you begin to visit that site or go to that place you know you shouldn't go, that is the moment when Christ will return, and no matter how good you may have been over the course of your lifetime, whatever you are doing at the time of Christ's return will speak volumes about what you have been doing when you thought that no one was watching.

Message:

We always like to believe that we would see the signs leading up to Christ's return. However, failed attempt after failed attempt by renowned scientists and theologians has proven that it is impossible to try to predict when Christ will return. This is because His knowledge of everything that has occurred in the past, is currently occurring, and will occur in the future is so much greater and so much more detailed than any understanding that we could ever hope to have. Therefore, any attempt to try to predict His return is simply a time-wasting exercise. The only action that we can take until that time has arrived, is to follow after Christ with all that we are, and spread the Gospel to as many people as we possibly can.

Share It!

Using these questions, reach out to your friends on social media and get the conversation started!

1. Where will you find yourself in that moment when Christ returns? Will you find yourself in a place where you would want to be seen by God, or will you be hiding your face from God?
2. What are you doing in your life and in the lives of others to prepare for the day when Christ returns to reclaim His church?
3. When you look at your life, whether it be the last four years, or yesterday, does it say, "I'm ready" or "Hopefully He won't come tonight"?

Reaching the Unreached

[40]And the King shall answer and say unto them, Verily I say unto you, Inasmuch as ye have done *it* unto one of the least of these my brethren, ye have done it unto me.

Matthew 25:40 KJV

In an era when it seems that we are more connected than we have ever been, with smartphones and social media constantly in an evolving state, we as Christians, and especially as Christian college students encounter thousands of people on a daily basis just in our classes and other interactions around campus. However, in all those interactions that we engage in, somehow, we still seem to miss so many opportunities to reach people, and those are people missing out on the chance to hear the life-altering message of the Gospel. From that guy that no one talks to in the dining hall, to that homeless guy that hangs around that store across from the school, we as followers of Christ have a duty, a responsibility to reach these people. These are the least of these, which Christ is talking about here.

No matter how much we talk to our friends, whether that be through face-to-face interactions or through the more common digital interaction, we are constantly, daily, ostracizing so many people who may have never been exposed to the light of Christ and the forgiveness that is available to them through His sacrifice on the cross. Imagine for a second if someone hadn't stepped out of their circle of friends to share the Gospel message with you. Maybe you came to know Christ at a church under a pastor's sermon. Imagine if someone had not stepped out of their circle of friends and invited your family, somewhere along the way, to that church. Where would you be? How can you know that you would have heard the Gospel elsewhere?

If you do not step out of your comfort circle and go into the world to seek out the least of these, such as the homeless, the hungry, the widowed, the orphaned, then who will? How long will you allow yourself to say, "Somebody else will buy that guy on the corner a burger; I don't have time"? How long will you allow yourself to pass that guy with the cardboard sign on your commute in the morning even though he is there every day as you go by? How long will you tell yourself that somebody else will give him something? Why not be that somebody else? Please understand that this author is not setting himself apart in this respect. It's so easy to 'Like' and 'Share' pictures on social media and feel as if we have done our part to show support to people, but in reality, we have done nothing.

As the church, we are called to go out into the world and to reach those in need. The sad truth about this is, that we no longer have to go on an expensive mission's trip halfway around the world to reach people with unbearable need. These people are in our backyard. We must decide to look up from our phones, even at stop lights when the guy with the shabby clothes and the long beard is looking right at us, and decide that we are going to be the ones who choose to act and reach the least of these for the cause of Christ.

One of the great things that sets Christianity apart from most other world religions, is that we are called to do good unto others, not so that we can get into heaven, but rather because Christ has already paid our price of admission into Heaven, and He now calls us to show love to these people because of what He did for us.

Who are we, to turn our backs on these people who fall into the same category as we do? We all came into this world as flawed human beings and we are all offered the same forgiveness as the guy on the corner. That could be us. No matter what college you may attend, or what career you are pursuing once you finish college, one has to wonder what would happen if that career suddenly vanished. While you would have a degree to lean on, that doesn't necessarily mean much today. Where would you be if suddenly your job was eliminated?

First, let me assure you that I understand how this sounds. Dialogues like this are common on social media when a crisis occurs in the world. However, it is something that deserves consideration. While some are wealthier than others, we all face the possibility that we could become the least of these at some point in time. There is no one with a job that can guarantee that it will be there tomorrow. There is no one, other than God Himself, who can guarantee that they will not face unexpected, unplanned events in the next twenty-four hours. If we were in the place of that guy holding the cardboard sign, who would stop for us? Who would go to the drive-thru and get us a burger? If you would want someone to be that person to you, then you must choose to be that person to someone else.

This is not only because it is the right thing to do, but also because it is what Christ calls us to do. Now the question becomes, will you be somebody's someone else?

Message:

If you're anything like me, at the beginning of this devotional, you were probably feeling like I do when I read those *Everybody Love Everybody* posts on social media. But through reaching the least of these by satisfying a physical need that they have, you will be able to open the door to sharing the Gospel with the individual and may possibly encourage them to do the same. While it may not be buying a burger, that person could reach people at the place where they may be staying by offering an extra blanket, or by sharing the same Gospel with someone else that you had shared with them at one point. While we often do not see the results of what we plant, we can know that the seed was harvested in that person, and that the harvest was passed onto someone else soon after. Reach the least of these, and maybe they will do the same.

Share It!

Using these questions, reach out to your friends on social media and get the conversation started!

1. Stop right now, put down this book, and message that person from your class or from your hall that seems like kind of a loner. Ask them how you can pray for them. Invite them to lunch.
2. What is one thing that you can do for those people around you that seem to live a life filled with struggle and always end up getting the short end of the stick?
3. Text five friends right now and set up lunch, but also send that identical text to that loner that you identified just moments ago. Be that individual's *someone else.* Be that person that gives them something to tell their family about when they go home.

Beyond the Stained-Glass Windows

[19]Go ye therefore, and teach all nations, baptizing them in the name of the Father, and of the Son and of the Holy Ghost: [20]teaching them to observe all things whatsoever I have commanded you: and lo, I am with you always, even unto the end of the world. Amen.

Matthew 28:19-20 KJV

In this passage, we find a call that goes out to all who choose to follow Christ. We also find a summary of every Christian's primary purpose in following Christ. As Christians, our purpose is to go into all the world and tell others about the love that we have been given as a result of the sacrifice that was shown through Christ's death on the cross.

Our purpose in following Christ is not to toss around a bunch of theological concepts at non-believers and expect them to come to know Him because of those. Our mission, once we have accepted Christ, is to go into all the world and tell others about the love that comes through Christ through the delivery of the Gospel both in action and in sharing the living, inspired, inerrant Word of God. In some cases, this means bringing light to some of the darkest places in our own community, where Christ may have never been shared with or explained to the people in that community, because so many people feel that this verse is telling them to go halfway across the world to be able to effectively share the Gospel. This verse does not say to go into all the world, except for that bad neighborhood on the other side of town, or go into all the world… except for the soup kitchen where people are afraid to volunteer because of the stories that have come from there. Christ tells us, in His own words, to go into ALL nations to share His Gospel.

It seems that sometimes, we sit at home as Christians and we watch the news, and we say, day after day, "This world needs Jesus", or something to that effect, but what are we doing as His followers to make that a reality? What are we doing to bring Christ and His message to the places where it is needed most and taught the least? What are we doing to bring about the change that we needs to happen in the world? We can share as many emotional videos on social media as we want to, but until we leave the couch and go out into those unreached communities, those people will remain in the dark about the message of Christ. It is so easy to sit back and watch TV and see those stories on the news about churches and other

Christian organizations going out and helping communities that have been destroyed because of some natural or manmade disaster. However, until we decide that we are going to go into the communities around us, and that we are going to be more than community service volunteers, that we are going to reach people with the Gospel at the times when they need it most, the only change we will ever see is going to be on a TV screen or on social media.

Christ's ministry was never meant to be contained within a brick building on a major highway. The ministry of Jesus was mobile, and it reached people in every corner of society. His ministry went to people who needed to know about the gifts that He offered. Today, it has become a popular idea that we, as the church, are supposed to make the people want to come to us. Churches send buses out into the community and load people into the bus, to bring them to a building, where there is fancy equipment, seating for thousands of people, and so much more that was never a part of Jesus' ministry. Granted, this is not to say that everything that was not a part of His ministry should not be in the church today. However, what this is saying is that the church is seemingly forcing people to come into the buildings with their name on it. Why isn't the church going out into the cities around them and standing in the middle of a public park somewhere and preaching the Gospel? Let us not be afraid to step outside of the walls that so often contain the church, and spread it beyond the comfy chairs and the slideshow presentations. Let us make it more about what Christ can do through us and less about what we can do to make His message sound or look better than it already is.

Message:

Christ does not need any help making His message more appealing to certain groups. He is not a politician or the CEO of some billion-dollar company. The message of Christ and what He has done is so rich and powerful on its own and the best way to add to this message is to hear from people who have been changed by it and by Him. Therefore, let us, as the church, be those people who shine forth the change that He has brought to our lives, and let Christ be the one in charge of causing the change to happen on the other end.

Share It!

Using these questions, reach out to your friends on social media and get the conversation started!

1. Think of your oldest friend right now. When you look at that person and the way that they are living, would you say that the world is able to look at them and know that they have a professing Christ-follower as an active part of their life?
2. What does it look like in your mind for someone to take the church and the love of Christ beyond the walls of that building that we pile into once, maybe twice a week? Is that the image that you see in the worldwide church today? What about your local church?
3. To what lengths are you willing to go right now to bring the Gospel and everything that we hear about, sing about on Sunday morning to those who are hungry for something that only the Gospel can offer?

Just Believe

Jesus said unto him, If thou canst believe, all things are possible to him that believeth.

Mark 9:23 KJV

How many times have we gone to the Lord in an attitude of prayer for something that we felt very strongly about, and the words that we were speaking contradicted what was going on in our heart? What was coming out of our mouth was 'God I know you can do this', but our heart was saying in the quietest voice, 'but I bet you won't'. From what this verse says, this attitude basically says that we are doubting what God is capable of, or feeling that the situation we are in is either too big for Him to handle or too small for Him to care. Therefore, while we may pray for the situation to be done according to God's will, we secretly wonder if He will even do anything about it, because, after all, what makes us so special?

The great thing about the love of God and His ability to act in a situation is that all that He asks of us, is that we just believe that He can do it, and He will act in the situation. Unfortunately, what this does not mean, is that, if we ask Him for a job, He may not give us that job at that top-notch company right away. He may bring you to a point in life that drives you to get a job bagging groceries and working a drive-thru, just so that you are able to pay the bills on time. If you ask Him to lead you to the right college so that you can get a degree that would enable you to compete in the workforce afterward, He may not send you that acceptance letter from one of your three choice colleges. He may send you an advertisement in the mail from the community college that is fifteen minutes from your house, whose biggest program is a degree that would allow you to become an auto mechanic. While this is not a terrible job, it is far from your first-choice major of becoming a teacher at an elementary school.

Just because we say that we believe God will answer our prayers in His perfect timing, it seems that we often fail to realize that in allowing this, we are allowing Him to answer our prayers differently than we may have originally imagined. Maybe you have just graduated with your degree in computer science, with a dream to create some major corporation one day, but your immediate concern is to find something that will get rid of that student debt. Soon, after weeks of prayer and listening for the voice of God, the phone rings one day and it is your roommate from college who graduated with you, and he tells you that he has heard about this job at an accounting firm as a data-entry specialist, and you have all the qualifications. It is basically a sure thing that you will get the job, but that is not what you were hoping for when you prayed for a job to come along. However, in the end, God did answer your prayers. With this job, you will begin to be able to pay for that student debt and have some money left over for the other stuff that comes with life. This is what you prayed for, but not necessarily the outcome you were hoping for. Due to your belief that He would act in the situation, He did, and your prayers were answered, but a condition of this verse is that we must agree to chase after the opportunities that God places before us, no matter what our original plans were that we had made in our junior year of high school.

So often, when someone has a sick family member, or some circumstance enter their life that tends to be very unpredictable, they spend hours on their knees praying for God to heal the situation, but when they turn around two weeks later, they're attending the funeral of the family member that was sick, or they are struggling to pay the bills even with this new job that they had been given. However, when God looks at that situation, He sees the reason behind those circumstances, even though we, as humans do not see it the way He does. Therefore, we have no way of understanding why He does things the way He does. If there comes a time when we do gain this understanding, it may not be until years down the road, or even at the end of life when we are surrounded by family that was instrumental in bringing us through those difficult times. Either way, when we pray about a situation that seems insurmountable at the time, we must put our signature on God's contract to accept the result that He presents to us. We must commit to following that plan and believing that, even in these moments when we wonder what God was thinking, he still has a plan and he is still leading and guiding us according to that plan.

Message:

We must remember when we pray for any situation, no matter how great or small it may be, that God has known about the situation from the time He created the universe. Therefore, it is likely that He will not deliver a result that will bring us pain and suffering without cause. We must understand that, when we pray to ask God for assistance, that He will bring us the help we need, if we just believe, but it may not necessarily be what we wanted or expected. It is important to keep this in mind when going before His throne. However, if you simply trust in His infallible ways, He will bring about a result that will make sense either today or sometime in the future.

Share It!

Using these questions, reach out to your friends on social media and get the conversation started!

1. What is one situation that is in your life right now or a situation in your past that you haven't quite given to God?
2. In your mind, what does it mean to *believe* that God can do something? Are you fulfilling that definition in your relationship with Christ today?
3. Do you believe that God can do anything, or do you believe that there are limits to what He is willing and/or able to do in the world and in the lives of His people?

Prayer is a Conversation

[2]And he said unto them, When ye pray, say, Our Father, which art in heaven, Hallowed be thy name. Thy kingdom come. Thy will be done, as in heaven, so in earth. [3]Give us day by day our daily bread. [4]And forgive us our sins; for we also forgive every one who is indebted to us. And lead us not into temptation, but deliver us from evil.

Luke 11:2-4 KJV

Let's take a second to imagine a scenario. Imagine that you are married to the person that you love more than anything. Now, imagine that you come home at the end of the day, and before asking any questions about his/her day or telling them how much you love them, you walk in the door, throw your briefcase on the table, and ask what's for dinner. Imagine the other person's response to this behavior. If you do not act this way on a regular basis, his or her reaction will probably be anywhere from a blank stare to the infamous silent treatment. Quite simply, to do this would be completely unacceptable in most households, and understandably so. Not only is this form of communication unacceptable, but it just doesn't convey that we are relating to someone who is supposed to hold such a special and privileged place in our heart. That's simply not how loving and nurturing relationships are supposed to work. It's not supposed to be all about what you can get from the relationship. It is supposed to be about what you can give that other person in return and how one is able to help the other grow. This means that the communication that happens between these two people should consist of words that build the other person up and make them stronger, as opposed to pulling them down and causing them to suffer. This is what relationships are ultimately supposed to do for those who choose to engage in them.

With that in mind, let's think for a second about the relationship that we have with Christ and what our communication with Him typically looks like. When you talk to God, you probably don't say, "Hey God, if you could give me this raise, that'd be great. Thanks". Most of us wouldn't even talk to our manager like that, so why is that suddenly acceptable when we're talking about the God of the universe? So often it seems that this is the trap that so many people fall into in their walk with Christ. We're busy, we're tired, and we just want things to get better and easier, so we bring that request before God, hoping that He will come through for us this time in a way that we approve of and that works with our plans.

However, it seems that we never take the time to stop, turn around, and notice how far God has brought us, despite our fatigue, our feeling of being near the end of our rope. Despite how close we seem to be to that infamous breaking point, God continues to be right there, pushing us forward and giving us the strength that we need to do the next thing, whatever that may be. He won't always give you that boost of energy that makes you feel like you can change the world in a day. Sometimes, He will give you the energy to get that assignment done before midnight the night that it's due. Whatever it may be, God will come through in some way. However, as we go back to the illustration that was made at the beginning, we need to realize that too often, this illustration closely resembles the way we approach our relationship with Christ. This is why, in this passage, Christ Himself gives us a template of sorts for how we should pray and communicate with our Heavenly Father. It's not just about the request, but also the conversation.

Our prayers to God should not sound as if we are sitting at a drive-thru ordering dinner. These conversations should sound more like a dialogue that we would have with a friend whom we love dearly because, in reality that is what Christ should be to us. Christ should not be a service that we use when we get lonely or when no one picks up the phone when we're stuck on the side of the road. This relationship should be a relationship that gives us something to look forward to, because we know that, regardless of what we may face when we get home, He will be there to face it with us. In knowing this, we should be able to face the world and all that it has to throw at us with a newfound confidence and excitement that we've never experienced. However, all this great stuff that Christ offers to those who love and obey Him can only become available as a result of a devoted, prayerful, communication-oriented relationship with Him. Therefore, before you rush to the "prayer phone" to call God and ask Him for that raise that you've been expecting all year, why don't you try to start the conversation by telling Him of your love for Him and how incredible He is, not only because of what you can get from Him but also because of what He has already given you?

Message:

What have you thanked God for lately? If you're having trouble answering that question, you may want to take some time to understand this passage a little bit better. In this passage, Christ does not tell us how to get the things from God that we want, or believe we need. Here, we find Jesus telling His followers that this is how they should *communicate* with God. This doesn't mean that we're sitting at our desk before that huge exam and praying for the A that it would take for us to pass the class. This means that we are sitting outside, or in our dorm room, and praying for God to guide our steps as we try to follow His path for our lives. This means that we wake up in the morning, and before we do anything, we stop to thank God for what He did yesterday, and what he's going to do today. If we begin to adopt this attitude toward prayer and communication with God, we will begin to notice that we are growing closer to Him and that the things which once seemed so critical in our mind have become irrelevant in comparison to what will come as a result of following Him.

Share It!

Using these questions, reach out to your friends on social media and get the conversation started!

1. When was the last time that you had a conversation, a two-way, intimate conversation with God?
2. What are some of the things that you talk about with God and how have you seen Him respond during those conversations?
3. How long do you wait for God to respond before you send that "Are you there?" message?

Simply Knock

⁹And I say unto you, Ask, and it shall be given you; seek and ye shall find, knock, and it shall be opened unto you. ¹⁰ For everyone that asketh recieveth, and he that seeketh findeth; and to him that knocketh it shall be opened.

Luke 11:9-10 KJV

It has almost always been the case that when we decide to visit a friend or arrive at a family gathering, that we knock before we enter someone's house. This is basically a simple way of asking someone to allow you to come into their house, and most of the time, that person will open the door if they know who you are and are expecting you to show up. You are allowing the person who lives there to invite you into their home so that they can visit with you and enjoy your company. However, this verse is not speaking of a physical house. The knocking that is being referred to here is prayer, and the one who allows us to enter is Christ.

When we go before God in prayer, the minute that we go before Him, He is standing at the 'door' to let us come into His presence. Christ basically tells us that we are more than free to come to Him at any time of day or night. However, it is up to Him to initially let us into His presence.

While this may not be a true demonstration for many in how they interact with their best friends, I ask that you still consider my point. Imagine walking up to someone's door and noticing that it is unlocked, so you decide to walk in and sit down at their table and ask what's for dinner. While some may say that this is how they interact with their friends whom they have known for many years, for the most part, it is still common practice to knock on someone's door when you want to come in. It's typically a common courtesy when visiting someone's home. To not do this is to deprive the homeowner of the privacy of their own home. Ultimately, knocking on someone's door is just a way of making sure that this is where you're supposed to be and that you are there at the right time.

On that same point, imagine just getting down on your knees and saying "Hey God, I really need this job to come through because I need the money, so if you could make that happen, that'd be great. Thanks". Now, I couldn't imagine speaking to anyone like this if I were serious about what I was talking about. Most people would not walk into their boss's office, put their feet on the desk and talk like this, so why would we go before the creator of the universe in this way? Fortunately, Jesus gives us the ideal mold for prayer in Luke 11:2-4. In this mold that Jesus creates, He doesn't begin by saying, 'God I love you and here is what I need from you today'. Approximately the first twenty words of the prayer laid out by Jesus are words of praise and admiration for God and just appreciation for all that He has done. While we may feel that this exam we have next week, or this project we have due is of the utmost importance to God, that is simply not true. While God most definitely does all that He can to allow us to be successful, He has more in mind for our lives than grades on tests and papers. Getting an F+ on an exam will never make Him love us less. Therefore, why make this the leading line of one's prayer?

While we do not necessarily have to copy the Lord's Prayer word-for-word, let it become a template for going before God and knocking on that door, so that He brings us into His presence. However, please understand this also. We also do not have to go before Him and deliver this prayer that makes our head hurt because we are trying so hard to remember all those words that we found in the dictionary to make it sound good. Go before Him with your burden and lay it at His feet, but also take a moment to look back at the life that you have lived up until this point, and realize the amazing things that He has done for you. Remember to take time to thank God for what He has done already before asking Him to do more.

Message:

Often, we feel that because God is all-knowing and knows our heart better than we do, we don't really have to tell Him how much we love Him and how thankful we are for Him. Often, we are so consumed in whatever is overtaking our lives at the time, that we forget that, had it not been for the grace and mercy of God, we would not have reached this point in our lives in the first place. Therefore, instead of launching immediately into, 'Here's what's wrong with the life you gave me' immediately, knock at the door and tell Him how grateful you are that He even let you in.

Share It!

Using these questions, reach out to your friends on social media and get the conversation started!

1. Think of one "door" in your life right now. Whether this "door" is a job opportunity, a change of major, a decision of whether you should attend graduate school, picture that door. Is it closed but unlocked? Is it standing wide open, or is it locked with no key in sight? If the door is closed, how hard are you knocking on that door? Has God answered it in any way?
2. How have you handled those closed, locked, and barricaded doors in your walk with Christ? Have you found yourself pulling out the crowbar, attempting to pry the barrier open, or do you trust that the door is firmly closed for a reason?
3. What are some interesting doors that God has opened in your life that you were not crazy about?

If You Only Ask

If ye then, being evil, know how to give good gifts unto your children: how much more shall *your* Heavenly Father give the Holy Spirit to them that ask him?

Luke 11:13 KJV

It is amazing the things that we request from other people at different times during the year. Every month there seems to be someone celebrating a birthday, which requires a gift to show that you didn't forget again. Every December, we say we are celebrating the birth of Christ, but so often, it turns into a commercialized two months in which businesses experience one of the best periods of the year. There are so many instances in life where we are almost obligated to give someone a bigger and better gift than last year. However, as the son of two amazing parents, I have had my mom tell me many times about the joy that is given to a parent when their child is ecstatic about the 'big' gift that they received that year, whether it be in size or in substance. It's an experience that I look forward to enjoying with my children one day in the future.

Here is something to think about. If you requested a new phone for Christmas, and you just had that feeling during those weeks leading up to Christmas that you were going to get the phone that you had asked for, imagine the feeling you would experience if you opened that box you had been sliding back and forth for weeks, to find that it contained a jumbo pack of notecards with a box of pencils. The chances are pretty good that you would smile awkwardly at the unexpected gift and give an unenthusiastic "Thank you", while you quietly panicked inside because you would be the only one at school who couldn't quietly access social media during lecture. The gift you received was not anywhere near the gift that you had hoped for. Your parents know that if you ask for a specific gift, that it is where your heart is set and there is no changing that. Your parents know that the gift would make you happy and that you would likely be a little bit happier because of that single gift.

Now transition to thinking about Christ and all the gifts that He has given to us over the course of our lives. Whether you have been alive for eighteen years or sixty-two years, the gifts that God has placed in your life are innumerable, no matter the form they may have come in. However, ultimately, the best gift that God could have ever given was the gift of His

Son. The difference, however, between this gift and the gifts that our parents have given us over the course of our lifetime, is that the gift of Christ and the salvation that His death brings, is that we didn't have to go before God and ask Him to send His Son to die for the sins of the world; He just did it. Imagine if you arrived home from school one afternoon, and there was a brand new, bright red sports car sitting in the driveway. You had done nothing to deserve this car. You had not given any money toward this car and had you purchased this car yourself, the price would have been yours to pay, but your parents freely sacrificed a massive amount of resources to get this car that you didn't deserve, but also, never asked for. Nevertheless, you enthusiastically accept because you are a young adult, and this is one of the best things to ever happen to you. But what happens when you go to your parents and ask why they bought you this incredible gift? They simply say that they did it for you because there was no way that you could have done it for yourself in your current state. They exercised grace in giving you something that you didn't deserve because they love you so much. There are two clarifications to be made here before we move on. The first is that Christ and a car are in no way comparable. The second is that you should not expect your parents to buy you a red sports car out of nowhere, as this is incredibly unrealistic for most college students. However, it did make for a good demonstration of the mercy and grace that was provided to us on the cross, when Christ, a sinless man, came to die a sinner's death to ensure that we would not have to face such a penalty in the future. This is the true message here.

If our parents can give us undeserved gifts, whether that be a smartphone or a car, what kind of grace does it take for someone who knows the mistakes that our parents may or may not know, to give us the gift of salvation if we only choose to ask for it? This is not a gift that is subject to answers such as "That is incredibly expensive and out of my price range", or "Maybe next year. I'll think about it". Christ is so willing to gift us with His forgiveness that we most definitely do not deserve, and all we are required to do is to ask for it. If that's not grace, then what is?

Message:

There are so many gifts that we receive over the course of our lives here on Earth, whether they be material or financial, that can be taken away if something were to go wrong with our finances or our conduct, or some controllable piece of life. However, the gift of salvation that God gives His people can never be returned or repossessed by the owner. This is a gift that we have ownership of for all eternity and the only term of service for the gift is to give your life completely over to the giver and agree to leave it in His hands for the rest of your life. Will you click 'I Accept' or 'Decline' on this gift?

Share It!

Using these questions, reach out to your friends on social media and get the conversation started!

1. We all have that one thing in our lives, which may or may not be a material thing, that we want, but the thought of asking God for that thing is probably a little terrifying? What is that thing for you?

2. What is one thing that you have asked of God? Is it a job? Maybe it's a way of paying the bills this month? Whatever it is, how much have you prayed about that? What results have you seen?

3. What is that thing that you really want to ask of God, but feel that you shouldn't? Maybe it's an upcoming test, or maybe it's for Him to rescue you from some addiction? What's keeping you from asking Him to give you that *thing*?

Give It All Away

[33]Sell that ye have and give alms; provide yourselves bags which wax not old, a treasure in Heaven that faileth not, where no thief approacheth, neither moth corrupteth. [34]For where your treasure is, there will your heart be also.

Luke 12:33-34 KJV

So often, it seems that we wait so long and go through so much to get some of the most critical material items in our lives, so that life goes smoothly every day. You spend four or more years of your life in college, so that you can get a job, so that you can live in a nice house and drive a nice car. All this is great. It is what gives us status and respect among those around us. However, when we look at this passage, it looks like Christ is telling us to give all that up. What is Christ saying here? He is saying to give all that stuff away. You may be thinking, *Well, He was only speaking to the people of that time. He doesn't expect me to do that.* Thankfully, all the words written in God's word are directed at both the people of His day and the people reading His Word today, so go ahead! Get to work on getting your stuff together and give it ALL to that rescue mission in the city. Chances are that you are still sitting in the exact same spot because you are terrified at the thought of selling all your stuff. Most people are, myself included.

We go to college, we get a good GPA, we try to get a good job. Why? We do this so that we can get more stuff and be more satisfied with life at that moment. The thought of giving away the car we use to get to work and other places we need to go is terrifying to most, and understandably so. Imagine if a pickup truck pulled up to your house, and out climbed a guy who was clearly homeless, and when he got to your door, he greeted you by saying, "Hey, I know that this is a little last minute, but can I have your house?". This would be laughable to most people, but imagine that you said yes. What would this mean? This would mean that this man would have a house where he could get himself back on his feet, and he would have new-to-him clothes, because… Oh, did I forget to mention that this was a "contents included" sale? This man would have all that he ever needed to get a job, be satisfied physically, and you could go out and get an apartment somewhere close to where you work. Most people would laugh at this, but Christ says that this is how we, as Christians, lay up for ourselves treasures in heaven. Now this is not to say that you need to dig up the deed to your home and prepare to turn it over to someone else. However, it is important to consider what types of possessions, what *things* in your life you would be unwilling to give up if someone needed them.

No matter the size of your house, or the prestige of your car, when all that has vanished, what will you be left with when you are standing before God one day? On that day, God will not care about how many degrees you have, or what your paycheck looks like. He will look at you and say, 'What have you done for me in the last [fill in the blank] years that I have given you on Earth?' What will your answer be? "Well, I closed that really big deal for my company and got them a really big payday!" When He asks what you have done to reach the least of these, what will you say? "I gave a dollar to that guy with the cardboard sign!" To this, Christ will ask why you thought that he, the Son of God, was only worth a single dollar. What will your answer be to Him?

This is not to say that, to please God, we have to live in poverty for the rest of our lives, but in a world where the best of the best seems to be the standard today, we can all afford to give some piece of our lives away to make someone else's better. It is important to remember that, whatever you do for those who are in need, the least of these, you are doing to and for God. This is something everyone should remember as we go throughout the lives that we are fortunate to be living.

Message:

Imagine that you are the one standing on the side of the busy highway with a cardboard sign. What would you want most? While answers would vary from food to cash, most of us would just want someone to show us the love of Christ that, if we were in that situation, we may have never heard of before. We wouldn't want someone to walk up to us with a list of questions and to ask us to sign something so that they can get community service credit for school. The love of Christ is not about a grade, or extra credit. Showing the love of Christ should be an activity that we engage in on an hourly, daily, weekly, yearly basis. The love of Christ is not about a credit, or a rubric. Showing the love of Christ is about telling, showing someone, whether they be the richest person in town or that guy sleeping under the bridge on your way to work in the morning, that true riches come because of Christ's love and grace. While we can work hard for the things that we want, how hard are we willing to work to give those same types of items to those who really need them?

Share It!

Using these questions, reach out to your friends on social media and get the conversation started!

1. *For where your treasure is, there will your heart be also.* With this in mind, where is your heart right now? Is it in your wallet? Is it behind the wheel of that car? Where is it?
2. What gives that thing that holds your heart its value?
3. What would it take for you to give that thing away or to lose it altogether?

Don't Get Comfortable

²⁶ If any man come to me, and hate not his father, and mother, and wife, and children, and brethren, and sisters, yea, and his own life also, he cannot be my disciple. ²⁷And whosoever doth not bear his cross, and come after me, cannot be my disciple.

Luke 14:26-27 KJV

So often, we feel that, because we follow Christ and because we are not living in a country where that is punishable by death, that we will never have to give anything up for the cause of Christ. We so often believe that Christianity will always mean a life full of blessings and prosperity. This is why so many enter a stage of life that seems to be filled with unfortunate, unexpected events, and they begin to turn away from Christ. Many people believe that life with Christ means that we will never have to give anything up. Sadly, this is an incredible misconception about living for Him.

Even in a country where our founding fathers guaranteed the freedom we have to exercise our faith in Christ, there will always be times in life when He requires us to sacrifice our finances, our family, and our home, to follow His plans for our lives. When we come to the point in our lives when we feel the conviction of Christ calling us to accept Him as our Savior, we probably are not sitting there in our chair or kneeling at the altar wondering if Christ will ask that we leave all that we know and love to follow Him. It seems that we are so overcome with the emotions that come with His convicting of our hearts, that we may forget what we are agreeing to. When we come to know Christ as our Savior, we are signing on that dotted line, that He now has complete control of our career, our education, our paycheck, and our family. When you think of it like this, suddenly the decision of coming to know Him is more than a five-minute decision in Sunday school. But what better way to spend one's time on earth, than following God's plan for their life that cannot fail and will never leave us in a place where we are on our own?

Why wouldn't you want to give all that you are and all that you have to the one who gave it to you in the first place? The answer is that after many years of life, we have grown comfortable in living life the way we have always lived it, and the possibility of changing that is quite honestly, terrifying to most people. If you have been living in the same neighborhood, in the same house, surrounded by the same people since you were born, it is likely that you would not be extremely fond of the idea of moving to Argentina, even though God may be calling you there to pursue missions. You would be starting completely over with your life in a place you know nothing about. In your current situation, you have it all! You have a job that allows you to live way above your means, you have a car that costs as much as some people get paid in an entire year, and suddenly, you are feeling the call of Christ to sell it all, and move to a place where the seasons are different, the people are different, the language is different, everything is different, and you don't know where to even start. But what if you just did it? What would you have to lose? You would be leaving behind your family, which would be the most difficult part, but you would be starting a whole new life and leaving behind your past to pursue this brand-new purpose that has been put in place for your life. Granted, this is not to say that this would be easy, but the Christian walk rarely is. God never promised that it would be easy. However, He did promise that He would walk with us through all its obstacles, as long as we choose to trust in Him and Him alone.

Message:

If you are coming into a relationship with Christ believing that this relationship will make life easier and get rid of trouble that may come your way, you are wrong and should not use this as criterion for coming into this relationship. There are many things that come from a relationship with Christ; forgiveness of sins, a place of refuge to run to in times of trouble, the assurance of knowing that everything that happens to you has been known about and planned around since the beginning of time, a relationship with the Creator of the universe, as well as many other benefits. Sadly, one of those is not the assurance that life will always be a smooth ride. As a matter of fact, when you exude Christ in your daily life and others notice, it could make life slightly more of a struggle at times. However, through all the struggle, Christ will be beside you to help you weather every storm that comes your way. Don't get comfortable, because change is always around the corner when you trust God to direct your path.

Share It!

Using these questions, reach out to your friends on social media and get the conversation started!

1. What is your biggest fear or apprehension when it comes to leaving your family and all that you know to begin chasing after God's calling for your life?
2. Is there a call that you have been feeling from God that you have avoided because it would cost too much in one way or another?
3. What is one thing that you would be afraid to leave if God called you to a place that required it?

The Power of One

[4]What man of you, having an hundred sheep, if he lose one of them, doth not leave the ninety and nine in the wilderness, and go after that which is lost until he find it? [5]And when he hath found it, he layeth it on his shoulders, rejoicing. [6]And when he cometh home, he calleth together *his* friends and neighbours, saying unto them, Rejoice with me, for I have found my sheep which was lost. I say unto you that likewise joy shall be in Heaven over one sinner that repenteth, more than over ninety and nine just persons, which need no repentance.

Luke 15:4-7 KJV

We live in a world today that puts so much emphasis on the power of the masses and the ability of a massive group of people to spark change for a cause that is trending at the time. Society has come to a point where it seems to assert that the needs and feelings of the many are more important than the needs of the individual. When laws are passed legalizing certain types of practices, it is because a majority of representatives for the American people said that this practice would be beneficial to society. This basically means that just because a few people are being harmed by this practice or have substantive concerns about the issue, they will just have to live with it, because the majority of the American people said that this was acceptable.

The interesting thing about this idea of the individual is that this is so much more than a slogan when we see it in a biblical context. Take, for instance, the family of God. When you become part of God's family, you become one of His sheep that He tends to day and night, as He watches over the herd to meet all their needs. If one sheep in a herd is not feeling well or is facing some sort of trial in life (we're obviously talking about humans at this point), He will run to that sheep and care for that sheep, even though He has ninety-nine other sheep to be concerned about keeping watch over. He runs to that one sheep in its time of need. He loves each one individually and is equally willing and determined to protect every single one.

Imagine that you are a parent, and if you are, imagine this scenario. You have been married to your spouse for the last five years, and over those five years, you have had, wait for it, ten children. After the fourth, you gave up on naming them after the apostles, so you began to get creative to distinguish each child in your mind. When children are young, they tend to be all over the place all the time. It is your responsibility as their parent to keep up with and nurture each child individually. If one child has a boo-boo, you care for it just like you would if it were one of the other children. However, what if you went outside to take the trash out, and you came back three minutes later, and during your routine roll call, one of the children are missing. Do you continue cleaning and just hope that the missing child shows up? Hopefully not. You probably drop what you are doing and go out searching for this child. When you find that he is reading a book in the treehouse in the backyard, you probably tell him to come down from the treehouse and you take him by the hand into the house.

This is similar to what Christ does to us as His sheep. Among the massive family of Christ, there is a lot of hurts, a lot of struggle, and a lot of wandering, and while the majority of the herd may be in a consistent pattern at times, there always seems to be those stragglers that can be seen breaking away from the herd, thinking that they will be undetected. However, Christ will always be right behind those people who begin to stray from Him because of some temptation to bring them swiftly back to them. However, there are also those people who run from God for fear of giving up their current lifestyle or addiction to follow Him. However, even in these scenarios, you can rest assured that God will be running after that one to bring it back to Him.

Message:

We all have and will face stages in our lives when we begin to wander or even run away from God either because we have done something we knew was against His will, or we have become involved in something that pulls us blindly away from Him before we realize what is happening. If you are attending a public college, or even a private college that does not teach Christian principles, it can be especially easy to find that you are slowly drifting out to sea and away from God and don't know how to get back without getting into more trouble. Maybe you've gotten into a crowd of friends that don't understand why you don't go to 'those' parties. Maybe that close friend of yours used to be a solid Christian, and He has begun to experiment with some dangerous stuff. These situations, if you stay in them too long, can pull you away from God, and into some deep water that you don't know how to handle on your own. However, Christ is right behind you coming to your aid in a time of great need. He will leave His herd of many, many sheep, to rescue you from your own wandering.

Share It!

Using these questions, reach out to your friends on social media and get the conversation started!

1. When you look at your life, your habits, your past, your mistakes, is there any part of your life that makes you think that God wouldn't chase after you? If so, what is that thing?
2. Think back to a time that you began to run from God. How could you tell that He was chasing after you? If this is you now, what are some things that you have noticed that would indicate this?
3. Think of one friend that seems to be running from God right now. Reach out to them and consider what you would need to hear if you were in that position.

Don't Become a Victim of Pray and Run
And being in agony he prayed more earnestly: and sweat was as it were
great drops of blood falling down to the ground.

Luke 22:44 KJV

Sometimes, when we go before God, we tend to be overly casual about it
because we have developed this idea today that because God is our friend,
we should speak to Him like we speak to our friends on our hall in the
dorm or how we speak to the people we hang out with. Some would say
that we should go before God and approach Him, the creator of the
universe, with phrases like, 'What up God? How's it going?' Yet we also
go to Him in the worst of times and praise Him (hopefully) in the best of
times, though the praise part can sometimes fall by the wayside when we
see successes that He provided us with. Sometimes it seems that rather
than seeking help or a better understanding of life's circumstances, we
treat this direct line to God as if it were submitting a ticket to the IT help
desk at our office or school. We go before Him, leave our request with
Him, and check out.

In this verse, Christ is in such fervent prayer with His father that has sent
Him to die at the hands of men, that He is sweating blood. How often are
we in such deep prayer with our Heavenly Father that we look down at our
shirt and notice drops of blood? While I would like to say that at least one
person has had that experience, I feel that is very unlikely, but this is not
to say that if you are not sweating blood, that you aren't doing it right.
What is being said, however, is that prayer should never be treated like a
box that you type something into and say 'OK' and then walk away and go
about life as usual. Prayer should remain constant in those times when it
seems that there is nothing left that we can do and quite simply, we need
help now. However, the same fervency of prayer in our walk with Christ is
expected during those times when things in our lives couldn't be better.

Prayer should not be something that you turn to when you have that test in
a week and you haven't looked at your notes once since the beginning of
the semester. Prayer is not a tool that you pull out of your belt when you
are failing a class and two weeks from the end of the semester, you begin
sweating bullets praying for a 'B' in the class. This is not how God
intended for this direct line to Him that is open 24/7/365 to be used. While
He intends for us to run to Him in times of trouble to become a refuge

from whatever storm we may be facing at the time, we must not pray for God to show up in our lives in a big way, while we sit back in our spiritual recliner and hope for the best.

God obviously expects us to follow Him through the hard times and the smooth-riding times that come our way with equal fervor and excitement. He doesn't want only part-time followers who only come around on payday or when the boss sends them an email that their performance is beginning to deteriorate. He wants us to come before Him and to remain at His feet when we get that raise at work or when we get that house and car paid off after all these years. He wants all us on the day you get that new job you have been looking for since you got laid off a year ago, and the day you find out that the company is closing its doors. He wants all you, all the time.

When Christ was on His knees praying to His father to deliver Him from this terrible circumstance, He did not tell God exactly what to do. In reality, He probably had the power to do that, but He chose instead to tell God that He would fully submit to His will, no matter the outcome. Let us also pray with such fervor while having an equal or greater amount of uncertainty about the results.

Message:

God does not ever deliver us into any situation without some a plan. If He sends a financial crisis your way and you don't know how you will make that tuition payment for the next year, you can bet that He knows exactly what will happen and the impact of that on your life. If you're struggling to find time to spend with your family because this job you are so grateful to have is consuming your life, you can rest assured that He has a plan for freeing up some of your time and allowing you to spend it where it matters most. Regardless of the situation, God will not bring you into it without some plan to bring you out of it. However, don't let the voice in your head tell you that God won't let you fail that class so don't even bother to show up. God expects that our fervent prayer be accompanied by effort on our part to ensure that we do all we can to ensure that His will becomes reality in the situation. God will always come through in some way, but we too must come through for Him.

Share It!

Using these questions, reach out to your friends on social media and get the conversation started!

1. When you pray, how do you view your communication with God? Is it a HELP button, or is it an ongoing line of communication to be invested in and developed over a lifetime?
2. When you face these moments of crisis in life, do you tend to sit at the feet of Jesus or run to Him and begin throwing everything in His lap in preparation to run?
3. What are some "Panic" button moments that have come into your life within the last few years?

Jesus is Not Your Emergency Plan

And the Word was made flesh, and dwelt among us, (and we beheld his glory, the glory as of the only begotten of the Father,) full of grace and truth

John 1:14 KJV

What an incredible truth this verse conveys! What we find in this verse in John is a single verse that shows us not only that Christ came to die on the cross, but that His ministry didn't stop there. He came to the earth to dwell among the people that He would soon die for. We so often remember His death on the cross, but forget all that He did before that day. He came down to be with us, to build a relationship with His people, with those who followed Him with all that they were. In that day, people were able to see Him in the flesh and yet, some still chose to deny Him and His stature as the Son of God.

How often do you see the dean of your college walking down the hallway observing the events of his school? Probably once or twice a year, and then you never see Him again until you get caught doing something or become a witness to something. Imagine if the dean of your school came into your classes and stood in the midst of the classes and pulled out that giant Bible that had been rumored to be on his bookshelf in his office, and began to preach in front of your class of four hundred students. While this would stun some at a Christian university, at a liberal university, this would likely be received with mixed reviews because this would clearly violate the status quo of that school and the tolerance and inclusiveness that it claims to stand for. This would not be something that would be seen as acceptable at most state-funded public universities.

Jesus came into a time on earth when people were used to worshipping inanimate manmade objects of wood or other natural material. Therefore, the concept that there was a man who suddenly came onto the scene claiming to be the only way one could one day see the face of God and gain eternal life was perceived as being utterly insane in the eyes of some. After hundreds of years of being told that there were many ways to Heaven if you acted right and said the right things, the sayings of Jesus were met with much tension and protest. If what this man said was true, this would turn these people's worlds upside down. This would immediately invalidate everything that they had ever been told up until that point. When these people began to hear that this man was saying that there was only one way to Heaven and that it was through Him, they were probably terrified.

Imagine that you walk into one of your classes on the first day of class, and your professor stands in front of the class and says that there is only one way to pass the class. This will likely be met with groans and complaints. The one way to pass the class is not to do a bunch of extra credit. You can't pass the class by doing a bunch of 'good' acts for the professor and fellow students. The only way to pass the class is to listen intently to the professor, come to know how he teaches the class and how he tests his students, and what he expects from his students. The only way to do this is to read and study the fifteen-page syllabus which contains all that you need to know and take intense notes on everything that he says because somewhere in those words, there is something that will come up at some point.

If you had a professor like this and ended up failing the class, how likely would you be to recommend him to other students? Probably not very likely. However, on the flipside, if you got to the end of the semester and passed the class with an A because you studied your hardest and came to know the professor at a deeper level by talking to him and developing a deeper understanding of why he does the things he does, how likely would you be to recommend this professor to other students? Probably very likely. What would you tell them about him? You would probably tell them that he is a difficult professor in that he requires a lot from his students. However, if you pay close attention to him and try to understand what he is teaching on a deeper level, you will be better able to develop a relationship with the professor and begin to understand why he says that there is only one way to pass the class.

Is this how we approach our relationship with Christ? Do we come into the relationship with the intention of studying His Word and listening for His voice in every moment or do we come into the relationship assuming that we will be okay if we just go to church and act like a good person? If we get involved in the children's ministry at church, we don't really need to know Him on a personal level, because he will see all the good stuff we are doing, and He will be so impressed that we won't really need to know Him on a personal level. We wonder why He does some of the things He does in the world and in our lives, but we will figure it out sooner or later if we wait around long enough. Does this make sense? To some people, it may, but to most, it probably sounds a little crazy. Unfortunately, this is how so many Christians lead their walk with Christ. Sure there are occasions when that lock-in at church comes around and you are doing five 'quiet times' a day and suddenly, you feel so close to God and you leave that lock-in on fire for God, and within two days, one of your best friends from school invites you over to watch that R-rated movie, and in those first five minutes when the first person is killed, that fire that was originally consuming your entire being had dwindled to a candle flame. The question is, how unquenchable is that fire that you got at that lock-in if you almost completely quenched it in two days?

When Christ came to this earth to tell people about how they could gain eternal life and a relationship with the God of the universe, He never intended for that relationship to last days. He wanted it to be a relationship that would carry that person from the day they accepted Him until the day that they met Him. He did not want it to last the entire weekend of that youth conference where everybody saw you raising your hands during worship. He intended for it to be with you through that busy week at school when you have five assignments due by Friday. He wanted that relationship to be with you through that month when you're trying to figure out how you're going to pay the bills because you had just been in a car accident and the bills are piling up faster than you can pay them. He intended for that relationship to carry you through the high times and the low times when you wonder what tomorrow holds. Don't let this relationship with Christ become an emergency option that you break out only when you need it. Let your relationship with Christ become a constant tool in which He dwells among you and all that you do, not just in the spiritual high times, but also in the spiritual valleys as well.

Message:

When Christ was sent to dwell among His people, He was not sent to the earth with instructions from God to just hang back and observe until somebody was in trouble. He dwelt among the people all the time. He desired then and desires now to be known among His people all the time and not only when they were facing some tragedy. He wanted these people who claimed to follow Him to know and to understand that He was there regardless of what circumstances may lie ahead. He didn't hang back until He heard a call for help. He was and still is an active God, who is constantly moving in people's lives, trying to make changes along the way, but first, those people need to get out of the way.

Share It!

Using these questions, reach out to your friends on social media and get the conversation started!

1. When God sent His Son into the world to dwell among His people, the goal in doing that was for Christ to eventually dwell inside those same people and become a part of their lives. Christ became like us so that we could become like Him. How have you seen yourself becoming more like Christ since you accepted Him as your Savior? If you haven't accepted Christ, what are some things that you are afraid He will change?
2. If you are a professing Christian, what are some ways that you have chosen to dwell among the types of people that Christ chose to intermingle with?
3. How has your service for the advancement of the Gospel changed your view of Christ's ministry on Earth?

You're Not Hiding Anything from God

[20]For everyone that doeth evil hateth the light, neither cometh to the light, lest his deeds should be reproved [21]But he that doeth truth cometh to the light, that his deeds may be made manifest, that they are wrought in God

John 3:20-21 KJV

How many people on the face of this earth would want to stand in front of the whole world on live television and admit to the world that you had cheated on that test in your freshman year of college? Who in their right mind would want to look their parents in the eye and tell them that you had been given a speeding ticket on the way to school? No one would likely want to do this because it would put us to shame and it would not be consistent with the values and lessons that our parents had taught us as we were growing up. This would be a source of shame (hopefully) to most young kids or young adults still under the authority of their parents. This would not be something that our parents would be proud of because it is something that causes them to question our judgment and maturity.

When we do something shameful, the last thing that we want to do is to bring it to the attention of our parents, because, let's face it until you tell your parents, you're not actually in trouble. Why do we feel this shame about certain things that we do out of the sight of those who love us and provide us guidance when we need it most? For that exact reason. When we spend our lives being given all this knowledge by our parents or by someone else who serves as an authority figure in our lives, we can't stand it at the time. We just can't wait to get out of there and back to our phone. But when we leave the house for college or when we finally get a job and are on our own in the world, we turn back to that wisdom and wish that we had listened to more of it when we had the chance. This is why, when we get in an accident or when we fail that test because we didn't take better notes in class, we feel shame having to tell our parents. We don't want to bring this kind of thing to light because we know that we will be reprimanded for it, whether that be a slap on the wrist or the loss of a privilege. The worst part is that we know that we had the wisdom to avoid the situation, but we chose to go ahead with it anyway.

Isn't this similar to how we approach our relationship with God? He has given us the tools of prayer and His Word to guide us through all life's situations, whether they are caused by us or thrown at us, and yet, so often we choose to ignore the advice He has given to us until we are backed into a corner that we don't know how to get out of. However, the worst part comes when we choose to try to get ourselves out of the situation, thinking that we don't need His help, and we just keep getting backed further into the corner, because we are so afraid to go before Him and admit that we strayed down the wrong path and now we're stuck. What's crazy about us doing this to God is that He doesn't care about insurance rates. God doesn't care about the money required to get you out of the situation. He only wants you to come before Him and admit that what you did was wrong and to seek forgiveness for it. The forgiveness that He offers is not an earthly forgiveness that says the act is forgiven but secretly sticks a note in your file so that he'll remember it forever. He permanently forgets it and does not hold it against us as is often the case with earthly forgiveness. On the flip-side of this idea, who would want to come before their parents and confess that you had made an A on that project that you had been working on for weeks, in addition to the paper that went along with it? If we were in a classroom right now, I'm assuming that every hand of anyone awake would shoot up immediately. Why are we so ready and willing to bring our good, virtuous acts to light? Because it shows our good side. It shows those around us that we have values that we stand for and that we can be successful. Most of us probably don't walk in the house at the end of the day slouching and mumble "I passed my hardest class with an A" [insert mournful voice here]. When we have successes that we are proud of, most of us can't get home fast enough to tell somebody about it. We can't wait to boast about what we did and to "bring it to light" as this passage says. However, why can't we be so forthcoming about our shortcomings? Why can't we walk in the door at the end of the day and tell our parents that we got a parking ticket today or we failed that test we didn't study for? We fear the consequences of our actions and this makes us hesitant to bring our actions to the attention of those we love and respect. While we want our positive, celebration-worthy actions to be emphasized, to have someone bring up that test that we failed or that parking ticket that we received, gives us that notorious knot in our stomach. Let us become just as eager and willing to lay our shortcomings and our mistakes at the feet of Jesus as we are to place our virtuous acts before men. Through doing this, forgiveness will likely come quicker, and we will not have that unnecessary burden on our shoulders that Christ died to alleviate.

Message:

Why hide the things in our lives that cause us to trip up? Is it because of pride? Fear? Anxiety? All these things are part of our human nature and all of them have their place in our lives at times, but when it comes to bringing your shortcomings before God, He already knows what you are going to bring before Him. To hide your sins and the other things in your life that cause you anxiety due to wrongdoing, is like trying to hide an elephant under your bed. You may think that He is unaware of it because you haven't acknowledged it, but He knew everything about it before it was even on your radar. In short, bring your failures and your successes before the Lord with equal haste and openness.

Share It!

Using these questions, reach out to your friends on social media and get the conversation started!

1. Over the course of your life, when have you had one of those moments where you openly and honestly brought your sin, your failure, your shortcoming before God with total honesty?
2. What are some of the consequences that you have seen because of not being open about your failures and shortcomings?
3. Where are some areas of your life that you find yourself tucking or stuffing things into the corner?

Make Room for God to Work

^{30}He must increase but I must decrease

John 3:30 KJV

Many times, as we scroll through our social media and we see people posting the second piece of this passage, it sounds good! It sounds like they are really submitting their life to God because they have posted this verse for the whole world to see. Soon, they begin to get all these positive reactions to the post and maybe even some people sharing the post because they so wholeheartedly agree with the sentiment of what is being said by this verse. However, regardless of how many times one has posted this verse, are we willing to make room for Christ in whatever venture we are currently a part of? Are we willing to give Him all the control over the venture and willing to live with the result? What if we are part of a major company and He takes away half of our employees? Will we remain decreased and allow Him to work or will we suddenly take center-stage again and do a reset of everything that God had done in the situation?

When we post that verse on social media, we probably think about its words for about half a second and then close the app and move on. We agree that for Christ to work, we must make ourselves less to make room for what He is going to do. Christ cannot work in a situation if we are there taking over every aspect of it ourselves. However, sometimes, it seems that we are only willing to decrease in certain aspects of the situation or even in our own lives. We want to see Christ give us success in that class we are struggling in, but we are afraid to give Him every part of ourselves so that He can do what needs to do to make that success come to fruition. We pray for God to shine forth in our small business, but we are too busy filling the city with ads, spinning signs on the highway and talking about all the education that we have, to give Him time to give us the success that we prayed for. Does this mean that you shouldn't do your part to make your situation better, whatever that may look like? No. However, what this does mean is that you should not become so busy doing things yourself that it becomes impossible for you to hear and understand what God is trying to do.

It's the same concept when we come before God for His assistance in a situation or even in life in general. Why would you spend night after night on your knees asking God for His intervention, and when He begins to intervene in the situation, we repeatedly tell Him how great our life is and how we have made our academics or our business so successful up until that point? Would you walk into a doctor's office and before he can get a word out, tell him all the possible conditions that you found on the internet? Maybe. But what if the doctor has a solution or a diagnosis that no one has ever heard of? What if God comes back with an opportunity to improve your business that you never even knew existed? If you refuse to decrease yourself and not make all that you are and all that you have become the focus of the conversation, you can never truly know how quickly God may come back with an answer.

Here's an example that some of the millennials will be familiar with. Imagine that your prayer is in the form of a text to a friend. When you send the text, you likely get some kind of notification when they read the text. However, as they begin to respond, you feel the need to say more, so they stop typing so that you can finish. As long as you continue talking and the more you feel the need to elaborate, the less of God's voice you will be able to hear. Until you decrease and let God become the center of your attention, you will not be able to hear what He is trying to tell you unless you take a backseat and begin to listen.

Message:

How willing are you to simply sit quietly and listen for God to speak in some way in answer to the question that you have been asking every day for the last year? Are you truly willing to decrease for the sake of God's increase in your life? Many would like to say that they are ready when He is, but too many times, this proves to be harder than they had originally thought. Don't be afraid to step away from the controls and give all control over to God. No matter your credentials, your pay scale, or your position, you will never be able to have as much of an impact on a situation as God will. With this in mind, why would you not *want* to give over all the control in a situation? Keep this in mind as you face what may seem to be an impossible situation, because when you are willing to decrease yourself in a situation, you are giving God so much more room to work, so that He can do what truly needs to be done instead of what you *think* needs to be done.

Share It!

Using these questions, reach out to your friends on social media and get the conversation started!

1. When looking at your walk with Christ up until this point, what are some areas where your influence over the situation attempts to stand taller than that of Christ?
2. What is the most intimidating part of giving God control of the situation you find yourself in at this moment?
3. What is that situation that you know you should give God control over, but aren't quite ready to do so?

Plant the Seed and Leave the Rest to Him

[37]And herein is that saying true, One soweth and another reapeth. [38]I sent you to reap that whereon you bestowed no labour: other men laboured and ye entered into their labours.

John 4:37-38 KJV

When you are in college, there is one thing that you can count on dealing with at least fifteen times over the next four years, and that is those dreaded group projects. Unless you get into a group with three or four of your best friends, you worry that nothing will get done. You worry that somebody in the group will slack off and not do their part, or someone will get sick the day you are scheduled to present. Therefore, rather than trusting that everyone in the group will always be available and trusting that everyone will do their part, many times, people will just decide that it is easier to do it themselves. It's a quicker and a more reliable way of doing the project. You always know how the project is progressing and you always have an idea of what needs to be done to get the project done on time.

Now, imagine this. You are given a group project, but you have never seen the members of your group. You don't go to the same school, and you may not even live in the same state or country, but you are given this project. This is often how it works when we witness to someone. We walk up to someone in the dining hall at school who seems to be struggling with something. You walk up to them and after learning about their situation, you ask if they have ever accepted Christ as their Savior. They say 'no'. After sharing the Gospel with this person and explaining to them what it means to have a relationship with Christ, you pray with them about their situation, and with a thank you and a hug, you go your separate ways. While you had hoped that there would be a decision made at that time, the person said that it just wasn't the right time. You have a sort of knot in your stomach because you fear there may never be a good time for the decision. However, during this encounter, you showed the love of Christ by listening to the person and praying with them about whatever situation they may be experiencing. It now becomes the opportunity for someone else to water that seed that you had just planted. This is where the group project concept comes into play.

You have to trust that God will bring the right person into their path who will water that seed and bring it to fruition. Often, this is the hardest part of the process of witnessing to someone. That person now has much more of an understanding of what it means to be a follower of Christ and to have a relationship with Him, and it is very possible that someone will show up at their door one night and reap the harvest of the seed that you had just planted. While you do not necessarily get that golden star in Sunday school for bringing someone to Christ, what you do have is the assurance that a seed has been planted in that person's life and that someone else will have the opportunity to see that person give their heart to Christ when they finally decide that they have had enough of their old life and that they are ready to give Christ full control of their future, their finances, their education, and everything else that makes up their life. Are you willing to put all your work and labor in the hands of some unknown person? Are you willing to trust that they will do what it takes to guide this person whom you may never see again to a place where they are willing to give their life to Christ? If your answer to this question is yes, then that is great. If your answer is no, then you may want to stop and figure out why you initially witnessed to this person? Was it so that someone would see you? Was it so that you would get that community service project done at the last minute? Maybe it was so that you could add a tally to your "People saved" chart on your wall. Either way, if your answer was anything other than to glorify God and expand His Kingdom, you may want to consider reevaluating your motives for doing what you did.

Message:

Witnessing is almost always a group project. When you witness to someone and do not bring them to the point of making a decision, it is not because your copy of the Gospel is defective or because you said the wrong words. If your witnessing encounter does not end in a decision, it is because God has placed another person or circumstance in that individual's life who will water and fertilize that seed, and at that point, it could take fifteen different people or one circumstance to bring this person to Christ. Either way, it is important that we as Christians realize that if someone does not come to Christ as a result of our delivering of the Gospel, God is not in Heaven turning our card. However, think about what the possibilities would have been had you not delivered the Gospel versus the outcome of doing so. In one case, you planted a seed to be watered and nourished through the delivery of His Word. In the other case, you did nothing. Never miss an opportunity to witness to someone. Whether you are the reaper or the sower, you will leave that person in better shape than you found them.

Share It!

Using these questions, reach out to your friends on social media and get the conversation started!

1. When you think of the Gospel -centered conversations that you have had within the last few years, how often have you considered yourself to be the one who reaps the seeds and how often have you been the one who had the privilege to sew them?
2. Who, in your own life, has been one who sews seeds of Gospel -centered truth in your heart? Who has been one of the individuals who reaped some sort of result from the seeds that had been sewn?
3. What kind of seeds have you been sewing in the hearts and minds of those around you?

In Christ, We Find Our Light
Then spake Jesus again unto them saying, I am the light of the world: he that followeth me shall not walk in darkness, but shall have the light of life.

John 8:12 KJV

Imagine that you are walking to your bedroom, and halfway there, everything goes black. It's so dark in the house that you can't even see your hand in front of your face. You are caught completely off-guard by the darkness that has suddenly surrounded and disoriented you. Until that time, you thought you knew your house like the back of your hand, but in the darkness, you are suddenly unsure of where to put your foot next for fear of falling down the steps or tripping over something. This is the kind of darkness that Christ is talking about here. He's talking about those times when it seems you have become spiritually blind in the world and you don't know where to go next because you worry that you will fall into unforeseen circumstances.

He's talking about those moments when you get that phone call that you have been laid off from the job that you were counting on to help with your student loans. You get a call from the doctor asking you to bring someone with you to his office as soon as possible. In these moments, it seems like darkness can quickly engulf one's heart. You look around and suddenly, you are confused by all that is going on around you. You fear every step that you take because one wrong step seems to be all that stands between you and a change of plans. However, what if I told you that there was good news? The good news is that there is a way to ensure that you will never again be left in such darkness, and His name is Jesus.

When one makes the decision to follow Jesus with their whole heart, that person can rest assured that they will never have to be left in the dark to fend for themselves ever again. You can know for certain that there will never come another day where you don't know where to step next in your walk of life. When you agree to follow Jesus, you can know for certain that He will be lighting your path all day every day. What this does not mean, however, is that you will always know where you are going. You will not always know why He allowed that call from the doctor giving you that life-altering news. You will not always know why He let that job be taken from you so suddenly. However, what you will always know if you follow Jesus, is that there is a road ahead of where you are right now. In that road, there will be bumps. There will be potholes that throw you off. There will be smooth roads that have not a single flaw. However, you may not know when each one is coming. Maybe you just finished that test that you thought you had failed miserably, and you get it back and have a B on it. Suddenly, it seems things are going well, and you return to the dorm, and you find an email that your scholarship has been suspended. To you, this may seem like a closed road, but to God, it could simply be a pothole that is simply used to encourage you to slow down and realize that He will make a way, no matter the circumstance. However, because of the light that Christ brings to those who trust Him for guidance and help in times of trouble, you have a light on your path that allows you not to be blinded by this circumstance. However, often, if we feel tempted to follow a path that Christ has not laid for us, but rather one that has been commonly followed by the world, the light of Christ will not always show us what we want to see, and therefore, you never know what you may encounter on that path. If God seems to be leading you to a job opportunity that pays slightly lower than the one that you lost, and suddenly, one day while you are checking your email, an offer pops up for a job that uses your degree and it pays double what you made originally, you may want to stop to consider why God hadn't laid this in your path. You ask yourself what the problem is with taking this opportunity. The problem is that taking this job would mean leaving behind the opportunity that God had originally been leading you to. This would be like taking your minivan on an off-road excursion. You're fine for a little while, but eventually, you will run into some unexpected obstacles. You interview for this job, and at the end of the interview, the manager says, "Well, I think we have found the perfect person for this job! Are you okay with drinking? We always have drinks with our clients". Suddenly you realize that there was a reason that God was not leading you to this company. You wandered from the illuminated path before you and ended up in unmarked territory that held some very unpredictable things. You strayed from His light and you became blind to what was around you. Therefore, if you only follow the illuminated path that God has set before you, you will never have to be concerned about what you may be stepping into. You can know that whatever may lie ahead is already included in God's plan and that He already knows how he's going to get you through it.

Message:

Basically, what this comes down to is that God has laid a path for us to follow before we were even born. He has prepared this path and given us all that we need to never stray from the path. Sadly, sometimes life will throw things our way that seem to be a continuation of the path, but in reality, it is an attractive distraction that is often disguised as part of God's plan, but is dangerously far from it. If you begin to follow the wrong path, you will find that you are constantly falling while chasing what seems to be the goal, when it is actually a cleverly disguised decoy. One of the greatest things about the Christian walk is, yes you will stumble occasionally, but God will never lead you into a situation where you can't see your next step. He may not give you a full view of the entire path from start to finish, but you can know with the utmost amount of certainty that He will never leave you blind in the dark.

Share It!

Using these questions, reach out to your friends on social media and get the conversation started!

1. In those moments when you encounter those unforeseen circumstances, where do you turn to find light to guide you?
2. Have you ever been in a situation where the light that you found turned out to guide you down the wrong path? What did you learn?
3. When thinking of Christ as being the ultimate source of light, how long do you have to linger in those moments of spiritual darkness before you begin seeking the light that He offers?

There's More to a Job than the Benefits

If the Son therefore shall make you free, then you shall be free indeed

John 8:36 KJV

Have you ever thought about what it means to be truly free from something? Freedom gives this idea of liberation. It suggests that someone has been released from some burden or punishment. When prisoners are released from prison, most of the time, they are free in only one sense of the word, because they are either on parole or they have to do community service to prove that they can handle being outside of those prison walls.

The freedom that is written about here is a complete and total freedom from every aspect of the burden that had once held down an individual. To most people, this is a sin. Because Christ died for the sins of the world, His blood broke the bonds that sin had placed on every person on the planet. His blood completely got rid of any trace of the bondage that came with sin. However, the problem that often keeps people bound to their sins of their past, present, or any sin that may occur in the future, is that individual's own mind. It seems that we often feel that it is impossible that Christ eliminated the power of sin on the world. That would be way too easy…right? We find it so hard to believe that we don't have to wake up every morning with that sin in the back of our mind. It's as if part of our human nature makes us want to carry all that unnecessary baggage around with us even though it has been taken care of.

What if you had just gotten out of the hospital and several weeks later when you went to pay for the time you spent there, you found a balance of $0.00 where the bill was supposed to be. Most people would be calling the billing department to figure out who had made the accounting mistake because you simply could not understand why that balance had zeroed out after your extended stay. When you finally reach the billing department, they tell you that a mysterious donor had paid the bills of many patients and you were one of them. What would you think about this? If you're anything like me, you would want to hand over the money just to be safe because you simply could not believe that your hefty balance had been taken care of.

This is how many people view the gift of salvation that comes only through Jesus Christ. People come into the relationship thinking, what's the catch? People find it so hard to believe that all one must do to see the face of God one day, is to give their life to Christ and to live for Him for the rest of their time on earth. There is no catch. However, soon people begin to understand what tends to make the Christian walk so difficult. We sign on the figurative dotted line agreeing to hand everything over to Christ, and when we reach a point in our lives when we crave control and realize that we have given it all over to Him, we realize that this whole living for Christ thing is a little bit harder than it sounded at first. However, no matter how hard it gets, we always have the assurance that we are truly free from the sin that once had such a strong hold on us.

We want the position of being a follower of Christ, but we don't want to pay the taxes that come with the job. Everyone loves the benefits of becoming a Christian, but when they realize that there is more to it than just the benefits, they begin to realize why so many people turn away from the relationship when they get older. Therefore, when you are sitting in that church pew and you begin to feel the conviction in your heart, take a second and ask yourself if you are only coming into the relationship for the job title and paycheck, or if you are willing to pay the taxes that come along with it.

Message:

Have you thought about it? Why are you in the relationship that you chose to enter into with Christ? Are you in it because you know that Christian classmate and they seem to be successful? Are you coming into it because you want to be able to go out with that witnessing group at your church without the guilt of not being a Christian? While these are not terrible reasons, they are mostly self-serving and those will not get you very far. However, if you examine the risks and benefits of a relationship with Christ, and you decide that you are willing to surrender all that you have, including your life for the relationship, then you have come to a point in your thought process where you have thought beyond the benefits and are also considering the risks of this life-changing decision.

Share It!

Using these questions, reach out to your friends on social media and get the conversation started!

1. When you came into this relationship with Christ, if you have done so, were there any "benefits" that you were seeking in the beginning?
2. What are some secret benefits that you still secretly hope to gain from this relationship?
3. When you look around at other Christ-followers, in what ways do you find yourself making comparisons between God's plans for the other person?

One Way

⁸Peter saith unto him, Thou shalt never wash my feet. Jesus answered him, If I wash thee not, thou hast no part with me. ⁹Simon Peter saith unto him, Lord, not my feet only, but also *my* hands and *my* head.

John 13:8-9 KJV

In this scenario, we are seeing Jesus down on His hands and knees washing the feet of His disciples. In this moment, Jesus is not a king sitting on a throne, but rather a servant who has humbled Himself to the point of washing these feet that probably haven't been cleaned in quite some time. This king that came down from that incredible place that we look forward to inheriting one day was now in the position of any other servant, and yet, these disciples knew with the utmost certainty that they were nowhere near worthy of having their feet washed by this man. They knew that it should've been them down on that floor, washing the feet of Jesus. However, what they failed to realize then, and what people fail to realize today, is that, when Jesus washed the disciples' feet, He demonstrated that He was, and still is, the only one who could truly cleanse us. He knew that, ultimately, there was no other way.

The interesting thing about this passage is Simon Peter's response to Jesus' service. For most people, to have the Son of God wash their feet with His own hands would be an incredibly humbling experience. Most would not have the breath or the words available to ask if they could do unto Jesus as He had just done unto them. However, we need to realize that Christ wasn't necessarily looking for someone to wash His feet because He wasn't there simply to rid the disciples' feet of the dirt and grime from the day's journey. He came to the disciples to wash them, to cleanse them in a way that only He was able to. Sure, had He not done this, the disciples would probably have washed their feet elsewhere. However, what we see in this situation is this image of Jesus demonstrating to His disciples and to the world what it looks like to serve those around them. We see this man who would eventually die for the sins of the world humbling Himself to the point of taking on a task that would today be seen as one of the most unsanitary and quite simply gross things anyone could partake in.

The interesting thing about Simon Peter's response to this was that he did not seem to understand that Jesus wasn't pulling a publicity stunt. He couldn't understand the idea that there was more to this act than getting rid of dirt. He didn't get that the Son of God Himself was giving these disciples a gift that they could never obtain on their own. Unfortunately, so many in the world today continue to live their lives in a way that says, "Wanna bet? Watch this", believing that there must be another way. Sadly, the only thing that eventually comes as a result of this is a bunch of good behavior that doesn't really lead to anything significant in terms of bringing glory to God. Whether it be going on that summer mission trip with your church or serving every week with that organization on campus, nothing that we can do, no amount of service or words or songs or anything else that holds such great value in the church today will be strong enough or good enough to become a substitute for the cleansing power of Christ. However, when we choose to implement these and use them as tools to help us grow in Christ and become more intimate with Him, we will be able to make these assets in our ministry, whatever that may be that will help us do what we are called to do as the church. We will begin to understand that it's not necessarily what we can do to receive the gifts because there's nothing we can do, but rather what we choose to do after we have received them that will have eternal significance. This will become a huge determinant as to the impact of these gifts on the world. However, first, we must decide to ask for them, and then to use them. Once we make this decision, we will be able to begin pursuing the path, the mission that God has set before us. However, to accept this mission, you must first be willing to understand and admit that when trying to reach these gifts and this mission, there is only one way, and His name is Jesus.

Message:

Have you ever found yourself in the place of being that person who was determined to be the exception to the rule? I think that it would be safe to say that we all have found ourselves in this position at one point or another. However, when it comes to being forgiven of sin, as if it has not been made clear by now, there is but one way and one way only and that is through the cleansing power of Christ Himself. Is this way necessarily easy? No. Is it worth it? Of course. Does this mean that people won't try to find an exception or an alternative? Definitely not. However, as the church, let us become intentional about sharing who Christ is and the lasting, unique, incomparable gift He so freely offers through the cross.

Share It!

Using these questions, reach out to your friends on social media and get the conversation started!

1. In this passage, we see Christ on His hands and knees serving His disciples through the washing of their feet. In your Christian walk, how do you "wash the feet" of those around you?
2. When you engage in these acts of service, what is your initial motivation? Do you find yourself with wandering eyes to see who notices, or do you find that you use this service as an opportunity to be a "little Christ" to that person?
3. What kinds of conversations have come from your acts of service?
4. Take a moment and open your social media. Post a status asking your friends and followers how you can serve them. Allow Christ to use you and to allow you to become His hands and feet even if it is only for a day.

Christ is Your Foundation

I am the vine, ye *are* the branches: He that abideth in me, and I in him, the same bringeth forth much fruit: for without me ye can do nothing.

John 15:5 KJV

Anyone with any basic knowledge of agriculture knows that the vine of crops such as pumpkins or grapes is the lifeline of that fruit and without that vine, any watering or fertilization that is done by humans or machines is done completely in vain because if that vine is severed in some way, that crop has lost its means of getting food and water. The vine gives support while the crop grows, it provides nutrients, and without these two processes, that plant will simply wither away and become worthless.

How often do you walk through the grocery store and see grape vines growing up from the ground? That does not sound like any grocery store I've ever been to. When grapes or pumpkins have reached their desired point of maturity, the person responsible for harvesting that crop cuts that vine, and at that point, the pumpkin basically begins to die because it does not have that connection to nutrients that was once there. Now that the vine has been cut, that pumpkin or that bunch of grapes has stopped growing and is basically dead.

In the same way that pumpkins and grapes rely on their vines to provide them with support and nutrients while they are in the process of growing to their full capacity, Christ serves as our vine, enabling us to grow through His pouring out of love and mercy upon our lives, and through His providing of support throughout our journey through the life that He has given us. As long as we stay close to Him, we have the privilege of enjoying His love and mercy and we are able to experience the growth that comes as a result of that. Unfortunately, there often comes a time, especially in college, when we are beginning to be exposed to different ideas and we begin to face storms that we now have to weather on our own, and when that time comes, we often struggle to stay bound to that vine that has been our support and our lifeline for a majority of our lives. When this happens, we often begin to question if we really know that God is even real because that one professor in our first class of freshman year said that He wasn't.

We often face opposition, some of it from the professor himself. It is in situations such as these that we can often become drained and we begin to have a more difficult time withstanding those storms. Eventually, it seems that our vine has begun to break, and we begin to realize that it is truly impossible to do anything apart from that vine that has been our support and our nourishment for so long. However, when you stay strongly bound to the vine that supports and nourishes you, you will begin to recognize that God was using those storms to give you strength for what lies ahead. This means that when you face that opposition from that professor at school, or when you struggle to share the Gospel with one of those outspoken atheists in your class, that God is beginning to train you through these experiences to be able to better reach those kinds of people in the world once you are outside of that campus, and that city where you go to college.

No matter where you work or attend school, there will always be opposition to your belief in the truth of the Gospel. This will occasionally tend to wear away at that vine of nourishment and support that God gives us through His Word and His plan. However, what this means is that you simply must dig deeper into your foundation in the Gospel to grab that nourishment and to keep yourself firmly rooted in the power of its truth.

Now, ultimately, as if it has not been made clear already, in this life as a follower of Christ, your vine will be weathered. Your roots in Christ will be tested by the world daily in some way. This is a truth that we simply must understand and accept. However, now you must ask yourself what you're going to do about it. What are you going to do to counteract that? Will you simply sit by and let the world take its best shot at you with no plan for recovery? Or will you build up your defenses against these types of storms so that when they come, you will be able to defend against and recover from them quickly? The choice is yours, but your decision will determine how strong your roots in Christ will be when those storms come. Will you be ready?

Message:

When you read this verse, you kind of begin to understand the scope of God's love and provision for His people. He doesn't bring us into the world and then leave us out there to fend for ourselves. He brings us into the world and from the time of our birth, He shapes us and molds us for a specific purpose. This purpose is not determined by what is printed on your degree or how many different cords you are wearing at graduation. The purpose that God is preparing you for will be something that, no matter how hard you try, you will never be able to escape. You will never be able to completely avoid the purpose that God has for your life. You may have grown up thinking that what missionaries do is admirable and an awesome cause, but you would never become one because you are afraid to fly. You may have spent those two years at community college and as you sat through biology, you knew that you would never become a doctor. However, one day, you get information from one of the state schools near you about their medical school. It's little things like this that God so often uses to mold you and prepare you for the purpose He has for your life. While you can always try as hard as you want to run away from God's purpose for you, applying for accounting positions along the way, you can never run so fast that His plan will not be able to stay ahead of you.

Share It!

Using these questions, reach out to your friends on social media and get the conversation started!

1. When considering this idea that Christ is our *vine,* what have you been doing to nourish and strengthen your connection to the vine?
2. Name one person in your life that pours into you to strengthen the roots that hold this vine in place?
3. How much are you taking off the vine and how much are you pouring into it?
4. Find one person on social media for whom you can help to nourish that vine and help it to grow stronger.

Show the Love to Others that God Has Shown to You

[9]As the Father hath loved me, so have I loved you: continue ye in my love. [10]If ye keep my commandments, ye shall abide in my love; even as I have kept my father's commandments and abide in his love.

John 15:9-10 KJV

There is so much to be unpacked within this verse, but first, we must stop and recognize the gravity of that first portion. What He is saying in this verse, is that the amount of love that the God of the universe has for His own child is the same amount of love with which His Son who died for the sins of the world, loves us. Let us also recognize how unworthy we are to receive such love. For this reason alone, this verse is so incredible.

Time and time again, as we read through the Gospel, we find example after example where God shows His love for us in unmatchable, undeserved ways. However, one of the biggest things about this love that Christ speaks repeatedly to His disciples and the crowds about is the fact that it is completely unconditional. He doesn't place any disqualifications in this verse. He doesn't tell us what we could do to lose this love that He so graciously provides. He only tells us what we can do to receive it. Like so many other instances, He doesn't tell us to see the attached terms and conditions for receiving this love and keeping it. He doesn't want to take away His love, just like a parent does not make a child sign on the dotted line at the time of their birth agreeing to the terms and conditions of a parent's love. This is because that parent does not want to withhold their love from their own child, and in most cases, they never do.

The only sort of condition that Christ provides for receiving this love that is being offered, is that we follow His commandments. Granted, doing this alone will not save someone. If this were the case, salvation would be through an action on our part, and not through something that He had already done. However, once someone has come to know Christ as their Savior, these commandments that are laid out throughout God's Word will serve as a template for living a godly life. Because it is a template, it is up to us to fill in the details, such as how we will love our neighbor, or how we will reach the lost and the least of these. Fortunately, God gives us a very reliable source to help us begin to understand how we can go about doing these things.

There is also a kind of difficult part about being on the receiving end of unconditional love. The difficult part about this is that not only are we the recipients of this love, but we are also called to spread that love and to do so just as unconditionally as it was and is spread to us. This can often be difficult for most people. There is always someone in everyone's life who they see walk in the door at work or in class, and they cringe because of something that this person has done to them or because of stories about that person's past. But God calls us to love that individual just as much as we love our best friend that we have been rooming with for the last two years.

There are so many people in this world who some people find hard to love. Some people see loving certain people as being almost criminal. However, it is important to remember that Jesus was hanging on that cross between two thieves, and as they begged Him for a place in His kingdom, Jesus tells these men in Luke chapter 23, that they will have a place with Him in paradise. He had every reason in the world to tell these men that they were not worthy of even looking in the direction of His kingdom. However, rather than doing that, He invited them in. He didn't tell them that because they were thieves, they did not meet the criteria for entering into His kingdom. Therefore, with this being the standard, we have no reason to deny anyone access to the Gospel that holds the key to a new life and access to the Father. We have no right to let someone's sin become a hindrance to their ability to have a relationship with the one who can heal any situation. Also, even if we did have that right, who would want to carry the burden of depriving someone of a relationship that could change everything for them?

Message:

The central message of this passage can be summed up in one word, and that word is *love.* Love is not something that you only show to those who you agree with. Love is not something that you only show to those who you approve of. Love is something that you show to those who do things that are not acceptable by society. Love is something that you show to those who wrong you in some way. Love is something that you show to those who do evil to you. These are all people to whom you should show love, because at one point or another, you have been at least one of these people to God. When you do wrong according to God's law, He still loves you. When do evil in the sight of the Lord, He still loves you. When you act in ways that God deems unacceptable, He still loves you. Therefore, if God loves you in all these situations, why shouldn't you do the same to those who are ultimately just like you?

Share It!

Using these questions, reach out to your friends on social media and get the conversation started!

1. How have you chosen to love those around you? Acts of service? Words of Encouragement?
2. When is it the most difficult for you to love someone? What do you usually do in these situations?
3. Think of one person that you may have the "cold shoulder" towards at the moment. Reach out to that person via text or social media and make this verse come to life!

WARNING: Tribulation (and Relief) Ahead

These things I have spoken unto you, that in me ye might have peace. In the world, ye shall have tribulation: but be of good cheer; I have overcome the world.

John 16:33 KJV

How often do we see those ads on TV advertising some kind of new product or medicine? In every instance where the person is seen after they have been taking the medicine or using the product, they always seem to be smiling and having the best time. How do they look before taking the medicine or using the product? They look completely miserable. The picture is always black and white and they're always doing things wrong for the purposes of the ad. Isn't that how we often imagine the Christian walk? Before we enter into the relationship with Christ, we imagine that we are walking around depressed and feeling down on our luck, and after we come into that relationship with Him, suddenly the picture fills with color and we are all smiles and life is suddenly good again. Is this accurate? For the majority of people, the answer is that this is far from the truth.

For many people, they may often consider their life before Christ better, by their standards, then the life that they are living after Christ. They look at the life they are living with Christ in the picture, and they wonder why they have been taking the medicine or why they have had the product, so to speak for so many months/years, and they are suddenly missing all that stuff that they were able to be a part of in their old way of life. This verse gives a little bit of an understanding of that.

When Jesus died on the cross, He didn't die to give us a perfect life with no trouble or circumstances that would occasionally test us and challenge our faith. He didn't die on the cross so that we would be able to live completely trouble free for the duration of our lives. He died on that cross to conquer the ultimate consequences for our sin. He did that so that we would not have to. Many are probably thinking, *Well, yeah. That's Sunday school 101.* However, what people so often fail to understand about this is that God never promised that because of His Son's death on the cross, or because of His nature as a loving and merciful God, that there would not be trials and tribulation in this life that we have been given on earth. This verse gives us clear evidence of that. He never said that any of this would be easy or that we would love every minute of it. Fortunately, He doesn't stop there. That comma in the middle serves as God's way of saying, "But wait! There's more!"

In the second half of the verse, Christ gives us that glimmer of hope that can so often push people through those hard times of the loss of a job or the loss of a family member or some other unforeseen circumstance. This second half of the verse is what makes it so incredible. He doesn't end the verse by telling us that we'll just have to figure it out on our own. He doesn't tell us that we'll just have to get over it. He tells us that He has overcome the world. He has removed that burden from us. He has taken it upon Himself to take care of the ultimate cause for all this pain and suffering that we experience almost daily in some way on this earth. He has taken it out of our hands and made it His priority to deliver us from these circumstances. He gives us that hope that, even in the midst of all the *stuff* that He tells us we will witness during our time on earth, from the pain to the struggles that so often seem to have no purpose, we can triumph over those struggles, not because of anything that we can do or say, but because He ultimately gave us an escape route from all that. He has given us an out for all that causes us pain on this earth. What's great is that it's free to anyone who chooses to accept it. Granted, sometimes He may not make that exit door immediately obvious, but when we trust Him to bring us through whatever circumstance we may be facing at the time, you will slowly begin to realize that the grasp that this circumstance or that situation has on your life is slowly beginning to loosen. However, it is up to us to decide whether we will take His perfectly planned escape route or if we will just start digging our way out to see where we end up. Which route will you take?

Message:

Struggle will always be a part of life until the day that Christ returns to bring those with Him who have put their trust in Him. As a matter of fact, He tells us that things will only get worse from here. The closer we get to His return, the worse the world is going to get. There is nothing that we can do to escape it, except to take the route that He has given. He tells us to trust in Him, live our lives according to His commandments, and to tell others about this escape route so that they too can experience the freedom from the grasp of sin. He calls us to tell them about opportunity to seek refuge from the struggles that so often plague this world we live in. Let us never forget that there is an escape available to us, and let us always remember that this escape is not meant to be kept a secret.

Share It!

Using these questions, reach out to your friends on social media and get the conversation started!

1. When have you found it difficult to believe this passage? When did you begin to see the validity of the second portion?
2. In your own life, where do you find yourself at the moment? In the tribulation portion or in the portion where Christ has overcome the world?
3. Reach out to someone on social media who seems to be going through a rough patch. Be that light, that relief to them that you have longed for in the past.

Keeping Our Promises After the Fact

And it shall come to pass, *that* whosoever shall call on the name of the Lord shall be saved

Acts 2:21 KJV

In this verse, we find a single verse that shows the inclusiveness of Christianity and Christ's message. Multiple times in the Bible, we find that word whosoever. This word means that there are no exclusions. If you only do this, you will have life through the blood of Christ. If you only call on the name of the Lord, you will be saved. While this is true about salvation by grace from sin, there is also another kind of salvation that is being referred to here. The other type of salvation that is being referred to is this idea of being saved from a circumstance that you find yourself in. The act of calling on the name of the Lord to deliver you does not become null and void when you become a Christian and have repented of your sins.

The idea of salvation that is brought forth in this verse is speaking more to the salvation that we experience in the midst of a circumstance that we cannot handle on our own. When you have reached that point at your job when you're on the verge of handing in your notice, go before the Lord and lay that situation at His feet, and in His time and in His own way, He will bring you salvation from that situation. It may not be tomorrow, and it may not be two weeks from now. It could be two years from now when you feel that you are at your wit's end. However, He will deliver you from that situation in one way or another. Now, this is not to say that if you don't pay the power bill, that if you pray to Him not to have the power cut off, that He will necessarily soften the heart of the person sitting at those controls. However, there are certain things that come our way in life that we cannot deliver ourselves from and we are often forced into prayer through these situations to ask for His provision in the situation.

One thing that we have in this verse that we do not often get in life, aside from those pesky infomercials is a solid, reliable guarantee. In this verse, it does not say that if you meet this criterion, you will be considered for salvation from this circumstance. It does not say that if you are within a certain salary range, that your salvation request ticket will come to God's desk. It gives us two words that form a guarantee: "whosoever" and "shall". It doesn't matter what level of education you have. It doesn't matter what your permanent record looks like. He simply asks that we pick up that direct line to God's office and ask for His help in this situation.

He asks the same thing of those who are ready to give their life to Him. He doesn't ask for a specific prayer. He doesn't ask for a specific level of biblical knowledge. He simply wants someone who will come and bow at His feet and say "Here I am, Lord. What will you have me to do?" This is often difficult for many people. So many people want to pray and repent of their sins and then run out of the door before they get an assignment they aren't too crazy about. So often, we go before the Lord in our times of desperate need, and when we begin to feel like He isn't listening to us, we begin to give our lives completely over to Him, but we do it somewhat blindly, as if we believe that He needs something from us before He will fulfill the desires of our heart. Before we know it, we are telling Him that we will do whatever He wants us to do, if He will only save us from this one situation. The problem is that, just like when we promise our mom that we will do those chores for a week to repay the cost of that money she put in our account, we get the thing that we had been asking for and we suddenly forget the promises that brought that became somewhat of a condition that was connected to our request. We become so relieved when we get what we have been asking for, that we forget what we had promised in return. Do not let your walk with Christ be defined by a long path of broken promises for services rendered.

Message:

In this verse, God makes a promise to His people. He promises that if we only call on His name, He will save us. What if He got so excited that we were calling on His name that He forgot to save us? This would leave us in a pretty bad spot and it would likely make us question everything that we thought that we knew about Him. With this in mind, imagine how He must feel when we make all these promises to turn back to Him if He will only take this thing or that off our back, and when that weight is absent from our lives, the promises that we made to turn back to Him or to be more devoted to Him vanished into thin air. The problem is that God remembers that broken promise, and we will one day be accountable for those broken promises when we stand before Him in heaven. That is a level of accountability that we can never truly escape. The great thing is that if we call upon His name to save us, He will, regardless of our past record on paying up on our promises. But imagine the joy that He will feel if we live up to our promise to worship Him because of what He has done for us and what He continues to do. Imagine what would happen if we gave Him the glory and honor that we promised Him for the rest of our lives. This would be the ultimate promise and to keep it would be the ultimate gift to your Heavenly Father.

Share It!

Using these questions, reach out to your friends on social media and get the conversation started!

1. When was the last time that you shared this message with someone who needed it?
2. If you have accepted Christ, how often do you refer to this verse in your own walk?
3. While considering the first question, take a moment and reach out to someone that doesn't seem to be following Christ. Whether it be on social media or through a text message, use that opportunity to share this message with that individual. You could be the first to expose them to this life-changing, life-saving message.

No Other Name

[11]This is the stone which was set at nought of you builders, which is become the head of the corner. [12]Niether is there salvation in any other: for there is none other name under Heaven given among men, whereby we must be saved

Acts 4:11-12 KJV

Do you ever feel that you are being constantly rejected by your own people? Do you ever think that there is no way you will be able to come out on the other side of this in a better place? This verse is evidence that there is hope beyond whatever circumstances you're in right now. Many translations of the first part of this verse say, "the stone that was rejected by the builders". This stone that Luke is speaking of is Christ. Christ was rejected by His own people because they didn't see Him as being a sufficient solution to the problems they were having. There must be a better way. They tossed Him aside as an insufficient solution because they knew there had to be something better that they themselves could do on their own. This is why they were startled and offended when He began to preach about being the only way to achieve true forgiveness of sins and having true access to eternal life. In John Gill's Exposition of the Bible, Gill considers this when he argues that these builders, priests, and other authorities within the church "[rejected] the stone of Israel, and instead of Him as a foundation, built themselves, and others, on the traditions of the elders, and their own righteousness"[1]. Here, we begin to understand how undervalued and misunderstood Jesus really was during that time.

Today, we find ourselves in the same place. Even though Jesus, as well as other voices in the Bible, tell us that He is the only way and that true forgiveness and redemption can only be found in Him, so many people today are so desperate to find another way that they can take care of themselves. People are willing to trust in everything but the one true source of salvation. People are willing to go to such surprising lengths to avoid giving their life and all that they are to Christ. Why is this? Is it because people believe that they are probably good enough to not need the forgiveness that Christ offers? Is it because people fear the life change that

---

[1] Acts 4:11 Commentary - John Gill's Exposition of the Bible. (n.d.). Retrieved January 04, 2018, from https://www.biblestudytools.com/commentaries/gills-exposition-of-the-bible/acts-4-11.html

so often accompanies giving one's life to Christ? Regardless of the answer to this question, it's a problem.

It seems that today, people are so insistent on finding another way besides the only way. This is where Christians often run into issues when they try to tell people about the gift of God that comes in the form of His Son, Jesus Christ. People think that they only have to believe that there is a God and they're set. They believe that if they do enough good, they will make their way to Heaven when they die, or when Christ returns. This poses an issue when it comes to witnessing, because how do you witness to someone who doesn't think they need what you are trying to share with them? This is not limited to high school or college students who say they are trying to figure out who they are. This issue expands even to older adults who may have spent their entire life in the church, but have never made a commitment to give their life to Christ.

Unfortunately, this is not a situation that can always be settled by sharing the ABC's of salvation. Though there is nothing wrong with this approach, when we encounter people who are callused against God, the chances are pretty good that they have heard it all: from the Roman Road all the way to the tracts that many hope will do work for them. When you approach people like this, it is important to sit down with them and figure out where they are coming from. What turned them away from God? When you begin this dialogue, you may be surprised by what you find out. However, it is very important that people understand that there is only one way to gain the forgiveness that is freely available through the death and resurrection of Christ. What if the person says, "I consider myself to be a good person"? In this situation, it is reasonable to begin dipping your toe into Romans to show them where they are wrong. However, the reason that so many ears have become deaf to what Christians have to share, is because so many Christians treat it like a game where they are trying to get the high score, rather than lives that they are trying to turn to Christ. Now, the other possibility is that they will politely sit and listen to you, and when you finish, they will thank you and you will go your separate ways. Do not consider this to be a defeat. In the end, you are not the one who will save this individual. Leave the saving to God. Whether you know it or not, when you and that person leave that encounter, you can bet that God will not let them forget it. However, make sure that they remember the encounter for the right reasons. Will they walk away with a bad "Jesus talk" aftertaste that has become so familiar to them, or will they walk away thinking about what you said and maybe even discussing it with their friends and family who may be in the same boat as they are?

It is important to remember that a conversation about Christ with a nonbeliever is unlikely to stop at that person. The question that you should ask yourself is what you want to be said about the encounter. Will they go home and tell their family that they talked to another one of those religious people or will they go home and say "I had a really interesting conversation with this guy/girl today. There was something different about them."? This should be our thought process before we even begin to talk to someone about Christ. Do we want it to be a conversation about how well we know our scripture, or about how much we want them to know Him?

Message:

Anyone who tells someone that there is only one way to do something is likely to have their share of turned backs. However, there will always be people who are willing to listen. However, you never know how long these people are willing to listen, so be sure that you use every minute to the fullest without overwhelming them to the point that they become deaf to your message. Ultimately, the question is who you want them to know more about. Do you want them walking away thinking about you or about the one whose message you were sharing?

Share It!

Using these questions, reach out to your friends on social media and get the conversation started!

1. Often, we assume that those who set Christ aside as a faulty solution are those who reject Christ in every way. However, how often do you find yourself putting Christ and His abilities on the back burner as an alternative?
2. What avenues are you prone to explore before employing the power of Christ in the situation?
3. What are some of your apprehensions about running to Christ first? What draws you to the alternatives as a first resort?
4. Reach out to one of your friends on social media that you have noticed running from Christ. Ask them what kind of solution they are seeking and why Christ is not part of that solution.

What Would You Do?

And they departed from the presence of the council, rejoicing that they were counted worthy to suffer shame for his name.

Acts 5:41 KJV

This is something that we probably rarely think about when we wake up late and miss the Sunday morning church service or drag ourselves to that prayer meeting on Wednesday night. We don't go into those meetings thinking that we may die doing that. This is the benefit of living in a free country, where we are free to worship the God of the universe without any government penalties. But why do we take this privilege so lightly? We live in a country where, if we want something, there is a way to get that, with obvious exceptions. We live in a place where people do not have to wonder if they will die because they were worshipping the Lord. However, what if we did live in a country where that was a concern? What would be our reaction? We would probably like to think that we would risk it and worship the God that saved us from our sins and the God who gives us freedom through Him. But what if it meant that there would be surprise raids on the house where you were holding church? What if you knew that there was a possibility that the government could come into that church and arrest, or even worse, kill you for worshipping the one true God instead of the state-sponsored god? Most people who were new to this idea would probably huddle in their homes or just go with the flow and go to the state-sponsored gathering required by law.

What about the people who chose to go against that custom without fear of the consequences? As a matter of fact, it wasn't that they were simply not afraid of the consequences. They actually felt joy because they knew that the suffering that they would endure would be in the name of the Lord. Would we be willing to take that risk? Would we still go to church every Sunday with our bright smiles, if we knew that we could die at this church service? If we went at all, the last thing we would probably want to do is to smile. This verse tells us that these individuals, after being tried and interrogated for worshipping Christ, left that encounter with joy in their heart. Can you imagine adopting this attitude after experiencing such strong persecution for worshipping the one true God?

It is no secret that around the world that there are millions of people who face this reality every day. The crazy thing is that they don't even limit their church to one day a week for forty-five minutes! Craziness, right? These people spend hours worshipping the God who they could become the reason for their death. Wouldn't it be easier to just submit to the government and worship the god that lives up to their standards? This verse tells us that the answer is no.

In this verse, we find that the apostles are just leaving a session where they were told not to spread the Gospel anymore and if they did, there would be consequences. For most people today, if we were told not to spread the Gospel for fear of death, we would probably listen, and slowly, if everyone listened, there would be no one on earth willing to spread the truth that sets men free. What's crazy is that it often only takes one person doing something, and then someone else joins in, and it suddenly begins a chain reaction. The disciples were well aware of this. They also had no intention of quitting their ministry simply because the government told them to. This is because their fear of the God that they were serving was so much bigger than their fear of the government. This is important for us to remember today. The closer that the world comes to Christ's return, the more the world will begin to turn away from Him. Today we see this in the government forcing people to embrace and in some cases, pay for practices that are spoken against in the Gospel. If we fail to pay for those practices through taxes and other types of charges on our health insurance statements, we lose our health insurance. Are you willing to surrender your health coverage for the sake of standing up for the Gospel? Most people would like to say yes, but in reality, most people cannot afford to do that. We simply write a check for the total and hand over our money. Now, this is not to say that every Christian should stop what they're doing and get rid of their health insurance. However, the point that is being made is this idea that, in the days of Peter, there were things that they were being forced to do that they refused to do for the sake of preserving the relationship with Christ. Now, when we think about this, we also have to think about the passage in Mark 12:17, where Jesus tells the people that they should give Caesar what is Caesar's. There will always be situations that come with being a citizen of the United States, where we don't necessarily feel that great about some of the things that we have to do. However, we are also called, as followers of Christ, to be ambassadors, representatives of Him. This means that, while we stand for the things that we believe in, we don't allow our protest to get in the way of the message of love and grace that we are supposed to be spreading.

Although life is much more valuable than health coverage, this is basically what Peter and these apostles were doing. Also, not only were they doing it, but they were leaving that session of intense judgment and retribution, and they came out rejoicing. Can you imagine that you stop paying for your health insurance, and eventually, one day, you go out to the mailbox and find an envelope from the government, and you open it and fall to the ground because you are so overjoyed by what's inside? Is it a check? No. It's a fine for failing to have health coverage. You stood up for your beliefs that what you were paying for was not morally right, and you lost your coverage, with a fine tacked on too. Why would anyone rejoice in this? This is a foreign idea to us in the United States today, but there are still people being executed, both by their government and by terror groups, for their belief in Christ. Many are tortured and beaten for their following of Him, but they come away rejoicing. To me, this is a big reality check.

Imagine that you are a student at a liberal state school (or if you are, there's nothing to imagine). Your professor assigns a paper about proving that evolution is fact. What do you do? Do you look for the evidence that the theory is true, because that is the assignment, or do you lay out your arguments for why it is false? If you take the first road, you are compromising the integrity of your relationship with Christ. However, if you take the second road, you risk failing the class and that will have an impact on your GPA. This is, on a small scale, the conflict that faces millions of people every day. It's terrifying to think about. However, the question still stands; which would you choose? An eternal life with Christ where you will be rewarded for standing firm in what He has done for you, or a life of conforming to a culture that worships a false god who only provides false hope to millions of people?

Please understand that this is not to say that if you don't die for your faith, that you are not in as good of a place with God. This is not the intent of this devotional. However, it is important to think about what you would do if you were forced to decide between abandoning God for your life or running toward Him at the risk of losing your life. Which would you choose? Your answer to the question could potentially tell you a lot about where you are in your relationship with Him. Are you in it just for the good times and fun, or are you in it for better or for worse?

Message:

If you came into your relationship with Christ so that everything would be settled for you and you would never have to do anything else to ensure you die happy, you may want to take a second look at the relationship. Are you willing to die for the relationship that you have with Him, or if faced with a choice, will you shy away from death and abandon the relationship you have with Him for the sake of living in submission to a government enforced religion? Are you in this marriage only for the fun, or are you also in it because you would be willing to fight for it if prompted?

Share It!

Using these questions, reach out to your friends on social media and get the conversation started!

1. What would you be willing to do for the relationship that you have with Christ? How strongly do you feel about taking this course of action?
2. Has there ever been a situation in which you have been required to defend this relationship that you have with Christ by putting your life on the line?
3. What is it about the relationship that you have with Christ that makes you willing (or not) to die for it if needed?

The Spiritual Cubicle

For I am not ashamed of the gospel of Christ: for it is the power of God unto salvation to everyone that believeth…

Romans 1:16 KJV

Picture something (or someone) in your life that you are insanely proud of. Now, imagine going through an entire day without mentioning the name of that person or talking about that item. Whether it be your home, your car, or in the realm of family and friends, it could be your spouse or your boyfriend or girlfriend, to think that most would be able to do this would be very unlikely. To be told that you had to go through all your daily activities without talking about that person or item would be a challenge that you probably wouldn't be willing to accept. You want to talk about that person or thing because you're proud of them and you want people to know all about them. Most of you probably have a phone overflowing with pictures of your family or significant other. Whatever the case may be, these people that bring you pride and joy in your life are likely very evident and prevalent in your life and in the way that you live.

When your parents talk about you with their friends and coworkers, they don't just walk up to that person and tell them your birthday and where you go to school. They want that person to know everything from what it was like to see you take your first steps to what it felt like when you got your license and your first car. They want that person to know the simultaneous heartbreak and joy that they feel every time they drop you off at college. They want to tell people about the moments in your life that make them proud to be your parent. Because they are proud of you, they want other people to know it and to know why. What if your mom had been working at a job for twenty years, and one day, you show up at her office to pick something up, and when her coworkers see you, they ask who you're here to see. You tell them your mom's name, and they have a perplexed look on their face and reply that they didn't even know she had any children, but they direct you to her office and you walk into a cubicle with no pictures, none of your drawings from preschool, not a single thing that would tell people that she was your mother or that she was proud of you.

Today, when we look at this image of what it looks like to be proud of those you love, one has to wonder if that image would carry over to one's walk with Christ. If you have invited Christ into your life to change you and to make you His child, why wouldn't you want people to know it? I don't mean wearing those t-shirts with Christian verses on them or putting that bumper sticker on your car. When I say proud, I mean that you are going throughout your day telling people about Him and resembling Him in everything you do. You are telling people about His work in your life and you are showing people how He has changed you since He became a part of your life. Your "spiritual cubicle", so-to-speak, is filled with evidence of His work in your life. You can't help but share moments in your life when Christ really showed up in a big way. However, when we look at the church of today, it seems that all-too-often, we are more likely to see a cubicle with empty walls than we are an office with evidence of Him and His presence all over the place.

If our lives were to resemble an office cubicle, most people would probably have posters of bands they follow, and they would have letters from their family that they may have received for birthdays or holidays. Some may even have a pennant from their alma mater. These are things that we are proud to show people as we go through our lives every day. However, where is Christ in this cubicle? If He is evident at all, it is probably in that Bible that you hide in the overhead storage compartment, but is it proudly displayed on your desk with the other things that you are proud to claim as a part of your life? Now, it is definitely a part of your life because it is up there in that overhead compartment, but it isn't a part of your life that you are proud of.

This is called shame. If you are not willing to proudly display something, it is probably because you are ashamed of it. Many will say that there isn't enough room on their "desk" for it. Many will say that they don't want to offend anybody with it, but that they will take it out before they leave on Friday so that they will have it for Sunday.

Let's revert back to our scenario. When we talk about a cubicle, we are talking about everything that makes up your life that is visible to the public. The things on your desk are the things that you talk about, the things that you tell others about yourself, and the things that you allow people to figure out on their own. You wouldn't work somewhere for twenty years and never tell someone that you had children. That would probably be an opening line on your first day. The first thing you would do is put out their pictures and tell people all about them. You would tell them about your spouse and what they do for a living and your family and where you are originally from. These are desktop items. You would probably set a family picture as your desktop picture. The question is, what are you keeping in that overhead storage?

The overhead storage is where you put the things that you can forget or that are unimportant. There is any number of possibilities in terms of what you may store up there. However, the one thing that should not be in that part of your public life is your love for the one who put breath into your lungs. This doesn't mean that you have to put I LOVE JESUS stickers all over your walls. However, in this spiritual cubicle, what are you showing people, and what is hiding up there in the storage?

Paul tells us in this verse that he is NOT ashamed of the Gospel of Jesus Christ. He tells us that, basically, it is because of Christ and His Gospel that we have the ability to come into a relationship with Christ. Because he had no shame in Christ, he basically spent the part of his life when he wasn't persecuting Christians telling the world about Christ. He didn't hide it for fear of backlash or of getting reprimanded by HR. He told everybody, whether they wanted to hear him or not. He didn't care! He wanted to share the message of Christ with as much of the world as he could because, in the end, if he didn't, who would?

Are we willing to be so bold for the cause of Christ today? Are we willing to share the message with those people who shut the door in our face, or call HR because we proudly display our Bible on our desk? What risk are we willing to take to carry out the Great Commission? Are we just going to wait for people to walk up to us and ask about the message that they know nothing about? If this is the approach that we are banking on, we will probably be waiting for a while.

Message:

Christ wasn't so ashamed of us that He didn't hang on that cross for the public to beat and abuse Him until after He was dead. There are Christians around the world who face the same thing today. What excuse do we have, as we live in one of the most privileged nations in the world, to not openly share and proclaim the Gospel for all to hear? We have no excuse. It is as simple as this: If you are proud of something in your life, you will talk about it. You don't speak of things that you are ashamed of. Whatever you choose to do with the message of Christ will fall into one of these two categories. There is no *but* provision. You're either proud of who He is in your life, and you will talk about Him, or you are ashamed, and you will hide Him away until you need Him for Sunday or for a problem you are having. It's your choice. Now, the question to consider is, what will your spiritual cubicle look like? Will the walls be all about the world, or all about the hope that is in you?

Share It!

Using these questions, reach out to your friends on social media and get the conversation started!

1. With a mental image in mind, what does your spiritual cubicle look like right now? What kind of things are on your calendar in that cubicle? What kind of pictures are inside? What kind of things are stored in the overhead compartment?
2. When was the last time that you cleaned out this cubicle?
3. When people walk by, do you find that they feel welcomed to come inside or do they stand at the door?

God Doesn't Play Favorites

[11]for there is no respect of persons with God.

Romans 2:11 KJV

Have you ever been in a situation where you felt that you were mistreated by someone because they liked someone else better? Have you ever felt that you were denied an opportunity because the person making that decision liked the other candidate better for personal reasons? The biggest question is this: Do you ever think that God is taking an opportunity from you and giving it to someone else because of their community service record or the frequency of their prayer life? Have you ever just been in a place when you thought that life wasn't fair and wondered why things (both good and bad) happened more to this group of people more than others? Well, regardless of your answers to the first questions, if you answered 'yes' to the last question, then this is for you.

When you were growing up in school, there were always times in your life when the teacher made a decision that you thought was not fair. As you grew a little older, you may have begun to get this idea that the teacher or maybe even your parent liked the other person better. Why is this? This is because you probably felt that you were the one who really deserved that opportunity to play video games or pick which movie the family would watch that night. However, ultimately, your parents or the teacher knew things about that other person and you that you may not have considered. It's possible that the other person may not be feeling good or may have something going on in their family, and the person who made that decision may have been trying to raise the person's spirits. Regardless of the reason, the deciding authority had some set of reasons for deciding the way that they did.

What about God? Do you think that maybe He gave that job to that other candidate instead of you simply because He liked that other person better? Do you think that He gave that huge raise to that other person who leaves at 3:30 every day instead of you because He just thought that he or she was just a little bit better than you? I would hope that this would not be your attitude, but if it is, let me assure you that God most definitely does not play favorites when it comes to His children.

When we look at situations from an earthly perspective, it can be tempting to assume that we know why God gave a certain situation to a certain person or family. Maybe they hit your mailbox last year and never apologized, so you just cannot understand why God would give them the ability to buy that new car in their driveway. Maybe they blow their leaves over on your yard, and you just cannot understand why the husband was able to buy that new lawn mower that you have been looking at for the last two years, hoping it would one day be cutting your grass. Whatever the scenario may be, you just cannot understand why God gave that to them instead of you. Well, here's a spoiler alert for you. There are reasons that God does things or gives things to people whom we may deem to be undeserving of whatever that thing or opportunity may be, and those reasons may not always make sense to us. However, we usually think that it is because of something that they did or said to Him to convince Him to give it to them. Alternatively, if it is someone we love going through a tragic situation, we ask, "Why God?" We just cannot understand what they could have possibly done to deserve such a devastating diagnosis or loss at a time like this when it seemed everything was going great. We think to ourselves that they didn't need that car or that new lawn mower, or that RV in their driveway; but how do we know that? Who are we to determine who needs something more than someone else? Who are we to say that we needed that position more than the person who actually got it? They've got a brand-new car and they just bought a new house. They are obviously not hurting for money. What evidence do we have for that? Well, nothing. What reasons do we have for their argument other than what we see in their driveway? None. Yet, somehow, we feel that we have the ability to be their undercover financial consultant and deem their belongings necessary or unnecessary. We look at that diagnosis that was given to someone whom we love very much, and we just cannot understand why God chose them. What did they do?

What if we looked at this from God's perspective? What if that neighbor one day came over to your house and apologized for the ways that they had wronged you. What if they explained that they were going to be doing a lot of traveling pretty soon and wanted to let you know that they were leaving the neighborhood? They go on to explain that they are having to relocate because the husband's job had been relocated and their son was diagnosed with a rare disease that only one hospital that is four hours away specializes in and is able to treat? They explain that their car was on its last leg, so they had to get a more fuel-efficient car for all the traveling they were about to do? Suddenly your attitude changes, but one thing that doesn't change is the last question we considered at the beginning: why does God allow things to happen to certain people more than others? Is it because He thinks that this person is better or more important than that person? No, of course not. We often face these types of internal debates in the world today.

We so desperately want answers to why the most wonderful people are often presented with an awful circumstance. We try to answer that for ourselves, but we only end up with more questions. However, at the risk of sounding cliché, the ultimate answer that leaves enough space for God is this: God has a plan for each and every one of our lives. Throughout the time that we spend on this side of heaven, we will meet people who leave us thinking, wow, God must really love them. They are truly blessed. We will also meet people who leave us in shock with the thought, why would God do that to them? Fortunately, there is good news and bad news. The good news is that, at some point in our lives, whether that time is in the past, present, or in the near future, we will be in that first situation. We will be the ones who leave people thinking that we are truly blessed by God because of all the good that is going on in our family's lives. We will also be the ones who leave people in shock, wondering why God would do such a thing to us and our family. These two scenarios describe everyone at some point in their lives.

Do you still think that God plays favorites? If you give Him time, you will be that person who will experience His goodness in your life in a big way. It may not come in the form of a new car, house, or job. It may come in the form of a good report from the doctor after you had that test done that had a 99% chance of coming back with not-so-good results. It could come in the form of getting an early raise from your boss because someone told them about the situation that you just came out of. It could come in the form of any number of things. For this reason, we must resist the urge to compare our lives with those of people whom we know very little about. This does not mean that you can't see someone's new car and say, "I'm going to make it my goal to save for that car". This does not mean that you cannot see someone constantly traveling and say, "When we retire, we're going to travel the world like that". Do not think that creating a goal is the same as questioning someone's worthiness of having a certain thing or opportunity. However, it is also important that we refrain from placing something of our own or someone else's at a lower value because we don't have it or because we feel that they don't deserve it.

Message:

God provides for different people in different ways at different times in their lives. Most people realize that this is true, but sometimes it seems that they don't completely understand what this means. God does not necessarily always deliver blessings in mass amounts to entire cities or countries. However, when looking at this verse in context, we see that God delivers blessings according to different factors in one's life. When people receive blessings, it doesn't always mean that they have been praying and reading their Bible every day. When people receive trials and tribulations, it doesn't mean that they have *not* been doing that. It simply means that God has a plan for each person's life and He will carry out that plan accounting for the free decisions that are a part of every person's life. There are certain things in life that God allows us to determine for ourselves. Therefore, He accounts for those free choices along the way.

Share It!

Using these questions, reach out to your friends on social media and get the conversation started!

1. Sometimes, it can be difficult to see God's blessings that have been planted throughout our lifetime when there haven't been any significant ones recently. When was the last time you saw God do something big for or through you?
2. What are some ways in which you have seen God's provision within the last year?
3. Think of three blessings that God has placed in your life over the last week.

Repent and Forgive Quickly and Often

[4]Now to him that worketh is the reward not reckoned of grace, but of debt. [5]But to him that worketh not, but believeth on him that justifieth the ungodly, his faith is counted as righteousness

Romans 4:4-5 KJV

The purpose of the book of Romans is basically to show us how worthless our actions are compared to the grace of God for the purposes of salvation. It tells us over and over that we cannot do anything on our part to unlock that door to eternal life. This is no secret to those who follow Christ and know anything about the Bible. Regardless of what translation of the Bible you use, by simply reading these verses, any reasonable person would conclude that this was true. However, in case there was any doubt, Paul wrote this verse, as well as numerous others to drive the point home.

If you are reading this and you know that you have entrusted your life to Christ and that He has complete control of it because of your trusting in Him, you probably know this. There are no right words or perfect process that can give someone eternal life. It isn't some digital code that you scan with your phone, and it suddenly puts a note on file that you are a child of God. To many, this would seem simpler than having to trust in Christ and giving their lives to Him. As has been mentioned repeatedly, God doesn't have a chart in Heaven counting your community service hours before He grants His forgiveness.

It is kind of funny sometimes the hoops that people are willing to jump through to gain what they assume to be true forgiveness of sins. It seems that we have made it more complicated than it has to be. There is no scavenger hunt to find the X that marks the destination of true forgiveness. Here's the problem that arises if this were the method to obtain forgiveness of sins; while accepting the gift of salvation is a one-time decision that we live out every day, there is something that is not only done at the altar or in your bedroom, or wherever you had that moment when you invited Christ into your life. This thing is called repentance.

Repentance is a decision that we must make every day, maybe multiple times a day. Repentance literally means to turn away from something. Whether that means turning away from a past that holds memories that you would rather forget, or whether it means turning away from a lifetime of small, yet significant sins, if we do not repent on a daily basis and choose to turn away from the things of yesterday, we will find that we are slowly drifting away from God, and before we know it, we find that we are not hearing His voice anymore and we find that we are not feeling His conviction when we do things that are against His will.

Imagine that you are swimming in the ocean this summer, and you begin to notice that you are being pulled out to sea. You notice that there is a lifeguard beginning to watch you a little bit closer, but you don't think anything of it. Suddenly, you begin to hear him blowing his whistle and telling you that you are too far out. What good would it do at this point to begin telling this lifeguard how grateful you are for what He is doing and how awesome it is that He is there protecting you? It would be useless. Soon, you would find that you had drifted so far out to sea that you could no longer hear his whistle or his voice. The only way to be able to hear him again is to heed the advice that he had previously given and to begin swimming toward shore.

In the same way that you eventually could not hear the prompts of the lifeguard once you drifted so far out to sea, when you stop listening to the voice of God, you find that eventually, you will be so far into the deepest parts of sin, that you will wonder why He has stopped talking to you and why He has suddenly left you stranded. The fact is that He has been talking to you all along. The problem is that you have drifted so far from Him that all you hear is silence. You can tell Him how much you love Him and post scripture on social media as much as your heart desires, but until you begin to swim toward shore, your words and actions will be useless.

The only way that we will be able to reach the shore again and hear the voice of God again is by obeying what He tells us to do. What reason do we have for not listening to Him? If there's any answer at all to this question, it is our stubbornness. We may believe that we can get back to the shore on our own, but all that will ever be accomplished through this will be more drifting. However, because of our pride, we are afraid to go before God to ask for His help. For some odd reason, we're afraid to go before His throne to ask for the forgiveness that He so freely offers. Even though He tells us over and over in His Word about the sinful nature that we are born with, we still seem to be afraid to tell Him about the wrong that we have done. Believe me, God already knows about what you did. He was there with you when you did it and even when you were thinking about doing it. He's not your mom or dad who have been at work all day and didn't pay attention to that fine you had to pay. He knows about everything that you do the minute that you do it. In this way, trying to hide sin from God is like trying to hide a new car in the garage. The world may not see it, but eventually, someone will find out about it.

In the other piece of this verse, we find the positive flip side. The other part of this is that when we simply live our lives believing on Christ for our salvation and repenting of our sins and drawing back to Him, we can know that we are in good standing with God. This does not make us perfect by any means. What this does make us is forgiven on a daily basis. The consequences of letting sin draw you out to sea and hoping that your good words and deeds will bring you back in will get you nowhere. However, if you live your life for Christ every day and constantly start each day with a new batch of repentance, you will be truly free from everything that happened in the past in God's book.

The other way to look at this is through a personal lens. Why would you want to continue to carry yesterday's burdens with you instead of confessing them? Most people who do this are miserable until they bring to light whatever they have done. Therefore, in addition to going before the throne of God to ask for His forgiveness, go before the person whom you wronged and straighten things out again. If you do not do this, you will spend months or maybe even years carrying a burden about something you did to someone, and that person may never realize it. If you spend your life doing this, not only are you withholding the grace that was given to you from someone else. You are also making your life so much worse for holding onto that thing that has been nagging you for such a long time. Why hold onto it? It will only bring you more and more strife when you think about it. Whatever burden you have for something that you did or something that someone has done to you, bring it to that person and allow them to ask for or provide the same grace and forgiveness that was once given to you. Do not let that person spend their life wondering what you may be holding against them.

Message:

God never asks us in His Word to work to a certain level before we come before Him and ask for forgiveness. It is one of the few things in the Bible that doesn't really require any homework on our part. The unfortunate thing is that we so often seem to assign extra credit to ourselves before we allow ourselves to accept His forgiveness. Do not make God's gift of salvation something that it is not. Also, be quick to forgive those who have wronged you. If they come before you and admit a wrongdoing, do not tell them that you will think about it or that they will have to earn your forgiveness, because if you do this to them, you are saying that God has the right to do that to you. This is not to say that forgiveness is always quick and easy. It isn't. However, do not attach conditions to your forgiveness, because at this point, it stops being forgiveness and turns into indentured servitude. Ultimately, be quick to ask and to give forgiveness.

Share It!

Using these questions, reach out to your friends on social media and get the conversation started!

1. When it comes to granting forgiveness to someone, what makes it so hard for you?
2. When was the last time that you had to ask someone's forgiveness for a wrongdoing? When was the last time that you gave that forgiveness?
3. How long do you consider a reasonable time to wait before you need to forgive someone?
4. Use this time as an opportunity to reach out to that person with whom you never really made amends after some sort of disagreement. Offer the forgiveness that Christ offers you, whether you consider yourself to be at-fault or not.

It's Not About You

[1]Therefore being justified by faith, we have peace with God through our Lord Jesus Christ: [2]by whom also we have access by faith into his grace wherein we stand, and rejoice in the hope of the glory of God.

Romans 5:1-2 KJV

What right do we have to have access to the salvation that Christ brings through His death on the cross? In case there's any confusion, the answer is none. We have done everything and given God every reason not to love us and offer us salvation and a relationship with Him, and yet He does so daily. We give Him every reason to not rescue us from the trials that come into our lives on a daily basis, but He still chooses to rescue us. Why is this? The answer is that it is not about us.

It's not because of us that we have salvation and the promise that we will one day be able to stand before Him and hear Him say "Well done, my good and faithful servant". It's not because of us that we have access to remission of sins. Our justification, our reason for having access to these privileges is not because of anything we have done, are currently doing or will do in the future. We don't have that magic access card that will get us into Heaven when we die or into a relationship with Christ while we are still here. Why? Because Christ is our justification. Christ is the one who holds that door open for us, so that we will enter into a relationship with Him if we only accept what He has done and who He is. Christ is the ultimate badge that will get us into that relationship with Him. Without that badge, you will hear words in Heaven one day that no person wants to hear: "Depart from me. I never knew you". Sure, you did all that community service and you served at that soup kitchen with your youth group, but was there ever a time in your life when you went humbly before the throne of God and confessed that you do not deserve any of the things that He freely offers, but that you acknowledge that it is through His Son that you can have access to them? Or did you think to yourself that if you soften Him up enough, maybe He would just give it to you when you died? So many people think this way, thinking of God as a system that can be played. Unfortunately, these people always end up being disappointed.

All this is not to say that this is the description that fits everybody on the earth. There are also those Christians in the world who have genuinely given their life over to Him and they have accepted all parts of the relationship. They understand that, without Christ, we have nothing. They understand that, without Him, God does not recognize us. Without Christ, we are lost, and to be found means that we find Christ and invite Him into our lives. However, so many people fall victim to this idea that they can negotiate God into a relationship that works for them too. Again, when you agree to a relationship with Christ, it is no longer about you. It is no longer about the things that you want or the things that you place value in. When you begin a relationship with Christ, it's about Him. It's about Him because we didn't have a right to the relationship in the first place. If you were on the operating table and in need of a heart transplant, and someone gave you that heart that you needed, you would hopefully be eternally grateful to that person, because, in their death, they gave you life. They did not leave posthumous requirements for you to have access to that heart. It was simply given to you as a gift that could only be repaid by making the most of the new life that you had been gifted with.

Something that is interesting to consider in this passage is the three main words that are contained within it. This verse tells us that, when we come into a relationship with God, that we gain three things: peace, grace, and hope. This sounds great in a social media post and it looks good on a t-shirt, but we never consider what this means. Through Christ, we have access to these things. This is also to say that, without Christ, we have none of these things. Sure, we can read those books and see those quotes that talk about giving ourselves hope, but that hope is fleeting. The hope that we find in Christ is a hope that only He can give.

The verse talks about peace. When we think of this word, again, there is the peace that Man offers by encouraging everyone to get along, and there's the peace that comes with knowing Christ and knowing that He will fight for us. We can have peace in the knowledge that He has given us everything that we will ever need, and He will never leave us in a place where we are in the middle of nowhere with nothing to defend ourselves against the battles that are placed in our lives.

This verse also mentions this idea of grace. Often, when we think of grace, we hear it described as the giving of something (usually good) that is undeserved. When we look at this in the context of our relationship with Christ, the entire gift of salvation is made possible by grace alone. It is because of the grace that Christ extended to us that we can enjoy the gift of salvation freely because nothing that we could ever do could ever be enough to compensate for this gift. This is why salvation is referred to as a gift. We did nothing to deserve it, but with it, we have a future that goes beyond the grave and a guarantee that we will always have a relationship with Christ and a place of refuge that will protect us and guide us in times of struggle and uncertainty.

Finally, this verse speaks of hope. Hope is what drives us to get out of bed in the morning. Hope is what makes us look beyond tomorrow and into the future with optimism that tells us that God has everything in control. Hope tells us that we can know that better things are coming. Now, that may sound like something that you would hear from one of those pastors on TV who probably shouldn't be called pastors, but it deserves consideration. When we come into a relationship with Christ, that relationship alone, regardless of whatever circumstances we may be facing, gives us hope that cannot be found anywhere else. This hope, if implemented in the right places and nourished in the right ways, should grow us, propel us forward and help us to continue pursuing the mission, the call that God has placed on our lives.

Message:

God's love for us is the ultimate picture of what it means to give grace and mercy to those who deserve it the least. In the grand scheme of things, we deserve nothing that he has blessed our lives with. However, it is because of His grace, His peace, and His hope that we have access to those things. No matter where you turn, you will never be able to find these three things in a purer form than they will be found in a relationship with Christ. This is not to say that we should give up all our earthly relationships. It is through these relationships that He extends that love to us and to others. As a matter of fact, these relationships that hold such a big piece of our hearts and lives give us opportunities to exercise this peace, grace, and hope that God has given to us. He doesn't give us those things so that we will lock them away and keep them hidden. He gives us these things so that we will apply them to our lives and share them with others. Is this easy? No. Will it make our lives a lot more bearable if we exercise it constantly? Most definitely. In the end, God gave all these things to us through His Son on the cross. Therefore, it is our responsibility to pass those things onto those who may have hurt us or who may be in the middle of an unpredictable circumstance. Either way, it is our responsibility to give away what has been so graciously given to us.

Share It!

Using these questions, reach out to your friends on social media and get the conversation started!

1. When you look at your Christian walk and the call that you are pursuing to reach others with the Gospel, do you see it as being a you-centered pursuit, or a God-centered pursuit?
2. What does grace mean to you? What about Peace? Hope?
3. In these college years, where can you see opportunities to reach others for Christ? Where do you see these opportunities leading you?

More Than a Heavenly Access Badge

[8]But God commendeth his love toward us, in that, while we were yet sinners, Christ died for us. [9]Much more then, being now justified by his blood, we shall be saved from wrath through him

Romans 5:8-9 KJV

Whenever I come across this verse, I feel that it is sometimes underappreciated considering what is being said here. Can you imagine being a father and having to send your son to die for people who do not even appreciate what kind of sacrifice that is? Consider the military. Parents watch their children go off to battle every day. They fully realize that they may never see their child again because of the circumstances that they are training for. They understand the sacrifice that is being made. However, the worst part of this seems to be the lack of appreciation that some people have for the sacrifice that these men and women are making every day.

Now, imagine that you are required to send your son (for the sake of argument) off, knowing that He will die and that He is dying for a people who call Him a blasphemer and a liar. This man is Jesus. We have all heard the stories in Sunday school and have heard sermon after sermon on the topic of Jesus' death from all different angles and perspectives. There are scholars who only study the resurrection and consider themselves to be experts on the topic. Yet, even with all this knowledge that we have about this event in history, we so often forget that we were the reason for that. We were the reason that He was nailed to that tree and died that slow, agonizing death. We were the reason for that, and today, it seems that, so many have forgotten the true meaning of the sacrifice altogether.

When Jesus died on that cross, of course, He knew that those who accused and convicted Him would turn their back on Him. It was happening before His very eyes. What He also knew, however, was that people who would come to live thereafter would do the same thing, even though they had been taught about every aspect of His crucifixion on the cross. Whether these people spent their Sundays within the walls of a church or in their homes, they would grow so accustomed and so used to hearing the message of Christ, that it would just become words to so many. However, if you read the first verse of this passage, the one piece that really sticks out is the words while we were yet sinners. He paid the ultimate price for the sins of the world, knowing that so many of the people living in the world would never pay Him back by accepting the gift that He so graciously offered.

Imagine that you are a judge in a courtroom. You have a defendant in front of you who has stacks and stacks of evidence against him for charges of robbery, but you do something many would call crazy. You declare this person not guilty and instead place yourself under arrest. Now, obviously this would make any judge look insane and it would probably cost them their job, but ultimately, you took the punishment upon yourself for this person whom you were 110% positive was guilty of all the charges against them. You knew this, and yet you set this person free and placed yourself in bondage in their place. You didn't have any reason to be counted guilty of robbery. By all accounts, you were innocent of that charge, but you took it upon yourself to face that charge, to give the defendant a second chance at life. You wanted to give them a second chance to turn their life around, to turn from what they had done and create a new life for themselves.

The question now becomes what the defendant will do with this newfound freedom. Will they use it to spread the word about the second chance that they were given, or will they go out into the world and rob another store or commit some other crime because they now have the freedom to do so? Unlike Christ, no one would ever know until that defendant showed up on their docket again, the impact that this decision had had on the person. They chose to sacrifice their job and their future to set this undeserving person free, and that person went out into the world and did not share about the grace that was given to them. Instead, they went out and told everybody about the "get out of jail free" card that they had been given and now they could do whatever they wanted.

Is that how we view the death of Christ on the cross? Sure, He freed us from our sins and sure, He gives us the ability to have a personal, intimate relationship with Him, but at least we won't go to Hell when we die. For so many, this is the basis for their entire salvation. The goal is not to have a relationship with Christ, but rather to avoid eternal pain and suffering. Granted, this is definitely a perk to Christianity, but that is not the only reason that we should come to that decision. We come to Christ because we want a new life. We want to leave that old stuff behind and begin to move toward the new things that lie ahead. It's about so much more than escaping Hell. Granted, I understand that a large majority of Christians come to accept Christ when they are young and before they have a complete understanding of what it means to follow Him, and at that time, they likely are doing it simply so that they will go to Heaven. However, as we grow and begin to understand more and more about who Christ is and what He has done for us, we should begin to understand that having a relationship with Christ is about more than simply going to Heaven or not going to the alternative destination. We should understand that the entire reason that we come to know Christ in the first place is that we want to turn away from the sin that has come to define us. Jesus died on that cross while we were still sinners because He hoped that doing this would give us a new view of the life that we had been given and He hoped that we would choose to handle this new life with care until we understood the value of it. Ultimately, the value of it can be summed up in this way: Christ gave His life to give us life. Now it is up to us to determine what we will do with this new life. Will we spread the message of it and the purpose of it to others, or will it simply be described as a free escape route from Satan?

Message:

It's no secret that we did nothing to deserve this gift of new life that has been placed inside of us if we have accepted Christ as our Savior. Something that may be a secret to some, is that this gift comes with responsibilities. It comes with the responsibility to handle your newfound freedom carefully and to not be reckless in how you use it. If you had been the defendant that was described earlier, would you want to make known the fact that you had avoided prison, or the fact that you have a new chance at life? This is the question that many Christians face today. Do we want people to know that following Christ will get them into Heaven when their heart stops or when Christ returns, or do we want them to know how that relationship comes into play while it is still beating? This is a question that should be answered quickly and honestly.

Share It!

Using these questions, reach out to your friends on social media and get the conversation started!

1. If you have accepted Christ, how has your view of this relationship, this second chance, changed since that time?
2. When considering the judge-defendant illustration, how has your walk changed since you started this new relationship?
3. When was the last time you used this "badge" to enter into the presence of God in genuine, intimate prayer?

He Loves Us Anyway

[10]For if, when we were enemies, we were reconciled by God by the death
of his Son, much more, being reconciled, we shall be saved by his life.
[11]And not only *so*, but we also joy in God through our Lord Jesus Christ,
by whom we have now received atonement

Romans 5:10-11 KJV

From the time of your birth, and even before, you were known by God.
Not only were you known by God, but you were loved by Him even
though you had not yet come into a relationship with Him. However, by
all accounts, from the time of your birth, you are born into sin and
therefore had a wall separation between yourself and the glory of God. At
that point in time, even though you had not begun an intimate relationship
with Him, He loved you and knew all that you would ever become and
ever do. With this wisdom, He had every reason in the world to put
Himself as far from us as He could until we made the decision to accept
Him as our Savior. This would be completely reasonable by our standards.
But because God is God, He does not operate to our standards. His
standards say that He will love us even before we choose to accept the
forgiveness that He so freely offers. To us, this is unthinkable. To think
that you would have the heart to love people who had cursed you, spit on
you and that you would even love their children is a foreign concept to so
many people today. But this is precisely what Christ did for us.

This passage should give us pause because it tells us that He loved those
who so often refused to love Him back. Can you imagine someone
walking up to you and throwing countless obscenities at you, and when
they finish, you simply tell them, "I love you anyway"? We'll let their
reaction be left to the imagination, but the chances are that there would be
some odd looks. Jesus received insults too. As He was hanging on that
cross with spit and shouts of hate coming at Him left and right, Jesus
simply hung on that cross and prayed to His father that they would be
forgiven. He didn't pray that God would have revenge on them for what
they had done. He prayed that His Father would have mercy on them. He
loved those people who had placed Him in the most unforgivable of
circumstances.

This verse urges us to think about that for a minute. Before we come to
know Christ and have a relationship with Him, we are considered His

enemies. We possess this sinful nature and everything that we do outside of His will is basically a spit in His face. When we think badly about that person in class or at the office, that is a spit in His face. When we listen to that music that curses in every stanza, that is a pain to His heart. When we choose to look to the world for our comfort and our fulfillment, that is painful for Him to watch; and yet He still loves us. This is probably unimaginable to most people because, were it us in that situation, we would likely remove those people from our lives. In some cases, we find it in ourselves to forgive the person, but ultimately, we usually end up going our separate ways. Fortunately for us, Christ refuses to do that because it is not in His nature to do so. Because He loves us in our most sinful form before we even accept His gift of forgiveness, we should not be surprised that He loves us even more when we make the decision to accept Him.

Unlike humans, Christ does not hold grudges against His people. When we do wrong in His eyes, He teaches us lessons, and when we repent of what we did, He tosses those sins into the Sea of Forgetfulness. Micah 7:19 assures us of this. He assures us that a sin forgiven is not a sin that has been buried in the sand and will one day reappear and haunt us down the road. A sin forgiven is a sin forgotten for all eternity. He doesn't keep a history of sins that He has forgiven, so He doesn't look back on all that we had done, and think, *Ya know, after all that they have done to me, I'm not sure I really want to love them.* The fact that He gave His Son as a sacrifice of forgiveness for all humanity that will ever exist is evidence that He doesn't care about our past. He only cares that we love Him and ask that He clear our history of sin. If we do that, He will love us even more than He loved us when we were enemies due to our sinful nature.

Message:

God *wants* to love us. The Gospel makes this clear repeatedly both through the actions of Christ and through the words that God Himself delivers to His people. Often, we feel that He doesn't love us because of the events that people face that can often cause people to drift from Him. However, these events are an attempt on God's part to bring us back to Him. No matter how far you drift from Him or how many reasons you give Him to not love you, He will only continue to love you more, despite your sin. To those who feel that they have a past that no one could possibly look past, turn to God. Those who have grades that they are ashamed of and feel like they have no future, turn to God. To all those who have things in their life that they are constantly ashamed of, turn to God. It's as simple as that. If you turn to Him and admit your wrongdoings, He will show you that, when you turn to Him, you will be able to lay aside that weight and continue pursuing whatever it may be that He has set before you. However, it is up to you to decide whether you will turn away from all the stuff that brings you shame so that you will be able to lay your eyes on what He has in store for you.

Share It!

Using these questions, reach out to your friends on social media and get the conversation started!

1. What are some of the things in your life that make you believe that God doesn't necessarily love you that much?
2. What have been some things in your life's journey that have caused you to turn away from Him in the past?
3. How have you seen God's love come to life in your own walk?

It Takes One

For as by one man's disobedience many were made sinners, so by the
obedience of one shall many be made righteous.

Romans 5:19 KJV

It only takes one. This standard applies to rule-making, as well as decision
making today. When a rule has been set, it is either because one person did
it, or because one person may try it at some point. It only takes one person
to mess everything up as well. When a system is working as it should and
there are rules and regulations for how to maintain this harmony in the
system, all is well until one person or one entity of some sort goes rogue
and puts the system into a tailspin.

The first instance of this was surprisingly at the beginning of time. This is
no surprise to you if you have read the Bible at all. God gave Adam and
his helpmate Eve a perfect paradise where they had all that they would
ever need. They had no reason to disobey what God had told them to do,
because all they ever needed was right there in front of them.
Unfortunately, one thing that God gave humans when He created them
was this little thing called freewill. Freewill is the reason that we are not
robots acting on some kind of programmed code in our brain. God gave us
the ability to choose for ourselves how we would use the resources He
gave to us. Surprisingly, it wasn't long until God found out the results of
this study of sorts.

It took one human to disobey God because of the work of Satan, and the
entire system went into a tailspin. Today, we see where that got us. In the
same way that sin began in the first place, it continues today. Sin often
comes in the form of what is often referred to as a slippery slope. One
minute, you will feel like you are on top of the world, and the next minute,
you find a notification on social media from one of those spam accounts,
and suddenly you find yourself looking at things that God expressly
prohibits in His Word. Maybe this is not the case for you.

Maybe you're at home one day, and even though your parents told you to
never invite people over when they're not home, your buddy texts you and
asks if he/she can come over. You make an executive decision that this
one time won't be any big deal, but when your friend gets there, he/she
has twenty friends behind them. Inside, you find yourself thinking that this
suddenly turned into something bigger than you expected. Once it began

to grow, you could no longer escape the possibility that you may be found out by your parents. The question is, do you call them now and explain what happened, or do you explain it to them when it's all over and you have been tagged by fifteen people on social media? Either way, this has snowballed into a huge mess that could have some serious consequences. Sin is like that. It begins with one small thing, and suddenly, you will find yourself in a predicament that can only be resolved through a third party acting as a rope to get you out.

Adam and Eve also found themselves in this situation. Once they had consumed the fruit, there was no turning back. They had no way out, except to come before God, which they failed to do, and ask for His forgiveness. The sad part is that, even with the thousands of pages of scripture that we have at our disposal today and the direct line to the God of the universe, we still do the same thing. We still think that God is as tuned in to what we are doing at home as our parents are while they are at work. We think that He doesn't know that we looked at that picture or watched that movie or listened to that music. We basically think that, sometimes, God is clueless as to what we are doing. We think that if we do this or that quiet enough, we will stay off God's radar with our sin. We think that if we can't see Him, then He can't see us, but in all honesty, aren't we glad that that's not the case? Isn't it great that our sin can't hide from God? Our first instinct is to say that we would rather that it be that way, but ultimately, God would not be able to forgive sin that He was supposedly unaware of. If He were unaware of our sin, He would not be able to help us. So why are we so afraid to bring our sin before Him and ask His forgiveness?

In the second part of this verse, Paul writes that sin also left the world through one man, that man being Christ. Imagine for a second that someone tells you that they will pay whatever debts you owe, including past, present, and future, no matter how big or small they may be. The only condition is that you tell that person about the debt that you accrued and would like for them to pay for. Now, they've set up an automatic draft system so that any debt that occurs will automatically be paid back, but this person simply wants to know about the debt, so that they can know that you are being honest with them. They will see the history on the account, so they don't need you to tell them, but they ask that you do, for the sake of the relationship. The question is, if you knew that the debt, no matter the size, would be forgiven, why wouldn't you bring it before this person for the sake of being honest with them? The answer is simple. The answer is pride. If we tell them about that debt, or that sin, that could be the last straw. If I tell them about this debt, or that sin, what will He think of me? All these questions are racing through our minds before we confess our sin before God, but what we forget is the fact that He saw us do it as if we were living in a glass house with fifteen cameras on it. We aren't hiding anything from God, because we often forget one tiny detail. If God did not know about all the sins in the history of the world, He would not have sent His Son to become a sacrifice for those sins.

Confessing of our sins is not to let God know that we did them. Confessing of our sins is to show that we are humbly coming before God to ask His forgiveness for what we have done. You are not hiding anything from Him, but since He knew about it early enough to have His Son die for it, you might as well let Him in on it and make your heart pure before Him again.

Message:

Do you want to know something crazy? God doesn't need us to tell Him what we did just so that He will know. God wants us to come before Him and confess our wrongs and our debts before Him, so that our hearts can be made whole again. It isn't about tattling on yourself. It isn't about putting your violation on file. It's about being able to come before God without any lingering transgressions on your chest. Refusing to be open and honest with God about our sin causes a breakdown in communication between ourselves and Him. It doesn't mean that He is blind to what you did. It simply means that He is disappointed that you didn't love Him enough to set your own pride aside and confess what you did so that you could restore your relationship with Him to its original state. Be open with God, because ultimately, you have nothing to lose and everything to gain, because whatever you have done, He already knows about and He has already satisfied it. He only asks that you confess it to Him yourself. He only asks that you be open and honest with Him so that you can enjoy the most intimate relationship with Him that you possibly can.

Share It!

Using these questions, reach out to your friends on social media and get the conversation started!

1. When looking at your "account" with God, when was the last time you saw an expense, a certain sin, and wondered, *I never reported that. How did He find out?*
2. Are there any unconfessed sins in your life that you consider to be too big for God to forgive?
3. What is that "closet" in your life that you tend to stuff the "undesirable" things inside and shove the door closed, hoping that God won't see?

Sin is Like a Computer Virus

[12] Let not sin therefore reign in your mortal body, that ye should obey it in the lusts thereof. [13]Niether yield ye your members as instruments of unrighteousness unto sin: but yield yourselves unto God, as those that are alive from the dead, and your members as instruments of righteousness unto God. [14]For sin shall not have dominion over you: for ye are not under the law but under grace.

Romans 6:12-14 KJV

If you have any basic knowledge of a computer at all, you know that it is important to maintain it both in its hardware and in its software. If you let any of these things fall by the wayside for even a short period of time, you could face some serious issues. Most of those issues concern viruses and other types of malware. If these things get into your system, you could be looking at a lot of damage and a lot of time that it will take to repair that damage. Basically, if you do not maintain your computer on a regular basis and do what is necessary to keep it in running order, any kind of malware that is on your computer will begin to overtake it and begin to change it, often to the point of no return.

The same thing is true of sin. We are born with the nature to sin. It is unavoidable and there is nothing that we can do to change that fact about our nature. Fortunately, God sent us a solution to this problem when He sent His Son to die on the cross. Because of Christ's death on the cross, we do not have to be completely consumed by our sin any longer, as long as we invite Him into our lives and repent of the sin in our lives. However, if left unchecked, sin, like malware, can begin to multiply very rapidly. Soon, it begins to overtake us in every aspect of our lives and eventually we find ourselves facing the cleanup that comes as a result of sin taking over one's life. Now, if we accept Christ as our Savior and invite Him into our lives to begin to make changes, He will slowly begin to chip away at the old sins of our past and the effects that those sins had on our lives. However, even though Jesus conducts a sort of full scan when we invite Him into our lives, that doesn't mean that our job is done. When we accept Christ as our Savior, we must remember to check ourselves internally on a regular basis to ensure that our relationship with Christ is working at its optimal rate.

If we accept Christ into our lives and after the initial thorough cleansing of our heart, we leave the upkeep to Him, slowly, temptations that we never knew were lurking around the corner and thoughts that we never thought were possible will begin to creep into our lives. We find that when we accept Christ into our heart, we become somewhat complacent in how we deal with sin. This first verse does not tell us that this warning expires when we accept Christ. This warning applies to everyone in every second of every day. Just because we invite Christ into our lives to make changes, this does not mean that our job is done. Once we have begun a relationship with Him, we have a clean slate. But when this clean slate is left out in the world and the stuff that it picks up begins to reach us, we may begin to find that we are allowing sinful activities of our past to make their way into our present. This is why it is so important to always be aware of what is lurking around the corner when it comes to your spiritual health. This verse tells us to basically keep a watchful eye out for sin that enters our heart, because like cancer, it spreads quickly without our knowledge, but by the time we know anything about it, the damage has been done. Fortunately, God is the ultimate expert in damage reversal.

In the next verse of this passage, we find something that is slightly more within our control. On a daily basis, we are faced with the decision of what we are going to do that day. These decisions range from getting out of bed, to what you're going to wear that day, all the way to whether you will talk to that person on the elevator on the way to your office or to class. These are decisions that we make somewhat unconsciously, but nevertheless, they impact the outcome of our day. In addition to these types of decisions, we have to decide whether we will go to that website or listen to this particular kind of music. These are decisions that we also make every day, but their impact is of a completely different nature.

Regardless of the nature of the sin that you may find yourself engaged in, this verse encourages us, as followers of Christ, to not give ourselves to those types of behaviors. There are many things that can often become an addiction in our lives that God intended to be for good. There are countless examples of this in the world today. This is not to say that God doesn't want us to have fun or enjoy ourselves. There are plenty of examples of people having wholesome fun in the Bible. What He does not want us to do is to let ourselves become engrossed in activities that can often turn very bad, very quick. Whether you attend a Christian college or a state college, you know what I mean when I say this. There are so many things that were used for wholesome, righteous purposes in the times of the Bible. Unfortunately, today it seems that the purpose and meaning of everything in existence is being redefined a little bit each day, including those things that were originally placed in the world for the purposes of doing good. This is why it is becoming more important than ever before that Christians stay on their toes when it comes to avoiding falling into sinful behaviors because the world is making it harder and harder to recognize those behaviors, even when they are right in front of our faces.

In the final verse of this passage, we have a result if we follow what is being asked of us in this passage. If we choose to follow the righteous path and refuse to allow ourselves to fall into these sinful behaviors that are so often trivialized by the world, we will have the power to escape the power of sin. We will have the power to overcome the temptations and the struggles that the world throws our way on a regular basis. Sadly, the temptations that come our way do not always look repulsive to the Christian. So often, Satan will use things that he knows to be something that Christians put a lot of stock in, to lure them in and bring them into a slippery sinful slope that they don't always recognize right away. It will often seem like a genuinely good idea at the time, but in the end, you will realize that it was not really worth the risk that it took to do this or that.

I will end with another computer example. Among the different types of viruses and malware, one of the most commonly known types is referred to as a Trojan horse. This type of malware disguises itself as a legitimate application, but it is actually ridden with all kinds of malicious code. Once it makes its way into your computer, it basically wages war on your system.

Sin left unchecked will usually have a similar effect. While asking Christ to forgive you of your sins is a great starting point in beginning a relationship with Him, that's only the beginning and you do not immediately become a perfect, sinless saint from that point on. You will still find yourself in sin on what seems to be a regular basis, because of your human nature. However, it is critical not to allow this sin to run rampant in your body. If you allow this, it will become difficult to manage the damage that had been done by that sin, and it will eventually reach the point of being almost impossible to repair.

Message:

God doesn't expect us to be perfect, because He knows that this is impossible. He doesn't expect anything close to that from us. What He does expect from us is that we remain open about the sin that can so often corrupt and overtake our lives. He doesn't want us to hide our sin from Him because doing so hurts both Him and us. The only thing that God wants from us is our open hearts, and He will take care of the rest. He wants us to lend our members to Him and allow Him to do as He will. Therefore, knowing that God is using these "members" of our body for His purpose should make unrighteousness something that we want to avoid at all costs. Therefore, be open about the sin that can consume your life, because doing so will ultimately result in a more intimate, more open relationship with your Heavenly Father.

Share It!

Using these questions, reach out to your friends on social media and get the conversation started!

1. When was the last time you ran a *full scan* on your heart and your relationship with Christ? What were the results?
2. In your personal walk with Christ, where does your sin usually start?
3. What steps have you taken, or will you take to ensure that sin does not begin to run rampant in your body and cause damage to your walk with Christ?

The Flesh is Conquered

[1]*There is* therefore now no condemnation to them which are in Christ Jesus, who walk not after the flesh, but after the Spirit. [2]For the law of the Spirit of life in Christ Jesus hath made me free from the law of sin and death. [3]For what the law could not do, in that it was weak through the flesh, God sending his own Son in the likeness of sinful flesh and for sin, condemned sin in the flesh: [4]that the righteousness of the law might be fulfilled in us, who walk not after the flesh, but after the Spirit.

Romans 8:1-4 KJV

Take a second right now to look up from reading this, and just look around you. Regardless of where you are right now, two things are true: You are alive, and the chances are pretty good, that in some way, you are serving the flesh, the needs of this world. In some way, you are doing something that you hope will benefit you in either the near or distant future. Whether that means that you are sitting in your dorm on your college campus, where you hope to get an education that will allow you to get a job, or whether you're sitting at a table somewhere eating, or whatever it is that you may be doing, in some capacity, right now, you are serving your flesh. If you think about it, serving our flesh, making ourselves more comfortable is probably the first thing that comes to our mind when we wake up in the morning. What am I going to eat today? What time do I get to go to bed tonight? Is it payday? All these questions and others that are similar race through our minds every day, sometimes before we even get out of bed. Before we even leave our house or our dorm in the morning, just minutes after waking up, our mind is filled with thoughts that ultimately come down to fulfilling some desire of the flesh. This is because, regardless of how good of a Christian you consider yourself to be, because of our sin nature that we are born with, our mind cannot help but to think of these things that make the body better rather than the relationship and future that we have with Christ. It's just who we are as human beings. Hence the reason Christ had to die to break this cycle. He came to make us free from the consequences of that deep-seated sin nature that comes with the package of human beings. Did He have to? Not at all, but He knew that someone who was sinless and spotless had to die in order for there to be genuine forgiveness and reconciliation for sins, and He knew that without this reconciliation, there was no path to a relationship with these people that needed so badly to be freed from their sin. He knew that only He could be that reconciliation, and He acted on it.

Now, as we rewind to the first verse of this passage, we see this idea of "no condemnation to them which are in Christ Jesus…" This was the whole reason for Christ's death in the first place! He promises no condemnation for anyone who chooses to receive this gift of life, renewal, and forgiveness. That is a guarantee, a promise to us and to anyone in this world who chooses to accept this free, non-perishable gift, that when the time comes for everyone on this earth to stand accountable for the sins that they have committed in their lifetime, we will be able to stand at the feet of Jesus, and hear Him say "You're good" (basically). No condemnation means that, as long as we are living in the Spirit, as long as we have made the decision to follow the plans that He has set before us, we can know that we're good in God's book, regardless of what may happen to us, to our flesh in this world today. That can never and will never change. Notice that there's not some kind of footnote attached to this verse that lists exceptions and exclusions. That's because there aren't any. If there were, they wouldn't be in a footnote and this sacrifice would no longer be considered unconditional and all-inclusive. Had there been conditions for the receipt of this gift, it would no longer be free, and it would no longer be given under grace, but rather as a result of action. This is exactly what God wanted to avoid. He wanted us to realize that this gift was only possible if it came from Him and no one and nothing else. He needed us to understand that He was, and still is the ultimate source of forgiveness through grace. Without having Him in the picture, we are left to our own devices when it comes to finding a way to save ourselves, which would ultimately lead to nowhere. See, God knew this, and the crazy thing is that His mind hasn't changed one bit to this day. He still wants a relationship with you. He still wants you to know Him and to want to live your life for Him. However, no matter how much He may want it for us, it's only through our wanting it for ourselves that we will be able to experience the change that comes with this gift.

Message:

Today, we put so much effort, time, and money into making our flesh better. However, sometimes we fail to realize that the flesh will eventually fail in one way or another, and when it does, we will find ourselves left with how we chose to glorify God through it and through our relationship with Him. Therefore, as we head out to pursue our daily routine, let us not neglect the nurturing and betterment of the relationship we have with Christ, simply because we get lost in our desire to make the flesh, the temporary flesh, just a little bit better for a little bit longer.

Share It!

Using these questions, reach out to your friends on social media and get the conversation started!

1. How have you fed your flesh (excluding food) today?
2. How has social media impacted your need to satisfy your fleshly desires?
3. What steps have you taken to combat these types of desires in your life?
4. Take this next week, designate an accountability partner, and commit to staying off social media for the entire week. To replace that activity, challenge yourself to write a letter to a different person every day. The only social media piece to this will be for you to identify the people that you plan to write to. For the first letter, write to someone asking how you can pray for them. This doesn't have to be the only thing included in the letter, but it should be included at some point. Go!

Christom Brings Life

[10]And if Christ *be* in you, the body *is* dead because of sin; but the spirit *is* life because of righteousness. [11]But if the Spirit of him that raised up Jesus from the dead dwell in you, he that raised up Christ from the dead shall also quicken your mortal bodies by his spirit that dwelleth in you.

Romans 8:10-11 KJV

Dead. That is what we are if Christ is not in us. Regardless of what you do for a living or how good of a person you consider yourself to be, if there has not been a point in your life when you admitted in the presence of Christ, that you are basically dead because of your sinful nature and the sin that you were born into, you are still dead. Basically, once you reach the point of accountability for your sins, you will remain dead until you place your life, your trust and everything you are in Christ. Sadly, there are people who go their entire lives and never do this. Therefore, if we follow the logic set forth in this passage, those people who have never placed their trust in Christ and received remission of sins through the blood of Christ have never truly lived. This passage tells us in a very logical way that, without Christ, we are dead. Until you come to this conclusion, you can never have a true relationship with Christ. However, like so many verses in Romans and throughout the Bible, Paul does not stop there. Paul also gives another provision here for those who have initiated a relationship with Christ.

In the second part of this verse, Paul tells us that the spirit is life. Without Christ, everything that we do, everything that we say, everything that makes up our lives, has no true significance. When you are dead in your sin, you go through each day, and sure, your job is helping the company to survive, but other than paying the bills, there is no purpose behind what you are doing, because that, purpose, that significance can only truly come from Christ. However, when you come to know Christ, suddenly, everything that you do in your life is for a different reason. After some time, you begin to perform your job at a level that makes others ask what is different about you. You live your life through your interactions with people and your activities in a way that makes people stand at the water cooler and wonder what's up with Steve.

So many adults have a past that they are not proud of. Some college students have a present that they are not proud of, but they do not see any way that they can change that. In a way, they are correct. There is nothing that you can do that will get rid of all that stuff that makes up your past and maybe even your present. There is nothing you can do. However, there is something that can be done. The healing power of a relationship with Christ is an amazing thing. The power of a relationship with Christ can bring someone who is spiritually dead to a place in their new life that will make people question whether that person had a secret twin. The power of a relationship with Christ will make some people figure out that they don't want to be associated with that kind of person, and that's okay. You will be amazed how many friends you will lose when you become a child of God and begin living your life for Him. You'll be amazed by the looks people will give you when they walk up to you and see you carrying a Bible instead of a smile that has gossip behind it. Will this change be immediate? Probably not, but it depends on how thirsty you are for the Gospel. If you do experience an immediate change, it either means that you are trying to put on a mask, or that you were so thirsty for actual truth instead of the made-up truth that people have been telling you, that having finally found actual, genuine truth has had a truly profound impact on you.

When I was initially saved at the age of five, I didn't understand the gift of God's grace or the sinful nature that I had been born with. I just knew that I had seen a lot of people do it and I wanted to do that too. Obviously, I didn't have much of a past at the age of five, and I hadn't really studied my Bible. All I knew was that the teacher asked a question and I wanted to answer it with a yes. However, when I reached a point in my life when the only evidence I had for my salvation was that my parents had told me that I was saved, I decided that it was time for me to do this for real. This didn't mean that it wasn't real the first time, but it did mean that I didn't know at the time what I was committing to. When I reached the age of eighteen and was away from home on a mission's trip, I had a moment during one of the sessions when I realized my sinful nature and my need to reconcile that sinful nature with God. It was at that moment when I truly put off that nature and began a renewed relationship with Christ. Granted, I didn't have much of a past and I still don't. Hopefully, that is your story too. If it's not, Christ's desire to have you in his family is still as strong as ever. When He looks at you, He sees a child who has run away from Him, and He so longs for you to come back to Him. It doesn't matter what you have done. It doesn't matter who you've hung out with. All that matters to

Him is that you make a commitment to Him that you will follow Him and honor that new relationship with your life.

Message:

The Bible tells us repeatedly that we are born sinners. The Bible also tells us that sin makes us all spiritually dead. Fortunately, it offers a solution. The answer is Christ's death on the cross, which in turn, gave us life. The incredible thing about this is the fact that we have a chance to have a relationship with Him. We have a chance to experience life through Him and only Him. It is not through any magical formula or any fancy words that we will be able to experience life through Him. This should serve as some good news considering the sinful nature that we just discussed. Ultimately, what it comes down to is that we are born dead in our sin, but Christ gives us a way to experience life through Him. The question is if you are ready to commit to that relationship. If you already have, how is your relationship with Him?

Share It!

Using these questions, reach out to your friends on social media and get the conversation started!

1. What kinds of truth have you been injecting into the veins of your relationship with Christ? Do you find that it leaves you quenched or looking for something more?
2. Where do you find your truth?
3. How are you able to identify truth in respect to your walk with Christ?
4. Today, we continue with the social media fast that was initiated yesterday. Today, write a letter to someone from school. In the letter, in addition to asking for what you can be praying, talk about truth. Tell them about how that truth is intertwined with the love that Christ has for us and the role that this love played in his sacrifice on the cross.

There is Freedom in the Name of Christ

For ye have not received the spirit of bondage again to fear; but ye have received the spirit of adoption, whereby we cry, Abba Father.

Romans 8:15 KJV

If you have been blessed as I have been to have a father to call your own, you will know the love that is shared by a father and his child/children. The love of a father is such that, if the situation demanded it, He would be willing to give his life for his child. A father holds his child's life in a higher regard than his own. Now, think about walking up to the God of the universe on the day that you leave this earth or on the Day of Judgment, and saying "Hey Dad". Most of us probably find the possibility of this both exhilarating and terrifying. So often, when we communicate with God, we think of Him as being more of a supervisor at a job as opposed to a father that calls us His own. Most of us could not imagine walking up to our supervisor at work and hugging him/her and telling them how much we love them and how amazing they are. We don't do this because we know that it would likely lead to HR involvement. However, if we walked up to our mother or father, whether you are still living at home or not, and said, "Hello sir. How are you doing today?" your father would likely be baffled by your behavior because this is simply not how that relationship usually works.

Why do we treat someone who would be willing to give their life for us different from someone who manages thousands of employees and signs our paycheck? We treat them differently because we have different kinds of relationships with both. Your father, who was responsible for bringing you into this world, wants your love. He wants you to show him how much he means to you. He wants to know about everything that is going on in your life. He doesn't expect you to come before him with a dictionary so that you can use fancy words to impress him. He wants you to come as the person he knows you to be.

In the same way that you wouldn't treat your father and your supervisor with the same kind of affection and respect, you should not feel like you need to come before God with a page-long prayer that you spent all day writing so that He would be impressed by you. He wants you to come before Him and tell Him about your fears, your worries, and your struggles. He doesn't expect you to be polished and perfect when you come before Him. That's why He died for you. He did that because you aren't perfect. He wants you to be honest about the things that you are struggling with, the things that make you worry every day and keep you awake at night. If you do not do this and you simply come before Him trying to come across as having it all together, you are only fooling yourself. God already knows what keeps you up at night. He already knows what you are struggling with, but if you don't feel that you can be honest with Him about those things, then you do not completely understand the scope of God's love for you.

The other part of this verse tells us that this relationship that we have with our heavenly father is not one that is founded on fear or uncertainty. That is what this relationship should help to alleviate. If we come before God to admit our shortcomings and our struggles because we are afraid that He will give us a spiritual spanking if we don't tell Him, I tell you again, you do not truly understand the scope of His love for us. Many times, the thing that keeps people from coming into a relationship with Christ is this idea that they have to have it all together before they are able to do this. They don't want to be tied down to practices and rules. The crazy thing is that this is what knowing Christ frees us from.

When we approach the throne of God in the same way that we approach the office of a manager, we cannot expect to have a relationship that is any different than that. We cannot expect to only share parts and pieces of our lives with the God of the universe and to have an intimate relationship with Him at the same time. To have an intimate relationship with Christ, we resolve to give over to Him all areas of ourselves and our lives rather than just those few areas that seem to need the least amount of work.

Message:

This verse shows those who walk with Christ the type of access that we have to Christ as his children. This verse tells us that He has adopted us. This means that He becomes ours and we become his. This means that we are in a new relationship with Him that gives us access to Him that we have never had before. However, this is a two-sided coin, because this means that, as our father, He should have complete access to all that we are; from our practices when we are alone to the people that we hang out with, in addition to the hopes that we have for our future. The problem that many have with this, is that giving Him access to these areas of our lives also gives Him the ability to make changes to those areas. Will you allow Him to have full, unrestricted access to your life, or will you give Him limited access with restrictions? Your answer to this question will determine the type of relationship you will be able to have with the creator of the universe. Will it be that of a father, or of a boss that you depart from at the end of the day?

Share It!

Using these questions, reach out to your friends on social media and get the conversation started!

1. What kinds of "permissions" have you given Christ in your relationship with Him?
2. What is your biggest fear/concern about your adoptive relationship with your Heavenly Father?
3. When have you had your most intimate moments with God?
4. On the third day of this social media fast, you are about halfway through! For today's letter, write a letter that discusses freedom. Talk about what freedom means to you, and ask what freedom means to them. Talk about how this relates to your walk with Christ. Additionally, if this individual is a non-believer, use this as an opportunity to share the Gospel with them!

No One is Immune to the Gospel

[16]The Spirit itself beareth witness with our spirit, that we are the children of God: [17]and if children, then heirs; heirs of God, and joint-heirs with Christ; if so be that we suffer with *him*, that we may be also glorified together.

Romans 8:16-17 KJV

Earlier, we discussed this idea that God is our father and that we should treat Him as such. We talked about how He reveres us as his children and that He wants to know about our lives. He wants to take part in our lives. This verse continues with that idea, but this verse looks more at the family aspect of our relationship with God.

When we make the decision to follow Christ, we become part of a family that expands far beyond those whom we see on holidays and birthdays. This family contains millions of people, some of whom you like and some of whom you might not be too crazy about. In this sense, it's somewhat similar to a nuclear or extended family. However, there is one major difference between the family of believers that you become a part of at the time that you enter a relationship with Christ and the family that you sit with at Thanksgiving. While there are a father and a mother at the head of your family that you are born into and there are smaller families that split off from this one when it comes to your family in Christ, there is but one head, and that is Christ Himself.

With Christ as the head of your family, no matter what may separate the members of the family, we all fall under on head and we all come from the same ancestor. It doesn't matter who your mother was married to or who your fifth cousin on your maternal grandmother's side was. Ultimately, when it comes to heavenly family, there is but one point of origin and that is God Himself.

If you've spent much time at all in church, you've probably been called brother or sister by members of the church more times than you can count. Sometimes, we view this as a term of endearment, which it is, but it also provides a sense of unity within the family of God.

Even though there are churches all over the place today with different names, denominations, beliefs, and practices, ultimately, they all fall into one huge family. Granted, there are churches that do not exactly align with the Christian belief, but those that do follow the Christian doctrine are all under one heading in the family tree of the Christian faith.

If you have ever seen a family tree on paper, the first names that appear are the names of the first parents that are recorded. Underneath them, there are a certain number of spots for the children they have had. If the church were a family tree, there would not be one set of parents for the Baptist church and one set of parents for the Methodist church and so on. With the parents representing who serves as the head of that church in the sense of the divine head, they would all fall under one head, with that head being Christ.

Regardless of what building believers choose to go into on Sunday, if they have professed a belief in Christ and asked for complete and total forgiveness of sins, they belong to the same family. This is sometimes difficult to grasp because of differences in theology, but when Christ is the head of your church and you are a believer and a child of God, you ultimately belong to the same Father as the other people on the face of the earth who have confessed their sins before God and begun a relationship with Him.

I fully realize that this sounds like one of those "Can't we all just get along?" speeches, but that is not my intention here. Unity in the church is something that can make or break the church in its individual segments and in the church. There are countless examples of this both in the world today and in the Bible. This is why it is important to realize that all who believe on the name of Jesus have become children of God and therefore belong to one family. This means that we all have the same point of origin when it comes to our spiritual rebirth and we all have the same point of refuge in times of trouble. This is not to say that there are not churches out there that teach unbiblical principles because there are. However, when it comes to Bible-believing, Christ-honoring churches, who believe in the infallibility of God's Word, then it is our responsibility as fellow believers to rally around those churches and unite with them in the good times and in the bad, and to love the members of that church just like we love the members of our own.

It seems that we have reached a point today where individual churches have become individual little colonies that only want their own people to dwell among them. This verse shows how incorrect that idea really is.

When you come to the same church for fifteen or twenty years, it can be easy to begin feeling like the doors are locked to anyone else who tries to come in. This is the danger that comes with confining a church to a building with its name on the windows and doors.

The church should be a single unit that operates as a whole. Because we live in the United States of America, we have the freedom to be that single unit without fear of retribution from our government. Sadly, it seems that we have closed our doors to the world and remain fearful to unlock them to allow the people of the world to come in. It's as if the church has become a sterile waiting room for those who are well and are waiting to see those who are sick. The problem is, we get so comfortable in the waiting room, that we often forget why we came there in the first place.

Our mission as followers of Christ is not to confine ourselves to the walls of a building for two hours, once a week. We cannot accomplish the Great Commission that Christ sets before us if we are not willing to leave the safety of our churches. We cannot do what God has called us to do if we refuse to realize that the people we are scared to talk to are in the same place in their lives as we once were in ours. Once we are able to establish that common ground, this mission that is set before us will become a little easier to start working on. This doesn't mean sending groups of fifteen people out on Wednesday night to give out tracts that people will throw away. This means meeting people out on the street or sitting down with that guy or girl on your hall, or in your class whom you believe is not a Christian, and talking to them. We so often forget that Jesus didn't go to every home in the community where He was and tell every house about an event that was going to be happening that Sunday morning. Jesus went into cities and would walk up to a group of people, and the more He talked, the bigger the crowd would grow. He didn't need tracts or flyers to attract people. He didn't need cotton candy and blow-up rides to bring people to hear His message. He simply began to speak, and people became naturally curious about what was being said. Sure, some people probably walked off because He may have said something that they didn't like, but the majority of the people stayed because there was something different about the message that He was delivering. He had a message of truth, but it was also one of hope. It didn't come in different translations for different denominations. There was but one message and people were drawn to it and changed by it, with no additional materials required.

Message:

The Great Commission, as it is set forth in the New Testament should be our sole purpose in the church. We should spend less time worrying about that family that left our Baptist church and went to the Methodist church down the road, and start worrying about that guy in front of our church on the highway that doesn't have a shirt to wear. That is what this verse is trying to tell us. Our focus has gotten so distorted when it comes to the church as a whole. Jesus didn't found denominations in His ministry. Jesus founded a church that still changes lives today. We must remember that if we want to see the church grow as a whole and expand beyond a building and an address.

Share It!

Using these questions, reach out to your friends on social media and get the conversation started!

1. When you look at your church and the part you play in it, do you find that it has become an "access-badge" church, or one that holds its doors open to the world in an effort to bring people to Christ?

2. When you leave your church on Sunday mornings, or your Bible study during the week, what are you doing to take that Great Commission, the mission statement of the church, into your community, your campus, your city? What more could you be doing?

3. When people look at your social media, your interactions during the day, your activities off-campus, do they see a message, a Christ, that they want to be involved with?

4. On the fourth day of this social media hiatus, the challenge concerns this idea of servant evangelism. Today, write a letter to one of the friends that you identified, and talk about service. What does it mean to serve someone? How does service play into the Christian walk? Ask them how you can serve them? Through this dialog, that individual will begin to see that there is more to Christianity than just going to church and being "good". Show them that this love that the Bible talks about is more than just a four-letter word that sounds good in songs.

The Ultimate Weapon and Defense

[31]What shall we then say to these things? If God be for us, who can be against us? [32]He that spared not his own Son, but delivered him up for us all, how shall he not with him also freely give us all things?

Romans 8:31-32 KJV

Have you ever considered this question? Sure, you probably hear it all the time, but have you ever really considered it? If we have God on our side to advocate and to fight for us, what have we to worry about? When I say this, I don't mean the verbal back and forth that comes from people on every side. This will always be a part of the Christian walk. Whoever told you that this walk was going to be easy was either lying or kidding, because this walk will be anything but easy. This is because this relationship with Christ that Christians are so blessed to be able to have is not based on practices or on rituals. It's based on grace exercised by a God that cannot be comprehended by the human mind.

God is over the entire universe and is outside of all time. He is outside of any realm of human understanding. Therefore, when we have God on our side, we have nothing to fear. Does this mean that we have a lifelong guarantee that our lives will never be in danger because of our belief in Christ? No. Does it mean that we know there's a reason behind whatever obstacles come our way and that we can continue to trust in God's plan for us? Most definitely.

God would not have put us into a world that is filled with sin if He didn't intend to become our advocate when that sin had an impact on our lives. The chances are good that someone reading this is in the midst of some kind of battle in their life. Whether that battle is one of health, or if it is one concerning your family, or if you are having uncertainties about your job, God would not have brought you into this battlefield without giving you the armor to weather whatever attacks, verbal, spiritual, or physical, may come your way. You will never be left alone in the battlefields of life without God being there to help you in your battles. This doesn't mean that He will always fight them completely for you. What this does mean is that you will never be left alone in these battles without a weapon that will help you withstand the attacks of the enemy.

If there is one thing that has been made clear so far, it is the fact that life is a battlefield and we will always have the assurance that God will be by our side throughout all those battles. We understand that He will help us to stand up against the enemies that come against us. The question is; what does the Bible mean when it says that no one will be against us? This verse is not necessarily trying to say that there will never be any opposition if you have Christ in your life. If anything, the opposition will grow greater when you begin a relationship with Christ. However, imagine that you are engaged in a battle, and the opposing side is five thousand people strong and they all have slingshots with rocks in them. However, you have a huge cannon with five cannon balls on standby. Just because the enemy seems massive at the time, this does not mean that the enemy is necessarily unconquerable. Just because there is more of them does not necessarily mean that they are stronger. If you thought of it this way, you would probably walk into the battle and think, *I wonder where the opponent is?* Your force is so much stronger than theirs because your force finds its strength in the power of a few strong ones rather than in thousands who do not have a lot of power to give. With the weapon that you have at your disposal, one shot will send everybody running. The enemy has been defeated with nothing close to an army of men. What you did have, however, was a few resources with a lot of power in them.

In the same way that the cannon would overcome thousands of slingshots, the God that goes to battle with you will be your best weapon in the battles of life. The battles of life, especially as a Christian, are numerous. On our own, we have no hope of conquering these battles. They leave us staring across the way and wondering how bad they will be able to defeat us. However, God is standing with us and He sees how minuscule the circumstance, the opposition really is when you have Him on your side. We must also adopt this same kind of attitude when we face battles in life that make us wonder how we will come out on the other side unscathed. The answer is that, without Christ, you will come out on the other side with a lot more damage than you would have incurred if you had simply asked God to advocate and to help you fight this circumstance that you are facing right now. Therefore, the question is, will you try to fight this on your own, and go into battle with no armor and no weapon, or will you go before God and ask Him to be your weapon and your defense in these trying times? Your answer to this question will determine your chances of success in whatever you may be facing right now.

God never intended for us to fight alone. If He intended for us to do this, then He would simply be a divine supervisor. God wants us to turn to Him when these circumstances that we face daily have become too big of a challenge for us to handle on our own. Unfortunately, no matter how strong of a Christian you consider yourself to be, I know for certain that at some point in your life, you have encountered a battle in which the enemy was so much bigger than yourself. During this battle, you likely found yourself without any defense, and the thought of asking God to go to battle for you likely disappeared from your mind as fast as it appeared there. We have this tendency to picture God in a way that makes Him nothing more than a heavenly man. We forget that His abilities and understanding are far beyond that of ourselves. We worry that He won't come through in time, but the God of the universe is never late. Usually, the problem is that we have become impatient. Ultimately, God will come through in a way that only He can in the battles that we face. However, we must remember to step back and let Him take over in every situation that is too big for us to handle.

Message:

Does God give us more than we can handle? Most definitely. Is there anything that God cannot handle? Definitely not. So why would you not go before Him and ask Him to intercede for you in whatever situation that you are facing right now? Once you have failed to conquer it yourself, what other options do you have? To give up? Why would you give up when you have a God who can take care of it for you? If you only ask God to become your ultimate weapon and ultimate defense, there will never be a battle in your life that you will not be able to conquer with Him on your side.

Share It!

Using these questions, reach out to your friends on social media and get the conversation started!

1. What is one battle in your life right now that you've been holding God back from attacking head-on? What would it look like for Him to have victory in that battle?
2. In those instances when you make God and His power a last resort, what makes the other options stand out ahead of Him?
3. When have you seen firsthand the results of God helping you to conquer a battle?
4. For the fifth day of the social media fast, write a letter to a friend, and in this letter, ask them how you can pray for them specifically in respect to a battle that they may be facing at the moment. Everyone has some kind of battle in their life. However, very few people are willing to openly admit that. Most are waiting for someone to ask. Be that person to one of these friends. Maybe they're fighting the same or a similar battle as yourself. However, you'll never know until you take the first step and ask.

There is Nothing Too Big for the Love of God

[35]Who shall separate us from the love of Christ? *shall* tribulation, or distress, or persecution, or famine, or nakedness or peril, or sword? [36]As it is written, For thy sake we are killed all the day long; we are accounted as sheep for the slaughter. [37]Nay, in all these things we are more than conquerors through him that loved us. [38]For I am persuaded, that neither death, nor life, nor angels, nor principalities, nor powers, nor things present, nor things to come, [39]nor height, nor depth, nor any other creature, shall be able to separate us from the love of God, which is in Jesus Christ our Lord

Romans 8:35-39 KJV

Love is a word that we often associate with a feeling that we have for someone. In the early years of our lives, love may be permanent, or it may be temporary, depending on who the person is and what the circumstances are surrounding the relationship. However, regardless of who the person is and what type of relationship it is that the two people are engaged in, the love that they feel, whether they admit it or not, has at least one thing that would cause that love to end. This one thing is going to be different for different people. For most romantic relationships, infidelity is a big one. For some, differences in religious or political views could be a make or break factor. For some, it could be differences in views on marriage. However, in the end, no matter how unbreakable you may consider the love to be between you and your best friend or you and your significant other, there is some hidden thing that would bring that love to a halt. Therefore, one of the shortcomings of earthly, human love, is the fact that, as perfect as it may seem at the time, human love is fallible and can be destroyed in one way or another, except for the love that a parent has for a child. This love, regardless of what that child does or says to that parent, continues to persevere through every obstacle that it faces. This is one type of earthly love that cannot be destroyed or lost very easily, if at all.

Now that we have established the parameters for human love and affection, let's turn to the passage above that talks about the true love and affection that comes from God through Christ. The passage opens with somewhat of a challenge question. It challenges us to come up with something, anything, that can fracture or eliminate the love that God has for His children. He challenges God's people to think about the unwavering nature of God's love; this love that we did nothing to deserve and everything to be deprived of. He challenges us to look at this love that we are given daily and to realize that, regardless of how many reasons we give God not to love us, He will never use any of them as an excuse to do so.

In the second verse, Paul tells us that we are more than conquerors. This is a very empowering thought. To be told that, through all the adversity that we face in the world, because of the love of God through Christ, we are not weakened, but rather, we are conquerors. Through the love of Christ, we are not worn down but rather strengthened. Regardless of the battles that we face, the struggles that we deal with on a daily basis, through Christ, we have the power to face each new challenge with renewed hope and strength. However, the hope and strength that we use to fight these battles is not the hope and strength that we get from self-help books or by attending inspirational seminars. The hope and strength that we use to fight these battles is a hope and strength that comes from knowing that it's not up to you to conquer whatever obstacle you have in front of you. It's not up to you to conquer this hurdle that you are approaching in your journey. We often forget that God doesn't put these battles in our lives so that we can prove how great and strong we are. He puts these battles in our lives so that He can show us how strong and great He is.

In these last two verses, we find an answer to the question which is posed in the first verse. In these last two verses, we find an extensive list that reminds us that the things in life that would fracture or eliminate the love that we have for so many people, would not even begin to touch the love that God has for us. The love that God has for His people is not a love that He felt one day and suddenly said, "I think I'm starting to love [insert name here]". The love that God has for us is an eternal love in both directions. This is a love that is strong enough to permeate every sin, every betrayal, every turn of the back that God endures from us over the course of our lives.

The love that God has for us does not reside in a building or in a special prayer. God's love for us can be found in Him and in Him alone. He also shows us that His Son is an extension of Himself in the last part of this passage when Paul tells us that the love of God, which is daily poured out upon us, is found in His Son, Jesus Christ, who came and died as a sign of that love for the whole world to see. You cannot take back the death of a child. Granted, He rose from the dead after the fact, but God could have rescued his dearly beloved son in a heartbeat if He wanted to, but He wanted so desperately to show us the love that He has for us in a way that would make sense to the world thousands of years later.

The love that we experience through Christ cannot be undone. It cannot be taken back. Regardless of what we do or what we say, God still loves his people as unconditionally as He does when those same people are in constant communication with Him. God's love for us is not something that is determined by our GPA or the grade that we make on that test or this paper. The love that we receive from God doesn't even count on our loving Him back. He wants us to love Him back, most definitely. He wants this more than anything, but in the end, He knows that there will be people who refuse to do that, and yet, He loves them still.

In the end, God's love is like a bulletproof vest. There is no circumstance, no words, no thoughts, no deeds that you can throw at His love that will make Him love you any less. It is important that we realize that the love God has for us is not the love that a boyfriend and girlfriend share or a husband and wife. The love that God has for us is a love that no one will ever be able to find anywhere else. This is an important thing to remember in those times when you may have just broken up with your significant other and you're feeling alone and unsure of what to do next. This is something that is important to remember when you feel that you are not doing your best in your academics because of some circumstance outside of the classroom. Whatever circumstance you find yourself in that makes you feel like hope is nowhere to be found, will never be too strong of a circumstance for God's love to handle.

Message:

You will never do anything big enough, bad enough or crazy enough to end up beyond the point of being loved by God. We often forget that He sent His Son to die for *all* sin. He didn't set a quota for the amount of sin that you could have in your life before He would abandon you. This doesn't mean that there shouldn't be a life change when you give your life to Christ, because there should definitely be one. However, God knows the sinful nature that each and every person was born into. For that reason, He will never expect us to be perfect and He will most definitely never attach this as a condition to our receipt of His love.

Share It!

Using these questions, reach out to your friends on social media and get the conversation started!

1. What kinds of boundaries have you been placing on God's love lately? How have those boundaries changed?
2. What is your biggest fear when it comes to wholly submitting to the love that God has for you?
3. Where does God's love and the relationship that comes with it rank in your collection of relationships in your life? What have you placed above it?
4. On the sixth day of this social media hiatus, the challenge is to write a letter to one of your chosen friends that talks about this idea of true love. In this letter, share what love means to you and what that looks like in your mind. Share with this person the love that you have for them. For this piece of the challenge, focus on using love as a verb. Sharing this kind of love with those in our lives who matter most has the potential to transform and renew relationships when both parties realize that there are no strings attached.

God is Not Clueless

O the depth of the riches both of the wisdom and knowledge of God! how unsearchable *are* his judgements, and his ways past finding out!

Romans 11:33 KJV

We've all had those days, weeks, months or even years when we found ourselves constantly saying "I don't understand". We've all been in those places in life when we look to God and the only words we can find the strength to say is, I just don't get it. These times in our lives are placed there for a purpose. There is guarantee after guarantee throughout scripture that we will face struggles in this life on earth. There is no escaping that. However, in the midst of these struggles that so often test us and try our limits, we must stop and remind ourselves where these circumstances come from. They don't come from some random combination of chance and circumstance. Whatever it is that may be plaguing your life right now, whether it be a sickness of your own or a family member, or whether it's some kind of financial struggle, it can become so easy to quickly turn to God and ask Him if He really knows what He's doing.

So often, we try to give God human qualities and limitations, while expecting supernatural results in the circumstances we face throughout life. We look at whatever situation we are facing at the time and silently tell ourselves that there is no point in praying for God's intervention in this situation. Whether that is a test in your hardest class or an issue that you may be dealing with on a personal level, the outcome will never be what you want it to be. This is our first mistake when we go before God to pray for a certain situation. While our words say that we are giving it to God, our heart has made the decision to keep its finger on that emergency stop button in case God's plan starts going south. We fear that if we give over every piece of the situation to God, that He will stick us in the middle of nowhere with no clue as to what we are supposed to do. Ultimately, what it comes down to, is that we have this often microscopic (or maybe not so microscopic) piece of doubt that believes that God doesn't know what He is doing. Because we fear that He may not know what He is doing, we hold onto an emergency ABANDON SHIP button in case anything happens that doesn't necessarily line up with our plans. We are willing to give Him control as long as it goes our way. Unfortunately, this course of action is not really what it looks like to give God control and to trust Him with the results.

What if we chose to genuinely give the whole situation over to God? What if, instead of praying for God to give us wisdom, but figuring out how an F would hurt our grade, we prayed for God to give us wisdom, studied to the best of our ability, and went into the test believing that God would come through for us? What if we made the decision to hand all our equipment, all our skills, all our assets over to God? What do you think God would be capable of then? What if we prayed for God to give us wisdom in this situation that we are dealing with, and actually believed with all our heart and mind that He would actually do what His Word promises? What do you think God would do with you if you placed all your trust and resources in His hands? The results may actually surprise you.

This verse tells us that His ways and His knowledge are beyond anything that we could even begin to imagine. He knows things about the past, present, and future that we could not even begin to understand. He knew from the beginning of time how everything that is happening in the world today would affect the plans He has for the future. While the presence of sin in the world definitely changed the plans that He had when He created the world and its inhabitants, He was not surprised by any of it. Does this mean that He made man sin and caused sin to enter the world? No. Could He have prevented Adam and Eve from committing that first sin in the garden at the beginning of time? Yes, He could have, but in doing that, He would have eliminated any free will that we are so fortunate to enjoy today.

God knows what He is doing at all times when He sends certain circumstances to certain people. He knows the impact that those things will have on the life of that person. He does not issue conflict blindly without any awareness of the impact it will have on people. If this were consistent with God's nature, He would be a dictator, not a God worthy of being worshipped.

This verse tells us that His judgments are infallible. The judgments that God issues in the life of every person on earth is not a judgment that is subject to appeal. God does not need us to tell Him what evidence or what facts He failed to consider. He doesn't need us to tell Him that He got this one wrong. When God looks at a situation, He knows everything there is to know about it. He knows things about the situation that we will never know. This is something that we must understand when we come into these situations in life that seem unjust or unfair. We need to remember this when we have a surprise job loss for no given reason or some other circumstance that completely blindsides us. While we may not know the reason that these things happen, there is One who has a reason, and we must rest assured that He would not bring it into our lives if He didn't have a purpose for it.

Message:

There is no fluff when it comes to God's plan for our lives. He never puts things into our lives that are useless. He didn't finish putting our lives together and end up with spare parts that He placed in random spots. There is nothing in your life that is random. Every triumph, every struggle, every journey in your life has a purpose in God's plan. Does this sound cliché? Probably. But this is because we hear things like this all the time, but never quite understand what people mean when they say it. Everything that you are facing or have faced has been placed in a specific part of your life, because without circumstance A, it is impossible for you to reach destination B. Sometimes, it takes struggles and conflict for us to end up where God wants us. Nothing you face is ever a mistake, no matter how unfair or unusual it may seem. Let us remember this when we face those uncertain times in our life's journey. Let us remember that nothing you are facing is a result of a God who does not know what He is doing. God has a plan for everyone on this earth and He has a plan for how He will make it a reality. Just trust Him.

Share It!

Using these questions, reach out to your friends on social media and get the conversation started!

1. Recall a time in your life when you found yourself questioning God and His motives. What kind of questions did you find looming in your heart during that time?
2. How have you seen God work through a certain "blindside" moment recently? How were you able to use that in your ministry to others?
3. On the final day of the social media hiatus, the final letter that you will write as a part of this challenge will somewhat circle back to the first day. Today, write a letter to the last friend that you selected asking them what challenge, what *blindside circumstance* you can be praying for on their behalf. Take this time to reciprocate and share a circumstance that is in your life and could use prayer.

What About You?

For the preaching of the cross is to them that perish foolishness; but unto us which are saved, it is the power of God.

1 Corinthians 1:18 KJV

This verse addresses something that is so often encountered by Christians when we attempt to share the Gospel with nonbelievers. In the world that we live in today, obviously, not everyone is a Christian. That has never been the case and probably never will be the case. However, not only is it the case that there are many people who do not follow Christ, but it is also the case that, so many are intensely opposed to following Him, mostly due to Christians' positions on social issues or, sadly, due to less-than-ideal interactions with Christ-followers. They simply write the Gospel message off as a fairy tale with no room left to consider evidence that offers an alternative answer. However, regardless of the reason that is used, the number of people against the message of Christ is growing increasingly larger as time progresses. With this in mind, what question should we, as Christians, be asking? You may be thinking that we should be asking how we can better reach them and how we can better share the Gospel. While these are great questions to ask, there is one critically important question that Christians should be asking, and it is about ourselves.

The question that Christians should be asking in a world where Christ is increasingly shunned from the government, the schools, and an increasing number of additional places in society is…What about you? What does this mean? What do the Gospel and the message of Christ mean to you? Regardless of how people react when you share the message with them, what does this message, which you claim to be living out every day, mean to you? This is a critical point in the witnessing process because before you can share it with other people, you need to make sure that you believe in the message of the Gospel yourself. This can often be challenging to Christians who have believed in the name of Christ for the majority of their life. But ultimately, why are you following Christ? Are you following Him to have a relationship with Him and to live in communion with Him, or are you following Him because your Sunday school teacher or pastor told you that it was a good idea?

These questions are important ones to ask yourself before you even begin to think about witnessing to nonbelievers. Why? Imagine that you go out on a Saturday afternoon, and you head over to the mall with the intention of sharing the Gospel with the patrons. You come across a young man who seems friendly, so you walk up to him and ask if anyone has ever shared the Gospel with him. He answers with a story of how he used to be one of the most dedicated members of his church. He follows this with the details of how he came to turn away from his walk with Christ, and to a life without Him. What do you say to this person? He delivers a very well thought out argument for why he did what he did, but how do you answer that? This man has heard every approach in the book. Would you be able to effectively bring him back to a point where he would be able to return to a relationship with Christ, or would he have defeated your entire toolbox of resources with a few sentences? It is critical that we as Christians do not make our top resource a list of questions that we received in a class or in church. These are great for those who have never heard the Gospel and are thirsty for truth that they can trust, but to those who have spent their entire life in the church and have turned away from Christ, it needs to go deeper than that.

When we think about this, it is interesting how this verse takes on a new kind of message. Often, we try to approach non-believers and believers who have strayed with Bible in hand and a mind full of Christian terms that would make any theology professor proud. These are great when writing papers for a theology class or to construct some kind of argument with a fellow believer, but this verse tells us that, basically, the Gospel is foolishness to non-believers. They do not regard it as being a book with any kind of authority. They usually view it as a book of feel-good stories with a good man at the center. For this reason, to go to these people with a book that they put no value in is a wasted venture. However, this brings us back to the first question. What about you?

When you approach someone to tell them about the Gospel, what do you bring to the table in your own life that makes that message one that they would want to hear and receive? The Gospel has a lot of power in its words, but to people who do not place any value in those words, it will take someone who has seen God work in their own life and has seen the difference that a relationship with Him makes in one's life, to show that person what it truly means to follow Him. It will take someone showing this person how they were once a victim of the sin that they were born into, but they are now free from that sin and are now able to have a relationship with the creator of the universe and can talk to Him at any time they would like. People who have fallen away turned away, or refuse to even acknowledge the message of the Gospel need to hear something from your life that makes them say, "I want that".

So often, people will have one terrible experience in the church or one bad encounter with someone who claims to be a follower of Christ, and they will find themselves thinking that a relationship with Christ is not something that they want to be a part of. At that point, it is up to those who follow Christ with all their being to bring that person from not wanting to have anything to do with Christ and the church, to a place where they find themselves wanting what you're having. This is why it is so important to evaluate what it is that brought you to Christ and what has made you stay with Him since that time. If you cannot answer this challenge with something that sounds like it wasn't written in five seconds, you may want to take a step back and figure out what your reasons are for following Christ. Once you have done this, it will become easier to generate a defense for the case that you are presenting. Once you can present evidence that this relationship with Christ produces the change that the pastor says it does, people will probably begin to listen just a little bit closer. Therefore, challenge yourself to become living proof, a living, breathing example of how Christ can take someone, no matter how broken they may be, and make them into someone whom He can use to accomplish something great.

Message:

There should be no doubt in the mind of believers that the Gospel is a true, reliable account of the events leading up to, during, and after Christ's life here on Earth. There should be no doubt in the minds of believers that this Gospel that they listen to several times a week contains infallible truth that was spoken by the Son of God and breathed by God Himself. This is where many believers forget that salvation requires that there is a conscious belief in order for one's acceptance of salvation to become genuine. Believers come to the decision to follow Christ (hopefully) because they believe in what the Bible says, and the things that God said and did. When one becomes a believer in Christ and the message of the Gospel, they are signing on an invisible dotted line that they believe what the Bible says and that they are willing to listen to those words. The Gospel is the truth that Christians are supposed to live by and base their decisions on. However, if we go before nonbelievers and we are not able to produce evidence from our lives that shows that the Gospel and a relationship with Christ works, then we are only continuing to feed the misconceptions that are held by nonbelievers that the Gospel is without value. If we cannot show nonbelievers that the Gospel and Christ *work*, then they will continue assuming that it doesn't. Therefore, before you head over to the mall to hand out tracts and tell people how incredible it is to have a relationship with Christ, you may want to stop and ask yourself one question; What about you?

Share It!

Using these questions, reach out to your friends on social media and get the conversation started!

1. When you engage with nonbelievers for the purposes of sharing the Gospel, what do you find to be your biggest obstacle?
2. What do you find to be the most difficult part about sharing the Gospel, aside from initiating the interaction?
3. What does the Gospel mean to you, and how would you share that with someone who may have never read it?

Our Plan Is Not God's Plan

[9]But as it is written, Eye hath not seen, nor ear heard, neither have entered into the heart of man, the things which God hath prepared for them that love him

1 Corinthians 2:9 KJV

How comforting it is to know that those who love God and live in communion with him have plans that were made specifically for them. How incredible it is to know that no person on the face of the earth can change that plan! So often, we face circumstances in life, whether they be changes in major, inability to find the funds to spend another semester at their dream school, or any other number of life-altering circumstances, which stop us dead in our tracks with no clue as to where we should go next. We find ourselves in this place where we never thought we would be, and we find ourselves wondering how these circumstances that we would have never chosen for ourselves could ever amount to anything close to good for us. We wonder why God would put these circumstances in our lives at a time when it seemed that everything was going right. We wonder why God couldn't have just let things stay smooth. Why would He do that?

I will answer this question like this. Imagine that you are on a six-and-a-half-hour journey to the most incredible vacation spot that you can imagine. You've been in the car for about three hours and so far, everything has been a smooth ride. Suddenly, you see a sign that says UNPAVED ROAD FOR THE NEXT FIVE MILES. Suddenly, it begins. The car is vibrating, and you can barely hear yourself think. The car is shaking so much that you can barely hold your phone in your lap. You are pretty sure that those are the longest five miles you've ever been through. Eventually, however, the shaking stops and you feel like you are riding on a cloud, but without the rocky piece of that journey, you would not have been able to appreciate the smooth-riding portions of the journey afterward. This is how it is when we go through life with Christ sometimes.

When we read this verse, Paul is telling us that, no matter how hard we try, there is no possible way that we will be able to understand the entire plan that God has for our lives. This is by design. He gives us pieces at a time so that we will be able to appreciate the incredible nature of each piece individually. Plus, if God laid out the entire plan that He had for our lives, it would be incredibly overwhelming. Think of it this way: Imagine that someone told you that they were going to build you a huge mansion free of charge. The catch, however, is that you will be responsible for retrieving the pieces and the builders for the house. He will put the pieces together and give jobs to the builders, but ultimately, you have a part in this deal too. Well, you get the list of builders and resources and some of the things that you are required to retrieve will bring you into what is considered the most undesirable parts of the city, but without those pieces and those people, this house will not be able to be built.

This house that you're imagining resembles your life. The builders and the materials represent your circumstances and the people that you meet along the way. You pray for years and years for God's will to be done in your life, but when the process begins to be put into motion, it becomes clear that you weren't quite aware of what you were getting into. The end result and some of the events along the way are somewhat pleasant, but there are also people and events along the way that you would rather forget. Why couldn't the house just come together right in front of us, so that we wouldn't have to go through all that stuff? The answer is that, without this stuff, you would not be able to accomplish God's ultimate purpose for your life, and without purpose, you are simply walking and breathing for the sake of walking and breathing. Without a purpose, you are not accomplishing anything for the betterment of God's kingdom. However, with a purpose, which is slowly revealed to you over time, you will encounter people you would not have met otherwise, and you will go through things that change you as a person. Because of the purpose that God has for your life, you become a tool, a resource that God will use to either bring people who know Him closer in their relationship with Him, or to bring people who have never heard of Him closer to knowing and loving Him. The question is whether you are willing to be used by God, or if you are okay just enjoying the smooth ride for as long as you can.

Message:

God has a plan. This is nothing new to anyone who has been through difficult times and has received this advice from friends and family. However, do you believe that? What do you think this plan consists of? Life will never be a smooth ride for anyone. If you are in college right now, you have plenty of proof to back this up. There will definitely be lows, but there will also be highs. The lows are difficult, and the highs are often incredible. However, you have to ask yourself what you are going to do in both extremes. You have to decide if you will try to reach out to others in your valley, or if you will sit silently and wait for God to rescue you. You will have to decide whether you will try to use your mountaintop to share the hope that you gained from your time in the valley, or if you will sit back and talk with other people about how good life is on the mountaintop. Whichever choice you make, realize that things change very quickly. Therefore, enjoy your mountaintop, but use it to share with people your story of how the valley helped you get there. Use your valley to share with fellow valley-dwellers the hope that you have because of Christ and how that hope is bringing you closer to the mountaintop. In the end, regardless of what mountaintop or valley you find yourself in right now, there is reason to rejoice, because God has a plan for your life that you will never be able to completely understand until you reach the finish line. Therefore, choose to trust Him when it can so often be the most difficult to do so.

Share It!

Using these questions, reach out to your friends on social media and get the conversation started!

1. When do you find it hardest to follow and trust God's plan for you?
2. When you put your plan for life and God's plan side-by-side, what differences do you notice?
3. Think of one moment, one period in your lifetime, during which you began to realize that God might know what he's doing. What was it about that moment/period that stuck out in your mind?

The Emergency Exit

There hath no temptation taken you but such as is common to man: but God *is* faithful, who will not suffer you to be tempted above that ye are able; but will with the temptation also make a way to escape, that ye may be able to bear *it*.

1 Corinthians 10:13 KJV

I'm going to take a wild guess and say that most readers perked up when they saw this verse at the beginning. This means that God will always make sure that our lives are free of trouble and He won't give us more than we can handle, right? Think again. If you watch enough inspirational speakers and read enough inspirational text, you may begin to think that God is just hanging out in the sky with a sign that says, "How Can I Make You Happy Today?" Let us establish right out of the gate that this is not how God works. Sure, He has a plan for our lives, but when it comes to "keeping our best interests at heart", those interests are not His sole resource when He makes these plans.

At this point in life, you've probably had your share of struggles and issues. This is probably something that is true of everyone, with some having had a larger share than others. However, what is also true if you are reading this is that you found your way out of the circumstances that you were in at one time. This is the promise that is made here. When Paul writes this, He is giving us the assurance that, yes, there will be trials and we will struggle in this life on Earth. Without suffering, we would have no appreciation for what it means to be in times of peace and times without suffering. Without trials, we would be living in a world where people would be able to easily turn from God and never look back, because they would have no reason to do so. Granted, this does not mean that God is a dictator who releases His wrath to get His way, because this would not be consistent with His nature of being a loving and merciful God. However, these obstacles that we encounter during our lifetime are there for a reason. They are there to strengthen us and to draw us closer to Him. They have a purpose.

When God places trials in your life, the trial may look like it's fifteen miles long and ten thousand feet high, but somewhere in that trial, there is an exit door. You are not locked in there without any way of getting out. However, if you submit to the idea that there is no way out and you refuse to fight to find an exit, you will never be able to find the exit sign that is somewhere in that struggle. If you choose not to look for a solution, for an escape, you will never be able to push open that exit door that may be just feet or yards away. However, on that same token, this exit door can be seen as a point during the trial, the temptation that God has placed before you when you have reached the point where you can no longer stand it. You have to quit now because you will never make it another step. This door, this exit that God provides gives us a way out. Now, this is not to say that if we get bored or a little tired during the struggle, the temptation, that we slip out of the emergency exit that God has provided and we slip back in after we have gotten some fresh air. We use this emergency alternative when we cannot imagine taking one more step, even with His guidance. Therefore, this emergency option should not be used lightly.

What is the first phrase after the colon? God is faithful. Does this mean that He is only faithful in that circumstance that is not as severe as this one? No. Does this mean that God is faithful only to this person because they go to the biggest church in the city? No. When the Bible says that God is faithful, it means that He is faithful in all things and to all people. God's faithfulness is not selective, and it is not biased in any way. If you are a creature of God and you love Him and honor Him with your life and all that you do, then He is faithful to bring you out of the circumstance that you find yourself unable to bear. He will never toss you into some unfamiliar struggle or conflict and leave you to fend for yourself. He will be with you through that circumstance, through that trial to fight right alongside you. Ultimately, as you have heard before in this book, there will be circumstances in life that you cannot handle on your own. That is no secret, but there will never be a circumstance in your life that does not offer some kind of emergency exit door that will rescue you if a rescue is needed.

Now that you know that God will never leave you out in the world on your own to deal with the struggles that you face, what are you willing to do for Him? God's plan and mission for your life are beyond anything that you can imagine. He has a mission for you to fulfill, but it is up to you to accept that mission. Will you choose to accept it, or will you hang out on the sidelines and play it safe because you're afraid He will ask you to do something beyond your ability? Your answer to this question could determine the outcome of God's mission for your life and your devotion to that mission. If you are willing to go all in, knowing that He will not leave you in a difficult situation with no way out, you will be better able to pursue the mission that God has set before you and you will become better prepared for the temptations and trials that you will face along the way.

Message:

God will never bring you to a place where there is no way out. If it were the case that He would do such a thing, He would be a captor and not a Savior. He does not want you to live a life of being stuck. His entire purpose for sending His Son to die on the cross was to set us free from whatever it is that our sin left us stuck in. Regardless of how dark and intimidating the maze of struggle that you find yourself in may seem to be, if you use God's Word and His guidance that He offers us through prayer, you will find that emergency exit sign that could be just around the corner. However, take time during this temptation, this trial to understand what it is that God is trying to teach you through it. God doesn't place pointless obstacles in our path just to slow us down. Every obstacle has a purpose. Therefore, while the emergency exit is there, do not let your search for this escape route make you blind to what God is trying to teach you along the way.

Share It!

Using these questions, reach out to your friends on social media and get the conversation started!

1. When have you experienced a situation in your life that almost demanded that you use the *emergency exit*? How did you respond? What did that emergency exit look like?
2. When you face a difficult situation, and make the decision to go before God to ask for refuge, do you tend to pray for:
   a. A way out
   b. God to bring you through it
   c. God to teach you through it
3. What kind of situations do you tend to be hesitant about asking for refuge from?

Because You Love Them

[1]Though I speak with the tongues of men and of angels, and have not charity, I am become *as* sounding brass, or a tinkling cymbal. [2]And though I have *the gift of* prophecy, and understanding all mysteries, and all knowledge; and though I have all faith so that I could remove mountains, and have not charity, I am nothing. [3]And though I bestow all my goods to feed *the poor*, and though I give my body to be burned, and have not charity, it profiteth me nothing.

1 Corinthians 13:1-3 KJV

Imagine that you have just been pulled from a car that had been rolled over due to a collision on a major interstate. You will never forget the face of the person that pulled you to safety. However, you go over to try to thank the guy that pulled you out, and you are met with "Dude, get away from me. I only did it because nobody else would". What would you think about the act that this person had just performed? You would probably realize rather quickly that this person did not do what they did out of love, but rather simply because no one else would do it and the car (did I mention) could have possibly exploded at any minute.

How often do we do this in our daily lives? We see someone struggling with their groceries in the parking lot of a busy grocery store, and we do everything to draw attention except for shouting "Fear Not! Super [insert name here] is here to save the day!" What we are doing is not out of love, but rather out of pride. This verse tells us that, without love, we have done absolutely nothing.

This verse brings to mind something that tends to fill the headlines from time to time; politics. While the circumstances of each election are different, there is one thing that is usually the same, and that is the campaign. Around the time of the elections, candidates will be seen greeting voters in those states that have a big impact on the outcome and acting like they just decided to show up there and greet those constituents. The real reason they do this? To get votes. If they were not in the election, they would be with their family in their luxury homes and watching TV. They do these things, not out of love, but rather out of a need of something for themselves.

Is this how we approach our interactions with strangers and acquaintances alike? We treat people well or do good for others, not because of the love that we have for that person, but because of some benefit on our end, whether it be social, financial or some other form of compensation. So often, we go into these worthwhile charitable acts without love, because our selfish motives leave no room for the love that should be surrounding that act of kindness.

The interesting thing is that we so often feel like if we do this or that, God will be impressed with us. We think that if we help the elderly lady with her groceries, God will put another gold star beside our name. However, so often, we forget that showing love to others is not an extra credit option in the Gospel. It's one of the main pieces of the Christian walk. This passage tells us that, without love, none of that typical *good* stuff has any value to God. If you go into that community service project over your summer break, and you find yourself thinking the entire time about the community service credit you will be able to get, you are doing it for reasons concerning self and not reasons rooted in love for others. Does this mean that you shouldn't do community service or that you shouldn't help people? No. Does this mean that you should check your motives before you even sign up for or commit to this project? Definitely. If you fail to do this, you risk making a project, a grade out of human beings to whom you should be showing Christ's love. If you fail to check your motives, you risk allowing yourself and those flawed motives to get in the way of Christ's love, which should be taking center stage.

In the end, when Christ was hanging on that cross, being constantly taunted to bring Himself down, He could have. He could have rescued Himself from that certain death. However, He chose death for our sakes, not because of some publicity that He might get, but rather out of love. His reason was love. He saw a world in pain, a world drowning in its sin, and He chose to eliminate that through His death on that cross. Therefore, before you go out to do another "look at me" project, check your motives, and ask yourself, *Is this for me, or is this for love?*

Message:

Everything that we have experienced in our lifetime has been a product, in some shape or form of God's love for us. He didn't do any of the things that we read about in the Gospel simply for the sake of getting it over with. He did it out of love for His people. He knew that His Son was the only one who could save us from our sin. He showed love to us in the form of His Son. He didn't have to make that choice, and yet He did it anyway. With this being set as the standard for what love looks like, suddenly, the gravity of our community service projects come into a new light. Suddenly, we realize that, when Christ becomes the standard and when we reflect on the sacrifice He made on that cross, we realize how important, how critical it really is for us to place love at the core of all that we do.

Share It!

Using these questions, reach out to your friends on social media and get the conversation started!

1. When was the last time that you engaged in an act of service for the sole purpose of showing love to someone? What was the outcome?
2. What are some of the flawed motives that you find to be at the core of your acts of love and service?
3. When you think about everything that you've done in your lifetime, think of one time in your life when you found yourself feeling genuine love for the people that you were serving at the time. What was it that made you feel that love? Is it still there?

Love Is

⁴Charity suffereth long, *and* is kind; charity envieth not; charity vaunteth not itself, is not puffed up, ⁵doth not behave itself unseemly, seeketh not her own, is not easily provoked, thinketh no evil; ⁶rejoiceth not in iniquity, but rejoiceth in the truth; ⁷beareth all things, believeth all things, hopeth all things, endureth all things.

1 Corinthians 13:4-7 KJV

Have you ever found yourself wondering what love was and what it looked like? You've come to the right place! In this passage in 1 Corinthians, Paul gives us this image of what love truly looks like. He tells us both what it is, in addition to what it is not. The problem that arises when we read this passage and when we begin to reflect on what he is saying here, is that we probably begin to realize that we have been doing it wrong. While we would like to think that we are basing our love for another person, whether that person be a family member, a spouse, a boyfriend or a girlfriend, on the ideal image that Paul is creating here, it is probably more often the case that we are eliminating the *not*'s in this verse and doing exactly what it tells us not to do.

In an age when social media leads to the beginning of many relationships, even among people who have been friends for some time, the things that we see on social media can sometimes skew our image of what love really looks like. One shining example of this is a collection of hashtags known as *#goals*. This hashtag is used on social media to depict what is often considered to be the ideal relationship. Often, these depictions even include common Christian principles, but so often, the things that are shown in these images have selfishness at their core.

Think about it in this way. Everything that Paul writes about here encompasses everything that we have in a relationship with Christ. Christ does not leave fruit or candy baskets on our porch. He doesn't put puff paint notes on our car. Not only did Christ die for us, but He also shows His love for us in the selfless way that He intervenes on our behalf on a daily basis. Does this mean that you should not do romantic things for your significant other? Not necessarily. However, what this does mean is that, when you decide to do those things, just like the last devotional talked about, figure out your motives. Why are you doing that? Is it so that she/he will post it on social media to tell the world how good you are, or is it because you genuinely want to show he/she how much you love them? This is an important question to consider when we think about this idea of love.

While this particular version of the passage (KJV) does not use the term *love*, the majority of translations choose to use that word in place of charity. This is the reason that this devotional focuses on love in the context of relationships rather than charity. This idea of love brings many images to mind, some of which were just mentioned, but beyond the love that will hopefully one day lead to a wedding, what about everybody else?

Assuming that you are in college, depending on what year you are in, you may have witnessed for the first time not seeing your parents for months at a time. In my experience, this gave a new definition to the word *love*. Suddenly, when you haven't seen them in weeks, you begin to realize the love that you had for them and that they had for you. The love that your parents have for you is beyond anything that you can imagine, and you hopefully realize this already, but if you didn't, now you know. This love is probably the best earthly depiction of what Paul is talking about here. They put your needs ahead of their own. They do not place any conditions on the love that they have for you. The comparisons can go on and on. However, do you want to know something mind-blowing? The love that your parents have for you and that you have for them does not even begin to compare to the love that God has for His children. This is a good thing to keep in mind when we think about love. Whether it be in the context of a romantic relationship, a family relationship, or even in the context of a close friend, let us all take it as a personal challenge to make this passage the framework for the love that we show to family, friends, and even complete strangers.

Message:

God's love for us is incomparable to anything we will ever be able to imagine. We, as His followers should live our lives with this as our guiding principle every single day. Every day, God fulfills this passage and this definition of true love in His love toward us. However, this love that He shows to us is not a one-way deal. If God's love were on a street sign, it would probably be an endless circle with an arrow at the top. God's gift of everlasting, unconditional love to us is not something that He gives to us with the intention of it staying inside of us. God gives us His love with the intention that we will let that love pour into other people. This means that, in the same way that God fulfills this passage in our lives, we should also fulfill it in the lives of those around us.

Share It!

Using these questions, reach out to your friends on social media and get the conversation going!

1. Think of someone in your life that you love. How does that person know that you love them if you don't tell them? How do you show them that?
2. How do you choose to love those in your life and even those who may not be extremely close to you?
3. In what ways could you love better? Where would you begin in pursuing this goal?

Spread the Love

[8]Charity never faileth: but whether *there be* prophecies, they shall fail; whether *there be* tongues, they shall cease; whether *there be* knowledge, it shall vanish away.[9]For we know in part, and we prophesy in part. [10]But when that which is perfect is come, that which is in part shall be done away.

1 Corinthians 13:8-10 KJV

What does love look like to you? This is an interesting question to consider. When you think of love, an image pops into your mind. What is that image? For some, it's a person. For others, it may be a memory. However, regardless of what may have popped into your mind, somewhere deep inside of you, there is an association with this four-letter word. For many, this association has come to define what they will look for in a spouse, how they will build their family, and what they want their future to look like. This kind of begins to show us the power of this word. It shapes us and makes us into this person that is hopefully somewhat consistent with the person that God wants us to be. Basically, this word, this four-letter word defines everything about who we are and who we want to be.

This passage tells us that love is one of the only things that we can know will be there tomorrow, next week, ten years from now. It's reliable because it comes from a reliable source that doesn't have the ability to fail us. For many, this is an incredible concept to think about because it is so hard for some people to imagine a love that is truly reliable and genuine. Maybe that's you. Maybe you find yourself in a position in life that leaves you looking for any scraps of love that you can grab onto and treasure. Maybe you have found yourself in a relationship where you thought you knew what love was and tried to convince yourself that this was it. Maybe you grew up in a home that made you think that love looked like something that meant disrespecting and hurting those closest to you. Now you find yourself in college, preparing for the future, and you are going into the world, into these new relationships, and you are facing the world with this false image of what it looks like to love your friends, your spouse, your family. Fortunately, Paul doesn't leave us hanging in this passage, wondering if we will ever get to experience this love. He goes on to say that "…when that which is perfect is come, that which is in part shall be done away". Paul is telling us that these images of love, whatever they may be, that have engrained themselves in our mind, will one day become history when the epitome of perfect, selfless, incredible love comes to reclaim us.

It's interesting to think about experiencing that love first-hand in the presence of Christ Himself. For us, it is something to look forward to, but for individuals such as the disciples, this experience was all-too-real. The thought of being able to stand in the presence of the Son of God and feel His love rain upon us is an experience that no human mind will ever be able to truly wrap their mind around until they, like the disciples, witness it first-hand. The concept of standing in the presence of the man who practically invented love is mind-blowing. However, it is also probably reasonable to say that this experience would be incredibly humbling. This is the kind of love that Paul is talking about here. Sure, the love that you have for your significant other and your family and your friends will last a lifetime, but the love that God has for you, it never expires. This love is not something that can be summed up in a card or in a poem. It's not something that can be placed in a box with a bow on top. It goes so far beyond that. In this passage, Paul kind of gives us something to look forward to. Not only does he tell us that the love that exists on earth, which is sometimes misshapen and misconstrued, will pass away. He also promises a new love, a perfect love that will overcome everything in this world that makes us hunger and thirst for something new, something different. Paul promises us in this passage that that is coming. However, while we wait, we have a job to do.

As we await the day that this love will come to earth and take us home, we have a responsibility. The responsibility that we have as followers of Christ is this responsibility to understand this love that He offers to His people and extend that love to those who need it the most. As the church, we cannot simply sit back in our pews and expect God to take care of the loving part while we wait for Him. He didn't put us here simply for us to await His return. He placed us here so that we could *prepare* for His return. If we simply sit in our churches and stare at the ceiling waiting for Him, we will continue to deprive the world of the love that he put us here to spread. We must make a unanimous decision as the church to take this message of love that we listen to week after week and share it with the world outside of those doors. The question is whether we will do that, or simply sit back and let everyone else do the work.

Message:

What are you going to do? When you look at this world today and everything that is going on, do you ever imagine what wonders it would do if someone decided to spread the love that Christ gave them to share? If you haven't ever thought about this, think about it now. Imagine a world where we showed those around us, not the love that the world promotes, but the love that Christ exhibits. Imagine the change that would take place. This is incredible to think about because so often it seems that we forget what it means to love someone like Christ loved us. We forget what that is supposed to look like. However, if we choose to draw closer to Christ, and begin to experience that love for ourselves, we may be surprised by the results.

Share It!

Using these questions, reach out to your friends on social media and get the conversation started!

1. When you think of the love that God has for you, and the ways in which He has chosen to show that love, how does that compare to the love that you have shown to others? How sustainable is that love?
2. Have you ever set love aside as a solution, believing that it would fail in this or that circumstance?
3. When have you seen proof of the unfailing nature of God's love for you?

You Don't Have to Fight Alone

[8]We *are* troubled on every side, yet not distressed; *we are* perplexed, but not in despair; [9]persecuted, but not forsaken; cast down, but not destroyed;

2 Corinthians 4:8-9 KJV

Regardless of who is reading this, the chances are pretty good that you need to hear this today. Have you ever or are you currently having one of those days where it seems that there is opposition everywhere you look? If you are a college student, do you feel that you are in a season of your college journey when it seems that you are constantly being challenged about your faith in Christ? At one point or another, you have or will answer this question with a firm yes.

In the world that we are living in today, it can often become difficult to be an open follower of Christ. From those who try to disprove what we believe to those who call us intolerant for the way we believe the world should be, it often seems that the Armor of God should include a bulletproof vest of courage due to the amount of struggle that we face daily. Granted, the opposition that is faced by Americans today is child's play compared to those who continue to stand firm in their faith at the risk of facing death for doing so. However, the opposition that Americans find themselves in is more of a verbal battle. We do not face the possibility of death for following Christ. If we did, how many would still follow Him? While we all would like to raise our hands, we all probably love our lives too, so the chances that we would all be sincere in saying that would be very slim.

This verse gives us this image of persecution that resembles someone going to battle armed with their Bible and all the apologetic knowledge that they may have gained over the years. However, what else are you taking into your battle? When you find yourself facing opposition because of the truth that you carry with you on a daily basis, what will you do to deal with that? Sure, we can say as much as we want that we are armed with the Armor of God, but are we really? Do we really believe that the armor that the Bible tells us about is going to be enough to bring us through the battles that we face? Well, if we only put on half of the armor, then no, it will not be enough to bring us through these confrontations. If we don't tighten it up and make sure that it is secure before we find ourselves in battle, it is bound to fall and put us in a scary situation.

It doesn't matter how much protection you have access to in your spiritual arsenal. It doesn't matter how great that armor is that you just bought if you don't know how to use it or the best way to use it. When we face struggles in our faith, because of the unexpected nature of these battles, we often find ourselves in the midst of the battle with the Helmet of Salvation on our head, but if none of the straps are tightened and the face shield is not covering our face, that helmet will not do us much good. If we wear the Breastplate of Righteousness on our chest but let it dangle loosely, our heart is left vulnerable and insecure. We can talk as much as we want about wearing the Armor of God, but if we don't know how to wear it so that it will protect us from the opposition, or if we take it off when we are in a Christian safe place, Satan is bound to attack us when we least expect it.

The battles that we face on a daily basis are exactly that. These battles are something that we face daily. There is nowhere that we can go where we will not face these battles that test us and try us in our relationship with Christ. This is another reason why so many people end up turning away from Christ in the years after they leave home. So often, we feel that this Christian walk should be easy and that we should never have to face doubt and struggles because Christ was supposed to take all that stuff away. We forget that Christ never told us that this would be easy. He tells us repeatedly that the opposite is actually true. Some people face more struggles when they come to Christ than they did when they were lost in their sin. This is because, when we make the decision to follow Christ with our whole heart and to give our lives to Him, Satan engages in this battle to reclaim our heart. So often, the battle that Satan fights to win our heart back may look more appealing to us than the life that we are living in Christ. Ultimately, this is what led to the fall man in the first place. Satan will make sin look more appealing than most people would ever expect. However, when we face battles in our journey with Christ, He doesn't turn around and run at the first spiritual gunshot. He stays right there beside you and He will fight alongside you if you just choose to trust Him.

Message:

So, now the rest is up to you. You have a choice to make. You can choose to defend yourself with everything that God has given you, including Himself, or you may choose to let the battles come to you and then figure out how you will defend yourself. One of these options will lead to success through Christ, while the other will only lead to destruction and struggle. Which choice will you make? You will face struggles in your walk with Christ. There is no way around this. What you do have a say in is how you will face those struggles. You can choose to do it on your own with only your memory verses to guide you, or you can choose to allow God to lead you and to bring you through the battle. The choice is yours.

Share It!

Using these questions, reach out to your friends on social media and get the conversation started!

1. When was the last time you saw a battle over the horizon and knew immediately that you would need God's intervention?
2. When you look at your armor, what condition is it in? Is it still the size that it was when you first came to Christ, or has it continued to grow with you in your relationship with Christ?
3. What kind of steps do you take to keep your armor in good condition?

A Shining Example?

[20]Now then we are ambassadors for Christ, as though God did beseech *you* by us: we pray *you* in Christ's stead, be ye reconciled to God. [21]For he hath made him *to be* sin for us, who knew no sin; that we might be made the righteousness of God in him.

2 Corinthians 5:20-21 KJV

Have you ever thought about this? Have you ever stopped to appreciate the fact that we, as followers of Christ are also representatives of Him and the grace that He extends to us? When we come to the point of acknowledging Christ and beginning a relationship with Him, we receive this duty of sorts that says that, as ambassadors of Christ, we should become a representative, a symbol, of what it looks like to follow Him with our whole life, our whole being. We should make it our mission to become the best representatives of Him that we can possibly be. This should make us stop for a moment and try to understand both the incredible nature of this, while also appreciating the amount of responsibility that comes with it.

It is no secret, especially today, that those who hold the power in our government are not always perfect and we may not always agree with what they do and say. However, they represent our country that people fought and are fighting every day to defend. For this reason, regardless of the mistakes that those representatives in the government make, those mistakes do not take away from the freedoms, the opportunities, and the sacrifices that make this country so great.

Just as the mistakes of a few officials in the government do not subtract from what makes America the place that it is, it is important to realize that, just because some Christian messes up, that mistake does not change who God is. Does this mean that we, as Christians can spend our lives assuming that none of our mistakes take a toll on how nonbelievers see the God that we serve? No. To nonbelievers, does this mean that if a Christian messes up in a time of struggle and weakness, that all Christians are like that, and therefore make Christianity something that should be shunned at all costs? No.

Ultimately, Christians will mess up in their lifetime, usually multiple times a day. Becoming a Christian does not mean that we lose that human nature, that sin nature that everyone is born with. However, a relationship with Christ should result in a change in that person. It may not be immediate, but it should be noticeable. This is something that we must remember when we go into the world every day.

The second verse in this passage should also serve as a huge booster for our motivation to become more like Christ. Ultimately, we should desire to become more like Christ because, due to our sin, He became like us. If He hadn't taken all that sin upon Himself, we would have no hope of the salvation that is freely available to us right now. If He had done as the spectators suggested and removed Himself from the cross, He would not have given us that hope. It is because He became like us and hung there for the sins of the world, that we can become like Him.

Now, take a moment to think. What kind of representation are you? Are you a representative that makes people want to join what you're a part of, or are you a representative that makes people question the legitimacy of what you are representing? We can often become so busy in the tasks of daily life, often doing the bare minimum of what is expected, that we forget that we are setting a standard, a precedent in the minds of nonbelievers. With this in mind, what kind of precedent are you setting for the case of Christ? Is it one that people will want to follow after and use as a template for their own walk, or is it a precedent that will make itself at home in the back of nonbelievers' minds and pull them further away from a relationship with Christ? It's ultimately up to you to make the decision of what kind of picture you want to paint of Christ and the grace that He extended to you.

Message:

Did you think about it? What kind of image of the Christian walk are you leaving behind in the minds of nonbelievers? Your answer to this question could be the same as so many in the church today. When we imagine winning souls for Christ, we often imagine sitting with a person that we have never met, telling them about their sin, and leading them to Christ on the spot. Unfortunately, that does not happen as much as it used to. Often, people's decision to follow Christ will not lie in memorized scripture verses delivered by someone going from door to door. More often than not, a person's decision to follow Christ will be at least partially based on what they see in those who claim to be an example of that relationship. Therefore, bear in mind that nonbelievers may be watching you to see how this relationship with Christ plays out in your life. What image are you giving them to answer this curiosity? Make them curious rather than confirming those negative assumptions that they have been keeping in the back of their mind.

Share It!

Using these questions, reach out to your friends on social media and get the conversation started!

1. When you look at Christ and do a side-by-side comparison, what sticks out to you?
2. In your mind, why is Christ the example that you want to follow and base your life on? How would you tell that to a nonbeliever?
3. How has Christ changed you since the day you made the decision to follow Him and give your life to Him?

The Company That You Keep

Be ye not unequally yoked together with unbelievers: for what fellowship hath righteousness with unrighteousness? and what communion hath light with darkness?

2 Corinthians 6:14 KJV

During the years of young adulthood, there are many things that consume our minds. However, among this list of items, most are probably wondering with whom they will spend the rest of their life with. With that in mind, this is obviously what this verse is talking about. Right? Not completely. Sure, Paul is partially talking about your romantic relationships in this verse, but what is the overarching theme? In this verse, Paul is warning us to take a critical look at all the relationships that we engage in, which include those friends that we have grown close to over what may have been many years. Many consider the possibility of losing these friends to be somewhat terrifying. They have probably become an important part of us and losing them would mean losing part of ourselves. However, these friends can often stand between us and God and hinder the relationship that each one of us has built with Him. For this reason, we must remain diligent about ensuring that we do not allow these people to come between ourselves and God.

We can often make the mistake of allowing our romantic relationships to have higher standards than our friendships because we feel that our romantic relationships will last longer than our friendships. There are two issues with this ever-so-popular reasoning. The first issue is that many friendships last much longer than romantic relationships. There is also the fact that our friendships so often either evolve into romantic relationships or impact the kinds of relationships that we will have in the future. Therefore, while this verse does warn us about the romantic relationships that we have, it also may call into question some of the friendships that have become a part of our lives over the last few years.

Now, in addition to figuring out what kind of people we should not make a primary part of our social life, there is also something else to consider as well. What kind of company do you keep? What kind of people do you avoid? The chances are pretty good that your answer will reveal that you're doing something wrong. While this verse tells us that we should not develop deep relationships with these people, we still have a responsibility to reach these people for Christ so that we will be able to develop stronger, Christ-centered relationships with those people. Therefore, do not assume that this verse goes against all those other instances where the Gospel tells us to reach the lost. However, when you find yourself in search of friends or "more than friends", keep this verse in mind.

This verse holds a lot of value because it gives us a small start to building a foundation for the relationships that we will build in our lifetime. The reason that we are given this sort of parameter for our relationships is that it gives us one of many principles that will help us to shape our relationships around what the Gospel deems to be godly standards.

We can often fall into a trap of looking for 'nice' people who look like good friends. We look for people who share our interests, without ever considering how these friendships fit into the template that God has given us. If they fail to fit into this template, it can often be like termites infesting a house. The damage may not be immediately apparent, but eventually, we will find that these friends we have made are slowly causing us to draw closer and closer to a downfall we are not necessarily prepared for. However, if we allow God to come into the middle of those friendships and relationships, we will find that He will bring people into our lives who fit into the template that has been set out in the Gospel. Are you willing to stick to this mold that has been given to us in the infallible Word of God, or will you risk breaking this mold and taking the risk of facing the consequences of ungodly relationships?

Message:

So much of our lives are determined by the friends that we have and the relationships that we engage in. These relationships can either help us to draw nearer to God and enhance our relationship with Him, or they can pull us away from Him and slowly deteriorate the relationship that we have. The choice is yours and begins, in part with the company that you keep. Therefore, take some time, look at those people with whom you spend your time and figure out whether they will pull you closer to God or further from Him. Depending on the outcome, it may be time to make some difficult decisions about where and with whom you are spending your time and energy.

Share It!

Using these questions, reach out to your friends on social media and get the conversation started!

1. After considering these guidelines for your relationships, are there any specific areas that don't quite line up? If so, what are those areas?
2. For the relationships that do *fit the mold*, so-to-speak, how do you feel after leaving that person?
3. How much time do you typically invest in engaging with Christ and growing in your knowledge of Him as your friend on a daily basis?

Enough

[9]And he said unto me, My grace is sufficient for thee, for my strength is made perfect in weakness. Most gladly therefore will I rather glory in my infirmities, that the power of Christ may rest upon me. [10]Therefore I take pleasure in my infirmities, in reproaches, in necessities, in persecutions, in distresses for Christ's sake: for when I am weak, then am I strong.

2 Corinthians 12:9-10 KJV

When we wake up on Monday morning at the early hours associated with the weekly routine, we look at the alarm clock, and we often wonder if we have enough energy, enough motivation, enough brainpower to get through the next busy week. We always seem to be wondering if we have enough, if we are enough, if we can do enough to make it. However, the Gospel basically takes that power out of our hands when it comes to being enough. The Gospel tells us that it is not up to us to make it through the week, the day, or even the next hour. It's not our job. The responsibility of ensuring we make it through the week, that we are enough, that we do enough, is up to Christ because Christ is enough.

This idea of being, doing, or having enough becomes very popular during the college years and thereafter when we enter into the work world. Will my GPA be high enough? Will my degree be sophisticated enough? Will I even have the finances to come back for the next semester? All these questions come down to one basic idea, and it is this: Will it/I be enough to do this, to accomplish this? The answer? No. You alone can never be enough to make it through everything that life throws at you. You will never have enough motivation, good enough finances, or a sophisticated enough degree to do what you want and need to do in your life. However, this first verse tells us that we don't have to be. The Bible tells us that we don't have to be enough on our own to handle this stuff.

When we travel through the Gospel, we find instance after instance where someone said that they could not do this or that. They would never be able to handle this. Fortunately for them, they had figured something out that many people spend their entire lives failing to understand. God never expects us to go into battle on our own. We cannot do this if we want victory in those battles. However, if we employ God's army to go to battle on our behalf, he will fight for us with every resource at His disposal. He will not leave us defenseless on the front lines to be taken down by the enemy, whatever that may be. Does this mean that we won't leave with battle scars? No. Does this mean that victory will always come in the shape that we expected? No. However, in the end, will we emerge from the battle stronger than before? Most definitely.

This first verse also tells us that, because Christ lives in us, we should celebrate. We should rejoice in the struggles, because regardless of what battles you are facing, have faced or will face when the battle is over, you will emerge stronger than before, with knowledge and experience you would not have gained otherwise. Therefore, if you find yourself in a battle that makes you wonder if you will be good enough, smart enough, or strong enough to emerge victorious, realize that you alone will never be able to do that, but with Christ, there will be nothing you cannot do.

Finally, at the end of the passage, we find a phrase that will hopefully make us pause and think. When the Gospel tells us that "when I am weak, then am I strong", it challenges us to employ the power of Christ at the times when it seems, in our minds, that it will be of no use. We must employ the power of Christ in those moments when it seems that nothing can be of help to us. We must always employ it every second of the day, because around every corner, there seems to be a circumstance we know nothing about and do not have the assets to conquer on our own. The assistance is available. The question is whether you will run toward it or away from it due to your pride. Will you, in those moments, be able to find the strength to go before God, and simply say "I'm not enough to fight this alone, but you alone are enough to bring me through this"?

Message:

What battles are you fighting today? What battles have you recently emerged from? The chances are good that you had a situation come to mind after reading one of these questions. Regardless of what the situation is about, without Christ, you will never be enough to conquer it on your own. However, with Christ on your side, you can guarantee that you will eventually emerge victorious in one way or another if you choose to employ the power of Christ in the situation. Therefore, what do you have to fear in letting Christ go to battle for you? There is nothing to fear, because He is enough where we come up short. Therefore, whatever battle you are fighting, put down your weapon and put Christ on the front lines.

Share It!

Using these questions, reach out to your friends on social media and get the conversation started!

1. When have you had one of these moments when you knew you weren't enough for a certain circumstance, but pushed God's intervention and guidance aside as a solution?
2. How has God shown you that you are enough? If you feel that you are not enough, what is it about yourself that makes you feel that way?
3. When you read the *Message* for today, what circumstance came to mind? How did you employ or are you employing God's power in that situation?

The Danger of Complacency

[20]I am crucified with Christ: nevertheless I live; yet not I but Christ liveth in me: and the life which I now live in the flesh I live by the faith of the Son of God, who loved me, and gave himself for me. [21]I do not frustrate the grace of God: for if righteousness *come* by the law, then Christ is dead in vain.

Galatians 2:20-21 KJV

We've all heard this passage during sermons, group devotional times and those yearly youth retreats at some point. It's one of those passages that probably makes some stand up and say "Amen" and some to shed tears. It's a passage with some powerful words that we all hope to apply to our lives daily. However, what are we really saying "Amen" to when we hear this verse? Sure, it makes for a good song and it has some powerful meaning behind it, but do we ever really think about the meaning?

When we look at this verse, most of us probably start silently humming the church hymn in our head. We probably look at this verse and think "Yes!" However, are we willing and prepared to do what is being asked of us here? Are we willing to let ourselves die, on a daily basis, with Christ? Christ died once and for all for the sins of the world. If you believe this in your heart and have accepted that gift, then your sins are covered and now, your job is to pursue Him. What this means, is that we, as followers of Christ, must wake up every morning with the intention of dying to ourselves so that we can live in Christ. This means that we wake up in the morning and strip ourselves of the sin of yesterday. In this sense, we are choosing to die to ourselves and to put on the person that Christ died to make a reality. However, what does this mean? How do we die on a daily basis? This is an interesting concept to consider because it seems that, when we think of this word, "die", we imagine one definition that can only occur once on earth. When we think of death, we think of someone lying in a bed, or someone in a bad car accident passing away after their heart stops. However, this passage shows us that there is another definition of this term that is not necessarily the most conventional of definitions definition.

Now, as we begin to think about this idea of being "crucified with Christ", there arises a certain question: what does it look like when someone dies? While I wish that I could assume that no one reading this could answer this from experience, most probably can. When someone dies, whether it be in an accident, from an illness, or simply from old age, the minute that that person stops breathing and their heart stops beating, their body begins the process of wasting away. In the same way that this is the process that takes place during a physical death, the same should be true about followers of Christ, in a spiritual sense of course, when we begin that new relationship with Him. When we begin this new relationship, this new life with Christ, this should be the point in time when we take all that we are, all our old habits, bad relationships, and other ungodly parts of our lives, and toss it all out the window to allow Christ to begin His work inside of us. Unfortunately, it seems that all-too-often, Christians fail to get rid of that stuff that Christ died to set them free from. The problem is, often individuals are not necessarily ashamed of who they were, or at least pieces of who they were before Christ, and don't see any reason to get rid of those things. However, I challenge each person reading this to take a few minutes to examine their life to figure out where those ungodly pieces may lie. If you are a follower of Christ, it should be relatively quick and easy to figure out what parts of your life don't necessarily line up with Christ and the person that Christ expects us to be. Once you have identified those things, whatever they may be, figure out what it is that is keeping you from letting go of it. It's very likely that, through this diagnosis, you will be able to determine what it is that you consider to be so great about this particular thing or activity. At this point, you should also be able to begin the process of figuring out what it will take to escape this particular piece of your life that you haven't quite been able to get rid of yet.

Now, I also would like to make an appeal to those of you who are reading this and have never actually become a follower of Christ. To you, I say this. The act of salvation is one that comes with a rather significant sense of urgency, because, as we have witnessed in recent days, there is not a single person on this earth who can guarantee without a doubt that they will see another minute, much less another day. This idea alone should give nonbelievers cause for concern and conviction. This passage speaks to you also.

Most of us have seen those infomercials that are filled with testimonials that talk about how incredible a certain product is. The commercial consists of people telling viewers how the product changed their life. This is all an attempt to make the viewer want this product that they may have never known existed. However, once you hear about the product, you suddenly wonder where it has been all your life and why someone didn't tell you about it sooner! Well, imagine that this is an infomercial for a new product and you may find yourself wondering where this offer of a new life, a new future, a second chance has been all your life! The answer is that it has been right in front of you. Unfortunately, so often, our sin and the deception that comes from Satan can blind us to the things right in front of us that have the capability to cure the human condition that we were born with. However, maybe you heard it here first. You have an opportunity to put behind you all the things in your life that made people reject you and made people kick you out of their lives. However, before you choose to dial that direct line to God and accept His offer, you have to decide how willing you are to die to all those things in your past and maybe even your present. You have to decide if this gift means enough to you for you to leave behind all the habits, the mistakes, the shortcomings, the sin that has consumed your life. That choice is yours, and if you allow yourself to become vulnerable before God and set aside all the pride that consumes every human in existence, God will eventually convict you and when you respond to that conviction, He will be standing right there in front of you with open, welcoming arms. What if I backslide? He will be right there encouraging you to regain that momentum that you had at the beginning. What if I mess up? If you didn't mess up, you wouldn't need salvation. What if I do [blank]? God will forgive you.

If you are a non-believer reading this, know that the God of the universe wants you in His family, and He will stop at nothing to make that happen. The issue comes when Man refuses to surrender to God and chooses to take their own path because nothing can be better than that! This is what so often lands both believers and nonbelievers in unfamiliar waters at times. This is what causes people to become stranded on the spiritual island with troubled waters on every side. However, when we give our lives to Christ, we become a point on His radar. Even when we have no idea where we are, whether that be in a spiritual or even literal sense, God has His eye on us and will rescue us in our times of trouble. However, on this same merit, God knows exactly where we are in those times when we don't necessarily want Him to find us. In these times, He will still be there waiting for us to come back to Him ready to repent and start over.

In the second part of this passage, we find further encouragement from the author to not become complacent. Complacency in the church can be and usually is dangerous. Complacency puts us in danger of wandering into a spiritual no-man's-land and not being able to find our way out, but also not being able to have the courage to fall before God and admit that we messed up. Complacency makes the phrase "It doesn't matter. It's fine", a phrase that becomes easier and easier to say and believe as time goes on. Complacency puts us in danger of drifting, and when we drift in our walk with Christ, not only do we move further from Him, but we also move into deeper waters that are not meant to be faced alone.

The last part of this passage warns us not to take the Bible out of our line of vision because if something stays out of your line of vision long enough, it will be forgotten. The question for you is this: Where is the Gospel in your line of vision? How long has it been there? If you have the Bible at the center of your line of vision, you will be better able to focus on it and understand it. You will be able to see it in ways that you weren't able to before because of the sin in your life. When you place the Gospel in the center of your line of vision, you will begin to understand it in ways you couldn't before. However, like getting used to a new pair of glasses, this new view of the Gospel takes time to get used to. How will you handle this new perspective? Will you adapt to it and begin using it in a new way, or will you throw it in the corner and continue to let it stay out of your line of vision? Think about it.

Message:

When Christ died for the sin that was engrained in us, He didn't do this so that we would look at His death and say, "Oh that's cool! Thanks Jesus!" and then turn around and go back to what we were doing. He suffered and died on that cross so that we could experience a lasting change in our lives. He died on that cross so that we would tell others about the change that He brings. If we do not make the Gospel the center of our line of vision, we risk letting the Bible and its message drift into the corner and become forgotten, and if this happens, we risk letting Christ's death become a venture that was done in vain, as we eventually forgot about it. Therefore, ensure that you not only tell others about the death that brought life and light to the world, but also ensure that you continue to recall His death, His sacrifice on a daily basis in your own heart and mind.

Share It!

Using these questions, reach out to your friends on social media and get the conversation started!

1. Where have you noticed complacency in your own walk with Christ? Have you done anything to change it?
2. How often do you find yourself thinking about the Gospel during the day?
3. How do you view Christ's death on the cross and the cost that it was meant to cover?

Welcome to the Family!

⁴But when the fulness of time was come, God sent forth his Son, made of a woman, made under the law, ⁵to redeem them that were under the law, that we might receive the adoption of sons. ⁶And because ye are sons, God hath sent forth the Spirit of his Son into your hearts, crying, Abba, Father. ⁷Wherefore thou art no more a servant, but a son; and if a son, then an heir of God through Christ.

Galatians 4:4-7 KJV

Have you ever thought about the unconditional nature of adoption? Regardless of where the child came from, the circumstances it came from or anything else that the child may have experienced prior to being surrendered, that child stands innocent and in need of love and a new life, which can be given to them by a set of parents willing to simply take them into their home. To those parents who choose this child, nothing that may be living in their past matters. They only want the child to live with them and to receive their love.

If you are a follower of Christ who has called on Him to forgive you of your sins and to give you a new life, you are that child who was sitting in that spiritual orphanage, waiting for someone to come and give you that new life. You did nothing to deserve or earn this adoption. There is nothing that you could have done to make yourself look more appealing or to make that one set of loving, hopeful adoptive parents want you any more than they already did. Christ adopted you into His family, not because you looked like a good person, but because His love that He had for you was such that it was able to look past what the world became blinded by. Christ adopted you knowing your past, but He was willing to wipe all that away and make it history. We are all born into a spiritual orphanage because we are all born into a sinful, flawed nature that makes every child look equally unappealing when Christ is set as the standard. We are all orphans, who are covered in sin and a past that is repulsive. However, the past is not repulsive because of what was in it, but because of the fact that Christ was not in it. However, one day, Christ came along and looked at us in our filthy, sinful, lost state and said, "I want this one". He gave us the right, the privilege to call him Father, Daddy, Papa. He took us out of our spiritual orphanage, cleaned us up, and made us a child worthy of being called a member of His family.

Now that we have established how unworthy we are to be a child of God and what a privilege it is to be in that position, what do we do with that? How do we handle this relationship and the freedom that it offers? Most people would answer that we should handle it carefully, but in reality, it seems that the way we handle this adoption looks like taking a box labeled FRAGILE: HANDLE WITH CARE, and tossing it on the floor. Before we have even completely unpacked and understood what was inside, we assume that having it is enough. We think that this is all that matters and that no further care needs to be taken with this privilege. However, this package, this relationship that we have with Christ is one that needs to be handled like the fragile object that it is. We must handle it in such a way that shows our Heavenly Father that we understand that this is more than our ticket to heaven. It's more than the title of "Christian". This relationship has the ability to change our lives, to make us that new person we want to become. However, when we set, or rather throw aside this relationship that we have with Christ, we demean the relationship, its value, as well as the One who gave us access to it in the first place. When we neglect this relationship, and leave it sitting in the corner with all those other things we keep meaning to get back to, it slowly turns from a relationship to a memory. It slowly becomes something that we simply lost interest in. This is the route that so many followers of Christ choose today, whether it be intentionally or unintentionally, and soon, they find themselves thirsty, longing for that relationship, that love to be back in their life again because they quickly remembered what their life was before they had this life-changing gift.

Now, here's the question for you. How are you handling your package? Are you carrying it with you everywhere you go to protect it, or are you tossing it on the floor every day and telling God that you will unpack it later when you have time? It seems that the majority of Christians today are so excited to get the package, but when they open it, they're not as excited when they see what is inside. However, unfortunately, the reason that people are becoming less and less excited about the privilege of being in God's family and becoming an adopted child who has the Holy Spirit inside of them, is because they forget to explore the contents of the package after they open it. Have you explored the package that you were given? Have you dived into the relationship you have with Christ, the adoption that He has gifted you with? Maybe you should take a second look to figure out what you may have missed.

Message:

The adoption that we receive from Christ is the epitome of unconditional love and forgiveness. There is nothing we can do to gain it or lose it. Sadly, to some, this is actually a deterrent. People want to think that they can earn their salvation because it puts them in charge. However, one of the benefits to the fact that we are not responsible for saving ourselves is the fact that, once we have been adopted into the family of Christ, there is nothing that we can do to allow this to be undone. We can never run too far, fall too fast or do anything bad enough to make God take us back to where we were. He forgot all those things that defined us before He adopted us. Those things can never come back to bite us on God's side because He doesn't remember that stuff. Therefore, if God doesn't remember that stuff, why should we?

Share It!

Using these questions, reach out to your friends on social media and get the conversation started!

1. The purpose of adoption is to bring someone from the point of not having a family to being a part of a family. If you have been adopted into Christ's family, what part have you played?
2. When you look at God, communicate with Him, think about Him, do you think of Him as father, or supervisor? Why?
3. One thing that is required in a family is communication. How frequent is your communication with your Heavenly Father? How does your communication with your biological family compare with that of your "Heavenly" family?

The Comfy Cage of Sin
Stand fast therefore in the liberty wherewith Christ hath made us free and
be not entangled again with the yoke of bondage

Galatians 5:1 KJV

Freedom is an incredible privilege and honor enjoyed by everyone living
in the United States today. This freedom is something that people died for
and continue to die for to this day. However, what if someone asked you if
you would give up the freedom that you enjoy today for 2 million dollars?
What would you say? On one hand, it's two million dollars. On the other
hand, you're risking the freedom that you have enjoyed your entire life in
exchange for money that you would not be able to spend without the
freedom that you are willing to give up. Either way, you have a choice to
make about the freedom that is so often taken for granted in society today.

Now, think about this. What if you could have all the money and
privileges in the world if you only gave up your new life that was found in
Christ? What if I told you that most of those who are reading this do so
practically every day, possibly without even knowing it? If you are a
Christian, you believe in your heart that Christ died on the cross for your
sins and rose again to conquer death, thus giving us eternal life, should we
choose to accept it. Through that cross, we gained freedom from sin, from
our past, from our pain, and from those things that once held us down. We
found freedom from those things that were slowly chipping away at us.
Now, I don't know what that may be for you. Everyone has their own
struggles that they deal with every day. However, when you gave your life
to Christ, He broke those chains that bound you to that sin, that past, that
burden. He broke the stronghold that this thing had on you. Now that you
have been freed from that, what do you do? Do you go running from this
thing, this person, this practice that has held you down for weeks, months,
years, or even your entire life? Probably not.

Have you ever been in a relationship with someone, whether it be
romantic or a strong friendship and something happened and suddenly,
you saw a different side of that person? I bet after you discovered that
thing about that person, you looked them straight in the eye and said: "See
ya"! Actually, you probably started walking away slowly, and when you
realized that they weren't changing before your very eyes, you started
walking back because it looked so much different from afar. You couldn't

stay away. Many of you have probably fallen victim to some kind of addiction, which can be different for everyone. However, one day, you got that feeling in your stomach, and you were done. You deleted the contact, deleted the app, or unplugged the computer. You knew that, at that moment, you had had enough. You were done; but then you went back to the computer hours or days later, or you picked up your phone when you heard an alert, and when you logged onto the computer or unlocked the phone, you realized that you had forgotten to close the page, or you saw one of those "Sorry to see you go" emails from that site you had just deleted your account from. Here is where you have to choose. Do you minimize the reality of the toll that this particular thing or person has had on your life and return to that place where you had once said that enough was enough, or do you recall to memory those experiences that you wouldn't wish on anybody and remind yourself why you walked away in the first place?

If you are in college or even beyond, you have had at least eighteen years of experiences that you hopefully learned from and some of those, you chose to never go back to. How many of those experiences have you returned to at this point? How many of those experiences are you still repulsed, disgusted by to this day? Would you go back if you had the chance? If you answered yes to this, then now would be a good time to stop and reflect on what caused you to walk away from it in the first place. Now would be a good time to ask God to remind you why He pulled you away from that thing, that person, that habit or that relationship. "Oh, but one [text, visit to the site, peek] won't hurt. Just one more time and then I will be good". If you found yourself saying this as you pledged to leave this hindrance behind, then you have not yet begun to grasp the quenching power of God's Love and His Word. So next time you find yourself heading for that computer or that app or to text that guy or girl, ask God to remind you why you stopped in the first place. Don't take the freedom from sin that Christ offered on the cross and jeopardize it with a text, a call or a visit to a site. Take the freedom that Christ has given you, step away from the cage that you have been living in, and run as hard as you can after Christ. When you do this, you won't have the energy to run back to those other things and maybe, just maybe, you will remember what it was about that thing that made you turn and run.

Message:

If you are a living, breathing human being and have been on this earth for any amount of time, you have had some sort of cage in your life. If you have accepted Christ, you have been freed from that cage and have hopefully left it behind. The question is how far you are willing to run with Christ outside of that cage before you shout to Him "I'll be right back! I left something at home!" Therefore, ultimately, there is one question and it is this: Will you place everything that you are and all that you have in Christ and run after Him, or will you leave a few pieces of yourself back at that place you are running from in case you decide to come back on weekends or in case you don't like this new life? The choice is yours. How much are you putting in Christ's hands and how much are you storing away for a rainy day?

Share It!

Using these questions, reach out to your friends on social media and get the conversation started!

1. Take a second to inventory your walk with Christ. As you walk with Him, are you leaving home and leaving the key inside, or are you packing a suitcase and a surefire way of getting back in?
2. What is your cage? Are you freed from it, and if so, how long have you been free? Do you find that it is still appealing or are you repulsed by it?
3. What are you using today to satisfy that spot in your life?

The Condition of Our Fruit

[22]But the fruit of the spirit is love, joy, peace, longsuffering, gentleness, goodness, faith, [23]meekness, temperance: against such things there is no law.

Galatians 5:22-23 KJV

Often, when we read or hear these verses, we flashback to those days in Sunday school when your teacher told you that it was good to be kind to people and if you were kind to people then you would be happy. There is definitely truth in this. However, what they didn't talk about with all the children in a circle, staring up at the teacher with hope and innocence in their eyes, was the rest of that verse.

What if we took this verse, and at the end, we added, even to those people you don't like? Let's take it one piece at a time with this in mind. The first concept that is mentioned is love. You're probably thinking, "Yeah, yeah. Love your enemy. I've heard that a thousand times". Well, my first question for you would be, are you actually doing that, or just simply accepting the fact that you should because you're a Christian? However, beyond that, I also challenge you to ask yourself what this love looks like in your life. This doesn't mean that you walk up to that guy who purposely dinged your car that morning and softly whisper, "I still love you". While this sounds nice on paper, it would probably come across as being just plain weird. The use of love here is not meant to be a noun or simply a concept to keep in the back of your mind. The use of love here is meant to be used as a verb. When the word love is used in the Gospel, it is there to encourage us to act. It's not there to make us stop and say, "Oh, I should start doing that". It is there to take us beyond the minutes or even hours that we spend with Christ on a daily basis. It is there so that, when we finish our devotions for that day, we get up from that chair or that bed, and we go out into the world and act on that love that we spent all that time reading about. It is there to tell us to show love to that person at the grocery store who bought one-too-many items, or that guy on the corner with the cardboard sign who just wants a hotel for the night. The use of love in the Gospel is not simply there for us to say, "That's cool!" It's there so that we will act it out and impact lives for Christ.

The next piece of this verse is this concept of joy. This is probably one of the biggest assets that we as Christians can use to bring people to Christ.

When someone looks at you during those stressful days at work, do they see someone who is calling clients or dealing with customers with an undertone of disgust that is more than evident? Maybe they see someone who looks at challenges and rough days with an attitude of joy because not everyone has the privilege to deal with the people, the coworkers, the life-changing tasks that you are able to encounter on a daily basis.

Maybe you don't have a job yet. When people see you in the library during those late nights, do they see a student who is blocking everyone out who tries to talk to them, or do they see someone who finds joy in the work that they are doing, regardless of the hours required for the work? When they look at you during those hours in the dead of night, do they see someone who understands how fortunate they are to attend that school, or do they see someone who cannot wait to return to hiding in their dorm? These small details in how we live can greatly impact others' views of the Christian walk and what it truly looks like to follow Christ and live life according to His plan.

The third concept mentioned here is the concept of peace. This one is a little more personal. How often do we as Christians experience true peace in our lives? What is peace when it comes to the Christian walk? We can begin to understand what this concept of peace looks like when we realize why it is considered a Fruit of the Spirit. The Fruits of the Spirit are things that can only become a part of one's life after they have accepted Christ as their Savior. The fruit of peace would have to be one of the major fruits, one of the major attributes that come with a new relationship with Christ.

What does it mean to experience peace in our walk with Christ? This means placing all our trust, all our assets, all our faith in Him. When we finally decide to do this, and actually go through with it, we provide Christ with the space He needs to provide us with true peace. This is because, when we surrender all control and resources to God, the results and the process is out of our hands and we can rest assured that the outcome of the situation will be one that is in accordance with God's will.

We also find this concept of longsuffering. This is one that Christians struggle with often. When we face those situations in life that make surrender look so enticing, we can be so easily tempted to turn and run to what may seem like a better, easier option. However, we must constantly remind ourselves that we are on this path because God placed us here.

When we wander from this path, we risk ending up in the deep, dark woods of sin and becoming distant from God. However, if we remain determined to stick to the path set before us, we can know with the utmost certainty that we will eventually end up where we are supposed to be.

What about this concept of gentleness? When we think of gentleness, the first image that probably comes to mind is this image of someone with a blanket draped over them on a couch, and someone is gently stroking their head, and it's also probably a grandmother. But what is gentleness when it comes to those people who may be struggling or hurting? When we encounter those people, we, as followers of Christ are called to comfort these people and to encourage them through the Gospel and through the hope that can only come through Christ. Gentleness means showing those who are hurting, those who are struggling, those who cannot see a way out of the situation they are in that there is a place where they can go to find help for, and refuge from whatever situation they are in. Gentleness means showing these people that you will listen to them, guide them to Christ and show them the hope, peace, and forgiveness that comes through Christ.

This verse goes on to mention goodness. What does it mean to us, as followers of Christ, to be good, or to exhibit goodness? All too often, people who do not know Christ as their personal Savior assume that it is enough to simply be good. However, this verse tells us that true goodness cannot be experienced apart from Christ. To exhibit goodness is an everyday activity. The goodness that comes through a relationship with Christ is something that should coat our inner being every second of the day. Now, is this to say that we will never have bad days when occasionally our goodness gets a couple of chips in it? No. However, this goodness should be something that people notice, hopefully in a prominent way through their interactions with you. Through their interactions, what will these people see? What kind of image of Christ will they begin to develop in their mind from their interactions with you? Consider these questions before you speak badly of someone or get caught going where you probably shouldn't be going. Remember that many people will get their first glimpse of Christ from what they see in you.

The next piece of spiritual fruit that is mentioned here is faith. This one kind of works hand in hand with peace, because without faith, you cannot truly experience peace, and without peace, it can become more difficult to exercise faith. This concept of faith is something that we often refer to in passing when we say things like "Just have faith" when what we really mean is "I'm not really sure what to say but this seems like a good *Jesus is awesome* response". Honestly, exercising faith can be hard when it seems that every side is telling us that we are wrong. Especially in a time when faith in Christ is slowly dwindling, it can be easier to surrender and give up on following Christ than to continue following Him despite the opposition. Faith means that you trust God to bring you through whatever you may find yourself in at the moment. Is exercising faith necessarily always easy? Nope. However, when you implement this "fruit" into your life, you will find that, when you face those circumstances that you didn't necessarily expect, you will be able to find rest, peace in Christ because you will be able to trust that He knows what He is doing, even when the future seems so uncertain.

The next to last fruit that is mentioned here is the fruit of meekness. This is somewhat of a duplication of the fruit of gentleness, which should be enough evidence to show how important it is for followers of Christ to resist the temptation to throw the Bible in someone's face while telling them that they are going to die a fiery death if they don't come to Jesus right now. First of all, this attitude will not make anyone want what you have in terms of your relationship with Christ. This is not to say that you don't have a close, intimate relationship with Christ if this is your approach, but if those who are lost cannot see that relationship in action, they will be less likely to accept the gift that you are sharing with them.

Finally, the last fruit that completes the realm of everything that comes from a relationship with Christ is the fruit of temperance. The one thing that many of these fruits have in common is that they focus on our ability to manage our reactions to the situations of life. This fruit is no different.

No matter who or how many people you talk to, every single person, whether they admit it or not, has faced some kind of situation in their life that has tested their level of self-control. The Christian walk is no different. When we make the decision to follow Christ with our whole self, this decision will not eliminate the struggles that come as a result of sin. As a matter of fact, often this decision only increases the tests placed on our self-control. How we handle these tests will determine how others see us and how they view the relationship we have with Christ.

Now, here's the question for you; What is the condition of your spiritual fruit? How often are you nurturing this fruit and taking it off the tree and allowing it to influence your life? If you forget to pull the fruit from the tree and if you only acknowledge that it's there and do not care for it, your spiritual fruit will begin to waste away and eventually you will begin to wonder where all this fruit went. Are you caring for your fruit, or are you simply letting it continue to hang on the tree?

Message:

The Fruit of the Spirit is something that should show in everything that we do every day. This fruit should be spiritual food, spiritual nourishment for us. This means that we should be exercising this "fruit" and exposing ourselves to this fruit if we want to see anything change because of it. Otherwise, the fruit will dissipate and will do us no good. We have to care for the fruit of the Spirit and put as much into it as it puts into us. This is a continuous process that should always remain in motion. We must never forget to both use and care for the spiritual fruits that we have been given. Now, ask yourself how you are using your spiritual fruit and who is being reached with it. Does this reveal any areas where you should consider change?

Share It!

Using these questions, reach out to your friends on social media and get the conversation started!

1. Often, Christians tend to judge the state of one's relationship with Christ based on the "fruit" that they bear. From the outside looking in, what fruit do you see in your life? Is there any that has been left to rot in the corner?
2. What do you consider to be your strongest fruit right now? What about your weakest?
3. Spiritual fruit comes from the tree that is our relationship with Christ. When you look at the tree, the roots, what state is it in? Well do you care for it?

But God...

[1]And you *hath he quickened*, who were dead in trespasses and sins: [2]wherein in time past ye walked according to the course of this world, according to the prince of the power of the air, the spirit that now worketh in the children of disobedience: [3]among whom also we all had our conversation in times past in the lust of our flesh, fulfilling the desires of the flesh and of the mind; and were by nature the children of wrath, even as others. [4]But God, who is rich in mercy, for his great love wherewith he loved us, [5]even when we were dead in sins, hath quickened us together with Christ, (by grace ye are saved;)

Ephesians 2:1-5 KJV

In this passage, we find Paul writing to us about what basically turns out to be a before and after picture of salvation that can only be found through Christ. He is basically telling us here that everyone is born in a spiritually dead state. We come into the world with sin engrained into our being. There is nothing we, our parents, or any of our ancestors, minus Adam and Eve, of course, could have done to change this. Because of the sin nature that each and every person carries around from the time that they come into the world, we grow up with this tendency to follow what the world tells us instead of what God instructs us to do through His Word.

We are born into a world where it is often so much easier to follow what the world says, which is right in front of us, whether it be through friends, media, school, or any other entity, because these instructions seem to be much more straightforward and in less need of interpretation than those words contained in the Gospel. This passage tells us that we are born not knowing how to be anything but sinful beings. We are born following the desires of our flesh, from wanting that candy when we are little, to wanting that girl, that guy, that tablet or that phone as we begin to phase into adulthood. We are born with this engrained in our being. However, the great thing about the Gospel is that, no matter what the situation is or how hopeless it may seem, there is always some kind of but God. There is always some point in the struggle, in the pain, in the battle when God steps in to show us how capable He is to handle whatever situation we may find ourselves in. Our sin nature is no exception.

In the fourth verse, we find those two words once again. This verse goes on to characterize why God is no everyday superhero that comes in with a cape at just the right moment. It shows us why the forgiveness, the grace, the breath of life that He gives to us through His salvation, is nothing that we can earn on our own. Have you ever heard of someone who was unconscious and was able to revive themselves? Probably not from any reliable news source. When someone is unconscious or even dead, there is nothing that that person can do in their own power that will revive them. This is why being a "good person" or doing "good things" is worthless when it comes to having a relationship with Christ. He is the only one who can truly provide us with the salvation that brings healing and life to those living in a state of sin and who are defined by worldly desires instead of those focused on the one true giver of life.

Finally, in the last verse, we find that Paul provides us with a sort of sticky note reminder. In this last verse, He tells us that it is only by grace through Jesus Christ that we can be saved. This seems to be his way of summing up the entire passage in five words. It's as if he's saying, "In case there was any doubt that salvation is not of ourselves and comes from God, here's one more reminder". Therefore, it would be reasonable to say that the ultimate message of this passage is that a dead person cannot revive themselves. They need someone who is alive and has breath and life inside of them to share that life. That is the only way we can truly experience life. The same is true of our spiritual state. If our spiritual state at the time of our birth were to be hooked up to one of those heart monitors, it would be a flat line. Because of this sinful state, it is only through Christ that we can make that flat line become active again. It is only through Christ, who is that breath of air, that saving grace, that we can truly experience a life that is not defined by the struggles, desires, and opinions of this world.

Message:

The Gospel makes it clear to us that we can't do anything of eternal value without God being in the equation. Without Him being involved in whatever *good* thing we may be doing, whether that be charity, volunteering to build a house for humanitarian work, or passing out tracts at the local superstore, we are simply doing that specific thing to glorify ourselves instead of Him if we fail to make Him the center of the operation. However, when we come to know Christ and we are cleansed from that grime and dirt that has built up over the years, we can know with the utmost certainty that He will be there to make the things we do for Him reap incredible results. However, it is up to us to get Him involved in the situation and to allow Him to work through it.

Share It!

Using these questions, reach out to your friends on social media and get the conversation started!

1. When was the last time that you had a "But God" moment or situation in your life?
2. When have you been able to see God the most clearly during your walk with Him?
3. It was mentioned that "If our spiritual state at the time of our birth were to be hooked up to one of those heart monitors, it would be a flat line". If your walk with Christ were on a heart monitor today, what would it look like? Would it be any different?

You Can('t) Do It

[8]For by grace are ye saved through faith; and that not of yourselves: *it is* the gift of God: [9]not of works, lest any man should boast. [10]For we are his workmanship, created in Christ Jesus unto good works, which God hath before ordained that we should walk in them.

Ephesians 2:8-10 KJV

What does it mean to give someone a gift? Does it mean that we go to that person in October and tell them that they better start making us feel special or making themselves look good so that they get this gift? Does it mean that we hand someone an envelope with $100 in it, and on the back, we make them promise to pay us back within the next six months? Of course not! When we give someone a gift, regardless of how much the gift is worth or who is receiving it, we don't ask them to fulfill a list of requirements or to pay the gift back later. The same goes for the gift that Christ gave to us on the cross.

Salvation is only available through Christ for those who make the decision to accept it. We are told repeatedly in churches and in the Gospel, itself, that the value of the gift of salvation is more than we can ever imagine or repay. The funny thing about this is that, even with that knowledge, so many people, including so many that fill church pews every week, feel like we don't really have to humble ourselves before God and confess that we are sinners to receive forgiveness and the rewards that come with that forgiveness. So many people feel that making ourselves look good before God is enough to get the job done. This is basically like taking a car from the junkyard and redoing the paint and bodywork on the outside while leaving all the junk and trash inside the car, and placing it on a car lot expecting someone to buy it. From a distance, everything may look okay, but upon further inspection, the stuff that we find is not very pleasant. But the outside looked good to the rest of the world! Who cares if the inside is messed up? This is the logic that so many people follow today when thinking about salvation.

How often do we walk down the halls at our school, at our job, even at our church, and see those smiling faces, those dry-cleaned suits, those polished hairstyles, and wonder how that person keeps it all together? How often do we see those people in the praise group at church and wonder how they stay so close to the Lord and how we can be more like them?

It seems that today, we live in an age where presentation is everything. It doesn't matter what you actually have, know, or can actually do, as long as you can make people think that you have, know or do this or that. When it comes to the Christian walk, all three of these apply to how so many Christians or supposed Christians live their life. From the music that they play in their car, to the shirts that they wear on the weekend when they are out running errands, to even the verses that they post on social media, we find ourselves at a time when it seems that the doing matters more than having salvation through Christ.

This verse tells us that it is through Christ, and Christ alone that we can have salvation. It doesn't say that, if we build up enough brownie points or get enough stickers in children's church, that we will get a pass on the whole confessing our sins thing. The Bible doesn't tell us that if we do enough, if we get enough Jesus dollars, we can go to the heavenly treasure box and pick out our favorite mansion in heaven. To many, this would be easier than humbly asking God's forgiveness that can only be found through His Son, Jesus Christ. If it was up to us to cleanse ourselves from our sin, it is very likely that more people would jump on-board. Fortunately, if this message of self-forgiveness sounds appealing to you, there are thousands of religions all over the world that will welcome you with open arms, but if you want true forgiveness, it must come from a source that is sinless. That is why Christianity is different.

The majority of religions out there live by this principle of, if you do this enough, then you're probably good, but we can't know for sure until it's too late. A relationship with Christ tells us that if we simply accept the forgiveness that is offered through the cross, then we can know with all certainty that we have a relationship with Him and have been cleansed from our sins. This is why following Christ is not only more secure but also, more difficult at times.

So often, it seems that the one choice that actually holds truth, regardless of what that truth is, is the one option that comes under fire the most. When Christ came onto the scene, He challenged every single belief that the people had held for many years. Obviously, this did not go over well. It cost Him, as well as many of His followers their lives. The reason for this is that He and His disciples were telling people around the world that they were not capable of gaining the forgiveness needed to enjoy a relationship with God and eventually eternal life. I don't know about you, but if someone came into my church and said that, after my parents, my teachers, my family, and the religious leaders of my church had been preaching it for as long as I had been alive, I'd be a little upset. This was a reality for so many people in that time-period. Unfortunately, however, there continue to be people in the world today who are outraged by the teachings of Christ. From fields of science dedicated to disproving Christ's existence and the validity of the Gospel to churches that refuse to give validity to the Gospel, Christ is still under fire for the things that He said thousands of years ago.

Even in that day and age, there were massive groups of people arguing that the Bible was wrong in saying that there was only one way to heaven. In this respect, it seems that history is in a period of repeating itself today, as tolerance takes center stage in almost every area of life. Today, it is no longer acceptable to teach the biblical account of creation in schools that has turned atheists to theists, evolutionists to creationists. It is no longer acceptable for teachers to share the Gospel in the classroom for fear of offending someone, or for fear of coming across as intolerant. Now, many of you are probably reading this and thinking quietly or saying out loud something to the effect of "Preach it! Ain't that the truth?" I want to warn you that this is the wrong response to what I write here. We as Christians have a calling, regardless of what school we go to, or what kind of job we are in, to fulfill the Great Commission. When Christ called us to fulfill this commission, He didn't include a disclaimer that said, "…But only if it's okay with management and HR". The only *if's* that we find in the Gospel are in the form of conditional statements. One thing that the Gospel does not do when it comes to reaching people for Christ is to give us a way out. There is no Escape key when it comes to sharing the Gospel.

I fear that because we live in a nation where it seems that nothing is off-limits when it comes to things that we can do that do not harm anyone or cause anyone to lose money, that we sometimes view rules and regulations in public places as persecution. Now, while I am not saying that being a Christian is always the easiest thing in the world, what I am saying is that Christ didn't die so that we could have it easy. Christ died to save lives, to save hearts. That mission is still in effect to this day. That mission has not been forgotten just because it has been a couple thousand years since it became possible to have a relationship with Him. We still have a job to do as followers of Christ. We should not be turning around and heading home every time we encounter someone who doesn't want to listen to us and chop it up to persecution. Those roadblocks that we encounter should only serve as a catalyst to encourage us to find another way to reach that person. Often, Christ may be using those roadblocks to see how devoted you are to the cause of spreading the Gospel. If you encounter an obstacle the size of someone turning their back on you and go home at the end of the day, exhausted from all the persecution, maybe you should dig into God's Word a little deeper and remind yourself of the people that lost family, homes, and money, and still chose to continue the mission. Maybe you should quickly remind yourself of what Christ is calling you to when He calls you to a relationship with Him. Once you have done this, you will hopefully begin to understand the resolve that is needed to genuinely follow Christ and to do what He has called you to do.

Message:

No one ever said that the Christian walk would be easy, but we didn't think it would be this hard! Why didn't someone warn us about this? Oh wait, they did, multiple times. When we go on mission for Christ, we must recognize that most people will not welcome a message that takes away the power to determine whether they can have something or not. However, depending on how long you have been a follower of Christ and how much you know about the Gospel, the chances are pretty good that John 3:16 and the Roman Road are not going to be enough to show someone that they need Christ. Most nonbelievers who live in the United States have probably heard every known approach to witnessing that any college (or younger) student can think of. Those who are lost in the world are looking for something different. People who are wandering lost want something that assures them that what they are doing is worthwhile. Therefore, it is our responsibility, as followers of Christ to show these people who are lost that the only mission worth pursuing, which can and should be pursued daily in whatever they do, is the mission that Christ set before us.

Share It!

Using these questions, reach out to your friends on social media and get the conversation started!

1. How do you manage persecution in your walk with Christ? What impact does it have on you?
2. What kind of results have you seen from your ability to persevere through persecution?
3. What does the gift of salvation mean to you? How does this impact your ability to witness?

Words Can Change Everything

Let no corrupt communication proceed out of your mouth, but that which is good to the use of edifying, that it may minister grace unto the hearers.

Ephesians 4:29 KJV

In a time when it seems that we can find opinions and feedback on just about anything through the powerful platform of social media, sometimes we could use some reminders such as this one that reminds us of the power of our words. The funny thing is that it seems like everyone recognizes this and understands what is meant when people say or write it on social media, but how often do we actually put this idea into action? Why don't we take a second and simply consider the power of words?

Think about what words can do. Whether they be in written or verbal form, words have the power to take life, and restore it. Words have the ability to bring someone into captivity and bring them into freedom. Words have the power to give someone hope and to also take it away. Words can make someone cry tears of joy or tears of pain. Words have the power to destroy someone's future, or to make it immensely better. Words have the power to do many things and influence many people, but it is up to us to choose how we use them.

When we look at the words of Christ in the Gospel, His Words were not only those that told people that everything would be okay eventually if they trusted Him. He told people of the future and about the things that they should be on the lookout for. With words, all that we see around us came into existence. With words, we were given the path to salvation. However, what was different about these words? What made these words different was the fact that they were not simply that. They were not just a bunch of words spoken by some guy. They were words that were spoken, but also backed up by truth and action.

Imagine that you go out to the grocery store after class one day, and someone stops you to ask you where the flour is. You are bewildered by this question because it seems that it would be common knowledge that it would be near the baking ingredients. However, just for laughs, you tell this innocent, lost person that the flour is in the frozen section. This person does not question you, and heads off toward the frozen foods. Those words influenced the direction that this person decided to go. Had you told them that the flour was with the baking supplies, that person would have received worthwhile guidance, but because you told them to go to the frozen section, they will now begin wandering lost looking for flour where there is none.

How often do we do this in our Christian walk? In addition to being encouraging in our conversations with people, we also have a duty as Christians to share the truth with them. The words that come from the mouth of a single, solitary Christian can change a person's entire opinion of not only Christians but also of what it means to have a relationship with Christ. How often do we encounter a nonbeliever outside of the church and find them craving something new, something fresh? How often do we find lost people, and instead of pointing them to Christ, we point them to that church across the street? We rationalize it by saying that they're not our problem anymore because we have handed them over to the professionals. We rest assured that they're somebody else's problem now.

Words are only words until they are backed up with truth and action. If Christ had said that He was going to die for our sins and conquer death forever, but never actually went through with it, what value would those words have? They would be worthless. If God had said at the beginning of time, "Let there be light", and nothing happened, why would those words matter? The answer is that they wouldn't. They would sound good on paper, but they would not have any value or give anyone hope. Now, what percentage of the words that you speak to people regarding the Gospel are backed up by action and truth? How do those words manifest themselves in your daily life? If you would give yourself a failing grade on that question, you may want to think next time before you speak and consider whether this guidance that you are about to give to this lost soul, is guidance that has been backed up with truth from the Gospel and tested out in your own life.

Message:

Words are important. Words are powerful. However, if your words are not being cemented through action, people will notice. If you find yourself sharing the Gospel in public, and telling people that they have to give their whole life to Him to truly enjoy an intimate relationship with Him, and yet you still find yourself sitting at the computer late at night watching that movie or scrolling through that page that you wouldn't tell anyone about, then you may want to think back to that advice that you gave to that person who had no point of reference and came to you looking for guidance. If you look at your life, and think back to those points in time when someone came to you for guidance, and you realized mid-sentence, that you should probably be doing that too, maybe it is time for you to turn to God's Word, and begin to integrate those words into your life, because we can know for a fact that those words are truth and have been backed up by action.

Share It!

Using these questions, reach out to your friends on social media and get the conversation started!

1. In addition to putting action and truth behind your words, it's also important that they have some sort of impact. What kind of impact are your words having in the lives of others?
2. How have you allowed the truth and action behind the words of Christ to become a guiding principle in your life?
3. Where are your words guiding people? Are they being guided to a source of truth and life, or are they only being sent further in the wrong direction?

What Do You Have to Lose?
For me to live *is* Christ, and to die *is* gain.

Philippians 1:21 KJV

What does it mean to have meaning in your life? Have you ever taken the time to give this question some thought? If you have, the answer probably looks different to everyone. For some, their meaning in life comes from their relationships with others. For some, this thing is their success in their job or in their fitness or in any number of other things. For college students, this may be a relationship, romantic or otherwise, or their academics. There's nothing wrong with finding joy in these things. It's natural for us to find happiness in things that we simply enjoy doing. However, in this passage, we find Paul writing from a prison cell where he is encouraging the Christian church to think long and hard about what this life is really about, and this verse begins to show us a piece of the answer.

In this verse, we find Paul driving home this point that, regardless of what hobbies and activities and job(s), and what kinds of relationships you have, regardless of this stuff that makes up our lives, if all these things are not centered on Christ and our desire to continue drawing closer to Him, they are basically being done in vain. See, the interesting thing about all Paul's writings, including this one, is that they are almost entirely written during a time in his life when he knew with the utmost certainty that he was going to die for doing what he is now telling other people to do. He knew that this thing that he was telling people to do, this act of spreading the Gospel to the world was an act that could and probably would get someone killed. However, the interesting and the great thing about this verse is that he kind of addresses this head-on in a very short, yet not so sweet way. In this verse, he tells us that "to die is gain". This piece of the verse serves as a sort of reminder, or maybe even an insight into what it means to be a follower and missionary for the cause of Christ. I mention that it may serve as a sort of insight for some because often it seems that we forget that when we accept this mission to follow Christ and to spread His Gospel, we are accepting the possibility that this mission could lead us to surrender our lives. If this is not our mindset when we go into the mission field, whether that field is our office, our hall, our classroom or even our home, then we need to take a step back and reevaluate why we are even doing this. If we look at everything that we are doing and labeling it as being for the cause of spreading the Gospel, and yet we find ourselves hesitant or even refusing to place ourselves in situations where our lives could possibly be endangered, then we are basically abandoning the piece of this verse that says, "For me to live is Christ".

In the other portion of this passage, we find the less pleasant, less social media friendly piece of the verse. "…to die is gain". When we see this piece of the verse, our mind seems to want to take an extra couple of seconds to consider what it is that is being said here. This idea of considering dying for one's mission to be a gain is an idea that we can often struggle grasp. Imagine this in the context of a battle. If a soldier dies, the troops within that soldier's unit and that soldier's family back home consider that to be a tremendous loss. However, when the public hears of that loss of life, that soldier becomes hailed as a hero. That soldier is seen as someone who felt so strongly about the cause that they were fighting for, the freedom that they were fighting to protect, that they would not even let their life come between them and completing that mission. Therefore, just as this soldier is forced to place their life on the line for the cause of a country's freedom, so we, as followers of Christ, should go into each and every day with the mindset of being prepared to go to whatever lengths we must to ensure that all people all over the globe have access to and an understanding of this message that gives its recipients something that cannot be found in any other source. This is where we take up that role of being a soldier for Christ, bringing people this message of freedom, of liberty, from sin. If we don't do this, we will be held accountable when the time comes that we will stand before God and answer to Him. Therefore, when you look at the various mission fields in your life, whether they be at work, school or even to the general public, what are some of the things that you find yourself placing between yourself and the fulfillment of the mission that has been set before you? What are you doing to impact these mission fields that you have been placed in?

Message:

When you look at the mission fields in your daily life, what are the things that are getting in the way of you placing everything on the line to do what it takes to spread the Gospel to those in that field? This can be a difficult question to answer because it can often be the case that something that God intended as a tool for fulfilling His mission has turned into a barrier instead. Additionally, when considering these questions, take some time to consider what this death that Paul speaks of looks like in your life. For some, it will mean sacrificing certain behaviors regarding social media, or certain relationships, or any other number of things. However, before you begin asking these questions and taking these steps, you must take time to simply stop and ask yourself if you are truly ready to die in every sense of the word to gain those eternal results. Your answer will have a significant impact on the outcome of your personal ministry in the years to come. Therefore, the choice is yours. What are you going to do?

Share It!

Using these questions, reach out to your friends on social media and get the conversation started!

1. What is one thing in your life that has become a hindrance, a barrier between you and your attempt to reach people for Christ?
2. Aside from your life, what is one thing that you would hesitate to surrender if it meant that an opportunity to share the Gospel were on the line?
3. What is one thing that you have given up for the cause of Christ in the last year?

Being the Light

[14]Do all things without murmurings and disputings: [15]that ye may be blameless and harmless, the sons of God, without rebuke, in the midst of a crooked and perverse nation, among whom ye shine as lights in the world;

Philippians 2:14-15 KJV

Mondays, assignments, projects, and the list goes on. These are just a few of the things that usually produce a sigh from college students and working adults alike. When we go in after that two-day break and we see that pile of work that we didn't want to do on Friday, it almost demands that we let out even a small grumble. This always seems like the best thing to do because it is usually the easiest thing to do. Plus, it is often the case that we aren't really sure what we are supposed to do in these situations where it seems that we are balancing the world on our shoulders. We come into the office knowing that this pile of work is waiting for us and that it will only get bigger as the day goes by. However, when we see this pile of work, tall as it may be, what if we took a second to look at that mile-high stack of paper, that calendar full of events, that inbox that is overflowing after only two days, and considered how we could go about using all that to bring glory to God? Now, depending on where you may be reading this, it is possible that all those things are towering over you, either literally or figuratively, and your mind is racing and trying to figure out how you will get it all done. However, this is where your mission field comes into play.

When we look at these stress-filled tasks that demand our attention daily, we never really take the time to consider how our handling of these tasks impacts the carrying-out of our mission for the cause of Christ. We so often fail to realize that, even in the midst of those busy nights, those days before that huge test, or the night before that big project is due, that there are people watching us as we face these times of stress and struggle. See, it is in these moments when Christ's role in our lives becomes extremely evident to those around us. It's in these moments that the world looks at us and sees, not our words, but our actions and how they reflect Christ and the relationship that we claim to have with Him. In these moments, we find ourselves being tested in how we will handle ourselves in these moments of trouble. Whether it be a car accident, some incident with our school or our employer, in these moments, we have the choice to be light in a dark world or to add to the darkness in how we decide to handle this situation. Does this mean that you are supposed to go around with a smile on your face all the time, acting as if nothing is going on in your life? No. However, when you find yourself being faced with some sort of struggle, whether it be in academics, relationships, finances, health, or any other variety of things, we must remain vigilant in how we conduct ourselves through these times.

Well, that's it! When stuff happens, just let it roll off and move on! Does that sound good? I didn't think so. It shouldn't. Therefore, when you find yourself facing these times of struggle, as I said earlier, take a moment to step back from the situation and look at how God is using the situation to lead you down this path that He has designated for you. Unfortunately, this is not going to be easy by any means. In many cases, it may take months or even years for you to be able to look back and see how God chose to use that situation for the betterment of you and His Kingdom. Maybe that means an unexpected diagnosis that blindsides you and your family. Maybe that means that you find yourself in an economic situation that brings your academic future into question. Maybe this relationship that you thought would be "the one" is beginning to deteriorate and you find yourself questioning everything that you ever thought about this person. Whatever it may be, eventually, there will come a time when you are able to look back at those situations that you faced, and you will begin to understand why it all happened the way that it did. The question is, will you be willing to stick it out, or will you turn and run at the first sign of trouble. It's your choice.

Message:

Imagine that God places this huge roadmap in front of us when we begin to follow Him. Wouldn't that be great?! If we had that, we could look at it and figure out where we needed to trust Him more, and where we could afford to slack off a little bit and chase after Him just a little bit slower. It would be great; and that is exactly why we don't need that roadmap. This walk, this relationship that we have with Christ is not like a workout schedule, where we spend more time doing it on the days we choose to splurge in some way or when we mess up in a big way. This relationship that we are a part of demands that we give Him everything that we have, and allow Him to do with it what He will. We don't get to tell Him how to handle the situation, and honestly, I'm not sure we would want that power. Granted, it may not necessarily be easy all the time, but if we continue pressing forward in this journey that we find ourselves on, we will eventually be able to look back and say "Oh! I see what He did there!" Therefore, regardless of how bad things may get during this journey, keep in mind that other people are watching, and that your actions and reactions in these situations will become a true indicator of where you really are in your walk with Christ.

Share It!

Using these questions, reach out to your friends on social media and get the conversation started!

1. When was the last time that you faced a situation in your life that tested your ability to keep a level head? How did you handle that?
2. Think about one instance where you found yourself in a situation that tested you in every way. What image of Christ did you paint in that moment?
3. We always hear that phrase *Walking with Christ*. For you personally, what happens when you are walking with Christ, and you happen to face a road closure, or you happen to "stub your toe" on some sort of inconvenient circumstance?

Think on the Good Stuff

Finally, brethren, whatsoever things *are* honest, whatsoever things *are* just, whatsoever things *are* pure, whatsoever things *are* lovely, whatsoever things *are* of good report; if *there be* any virtue, and if *there be* any praise, think on these things.

Philippians 4:8 KJV

What do you think about? That's vague, isn't it? What do you think about? Most would say that it depends on what they're doing, what time of day it is, who they're with, and maybe what happened that day. With that in mind, let's stick with that criteria. When you get back to your dorm or apartment at the end of the day, what do you think about in those moments when you are alone, or when you are tired, or when you're frustrated? Do you sit on the couch constantly recalling the way that guy or that girl on your hall looked at you or scoffed at you as they walked by? Do you sit at your computer thinking about the things that you would like to tell that teacher who assigned a ten-page paper on the one weekend you were supposed to be completely free from responsibility? The chances are that within one of these categories, you will find your thoughts in the last twenty-four hours or at some point during the last semester.

Because we are human beings living in a fallen world, the thoughts that find their way into our mind are not always extremely pleasant or pleasing to God. When we are in the library late at night doing an assignment that is due tomorrow, we become tired, we become anxious, wondering if we will make the deadline that is coming up in a few hours. In those moments of anxiety and sometimes fear, we can begin to wonder why we are even at this school. Why did God have to bring us here? Why did I have to choose this major or that concentration? In the moments when we become tired, anxious, aggravated, we can often begin to doubt pieces and parts of God's plan or the circumstances He has placed us in, simply because we have a lot on our plate.

What about the human impact of our thoughts, our anxiety, and our full plate? What about our parents who only want to see us succeed? What about our friends who have seen us at our worst and in those moments when our parents weren't there for us to vent? How does our stress impact them? What impact do those words we speak in moments of angst have on the relationships that we have spent months, maybe even years building?

In this verse, we find a list of qualities that should, and hopefully, do describe our interactions with people. One thing that is interesting about these qualities is the fact that, while they should describe our thoughts in general, these qualities should also show themselves in how we interact with and treat other people, both in times of rest and peace, as well as in times of stress and anxiety when it can sometimes be difficult to follow this principle. Ultimately, we can say that we exemplify these traits in our lives as much as we want, but until people see them on display, our claiming to possess these qualities will mean nothing.

Now that we have established the importance of what it means to let these qualities show in our daily life, what does that look like? Let's start from the top. When we look at the qualities expressed in this verse, we find that they all have one thing in common. All these qualities basically come down to being friendly and having integrity. In reality, how important are our thoughts in the grand scheme of things? It's not like we can knock someone over with our mind, right? That is correct. However, when was the last time that you left an interaction with someone and instead of thinking about how they had messed up that one time in high school, you thought about the words of encouragement that they had just spoken to you in your time of struggle? When was the last time that you saw that person at that gathering your friend had invited you to, and instead of thinking about how they had never paid that thirty dollars back to you from over a year ago, you felt your heart hurting for them because of the unforeseen circumstances that they had just found themselves in?

When we hear this verse and when we think about what is being said here, we should keep in mind that, when it comes to our thoughts and actions toward others, as well as in those moments when we find ourselves alone with our thoughts, we need to stop and realize that, when it comes to exhibiting these qualities in our lives, the standard eventually comes down to becoming more like Christ. Due to the fact that this is the standard for us as His followers, we will never, until the day we gain our place in His kingdom, be on point with all these qualities all the time. However, this does not eliminate our responsibility to strive to be more like Him in how we think about and treat others.

Message:

At times, it seems that we know how we should treat people and the forgiveness that we should afford them. However, actually acting on this forgiveness and grace is an entirely different story. Therefore, if you are ever having issues trying to decipher how long is too long to hold something against someone before forgiving them and forgetting altogether, think about it like this. Christ died willingly on a cross for sins that He didn't commit, but that He knew about before they had ever been committed. When we see our sin through this lens, hopefully, it will become a little bit easier to grant forgiveness to those who never intended to hurt us in the first place. Additionally, let us strive to remember the impact of our words. Let our words always be rooted in truth and backed up by action.

Share It!

Using these questions, reach out to your friends on social media and get the conversation started!

1. Think about the last interaction that you had with someone about your same age. What were your thoughts after parting ways with that person? How do these thoughts line up with the standard in this piece of scripture?
2. How do you typically approach interactions with nonbelievers, whether you know them or not?
3. How has God used some sort of interaction in the past for good in your life?

Christ Gives Life

[21]And you, that were sometime alienated and enemies in *your* mind by wicked works, yet now hath he reconciled [22]in the body of his flesh through death, to present you holy and unblameable and unreproveable in his sight:

Colossians 1:21-22 KJV

Have you ever had those moments in your life, specifically in a literal sense, when you looked around and realized that you had no idea where you were or how you got there? Have you ever felt like you were in a place where it seemed that you did not have an advocate and you were basically facing this impossible situation with no defense other than your words and your faith that everything will turn out like it's supposed to? This basically describes what it's like to live life without Christ. We look around and suddenly realize that we have no idea what we're doing, where we're going or in what direction we need to go to get where we want to go. Leading life in this manner is not only more difficult in comparison to walking with Christ. It also makes us more vulnerable to wandering into dangerous territory where we have even less of an understanding of what's around us. This is why we need Christ.

Christ is repeatedly referred to in the Gospel as being a light. Therefore, Christ is supposed to be our guiding light when it comes to our walk with Him. We can put as much of our own effort into the walk as we want to, but in the end, if we do not allow Him to take complete control, our journey with Christ can quickly become a walk away from Him and into total darkness. However, with Christ, we can experience true, genuine light that will guide and direct our steps as long as we choose to follow Him.

One thing that is interesting about this passage is the way that it depicts both angles of this walk with Christ. It shows us the side that we can experience with Christ in the picture, and it shows us the darkness and the loss of intimacy that we can experience when we become more distant from Christ. With these two options in mind, we are left with the decision of which type of relationship we want with Him. It is obvious when we read through the Gospel that Christ wants intimacy with us. Christ wants us to draw closer to Him and make Him our top priority every day. However, that is a decision that we must make on our own.

Let's look at this relationship with Christ in a different manner. The Bible refers to our relationship with Christ as a marriage. Can you imagine finding the woman or man of your dreams, and the day after you're married, you turn to this person, pat them on the back, and tell them that you will see them next Sunday, and if you feel like it, you may call them before then, but you're extremely busy so they probably shouldn't hold their breath waiting for that call. This is often how so many people approach their relationship with Christ. They look around and see other Christians, and they seem happy, so they get curious. Before you know it, this individual is reading their Bible for an hour every day and moving closer and closer to engaging in a relationship with Christ. Soon, this individual goes to the altar and accepts Christ in front of the entire church congregation. This basically represents the wedding. For a few weeks after that, the person is flooded with hugs, cards, gifts, and words of encouragement. However, soon, the words of encouragement and the cards come to an end. Now what? Is it still exciting? It should be. If it is not, then maybe you should reconsider your motives for beginning this relationship in the first place.

After the wedding or the day of salvation comes the honeymoon of sorts. After coming to know Christ, there are those weeks, months, or maybe even a few years, of intimacy when you spend every spare moment you have with God in His Word. However, soon, you get tired of having to block time out of your schedule for studying His Word and decide you could use that time for better things, like sleep or food. This is a pattern that so many Christians are familiar with. Some spend years walking in darkness, and when they find Christ and experience that light for the first time, it's like nothing they have ever experienced. However, eventually the high wears off and they find themselves drifting from God and back into the darkness. This is a path that can be very tempting for most people when they become fatigued or maybe even bored in their walk. However, if you continue to spend time in the light of the Gospel, you will be able to become more intimate with the light offered by Christ, thus leaving less room for a desire to return to the darkness where you once found yourself becoming increasingly comfortable.

Message:

A relationship with Christ is not all about the perks, and if you are in it for the perks, then you will find that those perks, like the candy in Sunday school will slowly become less than enough to keep you in a state of intimacy with Christ. However, if you dive into His Word and do everything you possibly can to stay in His Word, then you will find that you can never set aside enough time to spend with Him. When you finally find this intimacy in this relationship, it will become more like a marriage, in that you will *want* to spend time with Him, learning about Him, loving Him in new ways every day, and you will find that, suddenly, the world has fallen from your line of sight and all that is visible is what is in the light of Christ. Let this be what you set your focus on.

Share It!

Using these questions, reach out to your friends on social media and get the conversation started!

1. So often, in the world today, it can be easy to allow the light of Christ and His Word to become blocked by something in the world. What is that thing in your life? How easy is it to move it out of the way?
2. If you have begun this *marriage,* this relationship with Christ, how would you identify your intimacy with Him?
3. What is one piece of your walk with Christ that you find Him convicting your heart about today?

Mind Your Audience

and whatsoever ye do, do it heartily, as to the Lord, and not unto men;

Colossians 3:23 KJV

I want you to think about something for a minute. What is it that motivates you? What motivates you in your schoolwork? What motivates you in your walk with Christ? What is that thing that motivates you in your life in general? As with many of the questions that I have posed and will pose over the course of this book, the answers to these questions will vary from person to person. However, in the end, if we are honest with ourselves, the thing that usually motivates us in the work that we do in the various areas of our lives is our audience. Think about it. When you wrote that essay for that college application, you didn't write it in text lingo. When you wrote that résumé, you wrote it in a manner that would show that you wanted and deserved that job that you were chasing after. Regardless of what the situation may be, everything that you do in your life is ultimately driven by who the audience is. Now, with that in mind, what if God is your audience? In your job, it's approaching two o'clock in the afternoon, you're tired, you're ready to go home, but suddenly, someone walks into your cubicle. However, instead of your boss, you turn around and God is standing there asking you what it is that you are doing. How will you respond? What would He see?

In this thing that we call life, we can often forget that everything that we do is part of our mission field. Everything from our job to our extracurricular activities, to our academics is a piece of how others around us see Christ through us. Therefore, when we walk into the office after a long weekend, what image are these people around you, who may or may not be followers of Christ, seeing when you walk in the door in the morning? When you sit down at your desk and you look back over that report that you dedicated twelve hours to on Friday, do you look at it and think to yourself "what was I doing"? Do you find yourself in those late-night homework sessions, closing your eyes as you click "Submit"? Most of you are probably laughing right now as you reflect on last semester, last week, or last night when you found yourself doing just that, and the author of this book has two thumbs pointing at Himself because we've all done it. However, when we take a second to look at this life that we have been given, and we think about the many opportunities that we are presented with to present the Gospel to those thirsty hearts in the world today, we don't want these opportunities to be squandered by someone's observation of us turning in a halfhearted assignment that clearly was not well-done.

See, when we present this message of the Gospel and how it has the potential to change lives if people will only allow it to work, and then we turn around and see a pile of our own procrastination, it becomes extremely difficult to stand before these people that we are sharing the Gospel with and to tell them that we are a living example of someone who is living their life to glorify and honor God, when our work and anything that requires any kind of effort says otherwise. Often, this seemingly worldly piece of our lives, whatever that may be for you, can end up being center-stage in our ministry and in our lives.

In this passage, we are told that "whatsoever" we do should be done as unto the Lord. This means that we should be doing everything, our classwork, our work for our company, our various hats within our family, and any other responsibilities that find their way onto our plate as if we are doing them unto the Lord because ultimately, that is exactly what we are doing. When you walk into that job on Monday morning, you need to sit down at that desk with the realization that everything that you do reflects who God is and what He is ultimately worthy of when it comes to every area of your life. When you sit down in that 8:15 class on Monday morning, you need to sit down in that chair ready and willing to use these gifts that God has given you to reach people both through the direct sharing of the Gospel and through the indirect sharing of Christ's provision through how you do your work every day. It is through doing these things that we will be better able to serve God and others and spread His love to the world as they witness the shining example that He is making us be.

Message:

Now, what about you? When you go into the office, into class at 8:15, or into whatever mission field God has placed you in, what does He see? How are you using these gifts and assets that He has given you? In your use of these gifts, do others see Him through you? This is an important evaluation to make every day in your walk with Christ. This is important because if we are going into this job on Monday and we are not doing each task that we must do as if God is sitting in the CEO's chair, then we are not doing the quality of work that God Himself is worthy of. Therefore, if our work is not living up to God's standard, then how will others be able to see God through our work?

Share It!

Using these questions, reach out to your friends on social media and get the conversation started!

1. In this phase of your life right now, what is your mission field? How effective would you consider yourself to be at reaching that field?
2. When do you find it most difficult to be like Christ during your daily routine?
3. For you, what does it look like to be like Christ in your:
    a. Education
    b. Interactions
    c. Work

The Sword

For the word of God is quick, and powerful, and sharper than any two-edged sword, piercing even to the dividing asunder of soul and spirit, and of the joints and marrow, and is a discerner of the thoughts and intents of the heart.

Hebrews 4:12 KJV

How often do we open God's word, whether it be for an assignment for one of our Bible classes or simply for the purposes of study, and view it in this light? Most of us would probably be the first to admit that more times than not, we open our Bible in church, listen and read along, and close it without considering the power that is contained within that book. We don't think about the fact that it is considered a weapon and an asset for winning souls for Christ. So often, just as many scholars, Christians fall into a mindset that leaves them viewing the Gospel of Jesus Christ as being a book and nothing more. However, what if we took just a second to view the Bible and the truth it contains in this light? What if we handled and read the Bible as if it were a weapon and an asset for the purposes of reaching the world for Christ, and used it and shared it as if we truly believed that it could save lives? If the church made the decision to commit to handling and sharing the Bible in this manner, imagine how the world would be changed. However, what does it mean to share the Gospel?

When thinking about a sword and the power that it contains in the right hands, that sword has the power to defeat or slow down pretty much any threat that may be thrown in its direction. That sword does not encounter someone who may not be interested in a battle that day and decide not to engage them. That sword does not only work one or two days a week for a couple of hours. That sword is going to do its job on a daily basis, every second of the day. This sword doesn't take days off or avoid certain people for fear of confrontation. This sword does its job when the job needs to be done. Ultimately, the Gospel is a tool that is to be used every day and shared with everyone we meet. This is the only way that it will be able to truly do what it's meant to do.

As we continue with this idea of the power contained within that sword, there's a question that begs an answer. Is there anything that this sword cannot conquer? This verse basically tells us that there are no boundaries to the material that this sword can cut through. There are no limits to the circumstances that this sword can conquer. Now, you're probably thinking, *Well, what about that guy in class who cusses constantly and doesn't respect anyone?* The Gospel can conquer that. *What about that atheist in my biology class that speaks against God every chance she gets?* The Gospel can handle that. *What about that professor who failed me on that paper because I spoke of Christ?* The Gospel can win that battle. The Gospel can stand up to any challenge. There's no doubt about that. The Gospel has the ability to save lives because of the truth contained within its pages. However, while the problem is not within the Gospel itself, there is a problem, and it can be summed up in one word; *us.* So often, when God wants to reach people for Him and wants to use us to do that, the things that get in the way are our fear, our laziness, our uncertainty, our insecurities that they may turn us away. We fear that we will be turned away, so we completely avoid sharing the Gospel altogether. We let the fear of getting our feelings hurt get in the way of sharing the gift of salvation that Christ died to make possible. What if we chose to set our feelings and our fears aside, took up our sword, and went to the battle lines to share this gift of salvation that is offered freely to anyone who will accept? Can you imagine the impact the church would have on the unsaved population if the church did what it was supposed to do and shared the Gospel regardless of the penalties? Maybe it's about time that we stepped away from our feelings and decided that it's not about us, but rather about Christ and the lives that He died to save! What could the church do if it chose to adopt this mindset? You may be surprised.

Message:

What fears are you allowing to get in the way of sharing the Gospel with the world around you? What is holding you back from giving the world that is hurting, something fresh, something that can give hope and promise where there so often is none? We must remember that when we share the Gospel and spread the word about what Christ has done and is continuing to do, it is not about us. It's not about our feelings or what may or may not be acceptable. It's about what Christ has called us, as His followers, to do during our time on earth. We are not here simply to enjoy life. While this should be a by-product of many of the things that we do, this is not our main mission on Earth. Our mission here is to win people to Him and if we do not do this for fear of discomfort, we are not fulfilling our purpose that has been set before us by Christ.

Share It!

Using these questions, reach out to your friends on social media and get the conversation started!

1. When thinking about this concept of the Gospel being a sword, we understand that the sword itself can do more than enough damage. However, is there anything that you may be adding to it that could be getting in the way?
2. What are some instances where you tend to conceal your sword for fear of being confronted?
3. How has that *sword* impacted or penetrated you in your own walk with Christ?

Leave Your Pride at the Door

Let us therefore come boldly unto the throne of grace, that we may obtain mercy, and find grace to help in time of need.

Hebrews 4:16 KJV

If we were completely and totally honest with ourselves, most of us would be the first to admit that one of the hardest things for anyone to do is to ask for help. For those of you who are reading this inside their college dorm or library during a study break, you are among this population of people who are in a phase of life when you're expected to be figuring your life out and you are beginning to make decisions that will impact you for the rest of your life. Therefore, these decisions should be made carefully with a lot of counsel. However, how easy is it, especially for the guys out there, to come to their parents, or a mentor, or maybe even a teacher to ask for help with something? That can often be one of the hardest things students have to do. Often, we have to reach out to someone with more experience, more wisdom than ourselves, and we have to admit that we do not know everything under the sun and we are seeking wisdom from experts in this area or that field. We have to admit that we need help, and to most college students, this is like getting teeth pulled. However, how does this act of asking for help play out when it comes to our relationship with Christ?

Whether you are a college student or a grown adult, everyone has a different story and has been in a relationship with Christ for a different amount of time, if at all. Therefore, some individuals will have more experience and more wisdom than others. However, one thing that no amount of experience will ever get rid of is the need to seek intervention from God in situations that we face in life. Regardless of how long you have been saved or how much knowledge you may have about the Gospel, at some point, you will run into a situation in your Christian walk that will force you to your knees and make you ask God to guide you because you have found yourself to be basically blind as to where you should go next. We will all reach the point when we have run out of answers and have more questions than we can count. It is in these moments that we become weak and vulnerable and ask God where we should go. It is in these moments that we humble ourselves and seek guidance from the one source we know will point us in the right direction.

Now, we understand the importance of asking for help, but for many, it is not necessarily the act of asking for help, but how they do it that can be a problem. When we ask for help, we tend to do so in an attitude of humility because we don't want to make a big deal about the fact that we have figured out that we cannot do this or that on our own. When we ask for help, so often, we do so quietly, and we hope that the help that comes is in a form that makes it look like the result was only by our own efforts. We don't want people to know that this product was the result of advice and guidance from a respected mentor or that we prayed and asked God to guide and direct our steps in this particular venture. What this verse tells us is that, when we seek guidance from God, we should do so boldly. We should come before God's throne with an attitude that says that we know that we cannot do this on our own, but that we can conquer it with God's intervention. We should not try to hide this acknowledgment of our weakness and insufficiency. We should be open and honest about the fact that we would rather admit our weakness and seek guidance from the ultimate infallible source instead of relying on our own fallible efforts. Through doing this, we will be able to know that the result is what God wants and that it will honor and glorify Him.

Message:

How do you approach God's throne? Do you approach it with an attitude of wanting Him to intervene, or do you approach His throne with a sense of dread and a hopefulness that He may not answer you? Once you identify the attitude with which you are approaching His throne, you will probably begin to figure out why you may or may not be getting the results you may be seeking. This is a critical step to take in the Christian walk because it can often help to diagnose so many of the issues that tend to plague the Christian life. However, it is critical to take that initial step of being able to understand and acknowledge that help is needed and that one is able to accept the help that is being offered. Once this has been accomplished, we must agree to allow God to work and to do what He asks of us. Once this decision has been made, it is up to us to do two things, and those are listen and obey.

Share It!

Using these questions, reach out to your friends on social media and get the conversation started!

1. When do you find that you have the most difficulty asking God to intervene in a situation? What do you attribute that to?
2. Have you ever had a situation where you were practically forced to seek help from God in a situation?
3. Who is one person in your life that makes it easier to ask for help? What is it about that person that makes asking for help so easy?

Standing Strong

Let us hold fast the profession of our *faith, without wavering; (for he* is *faithful that promised;)*

Hebrews 10:23 KJV

If you are a Christian who has been saved by grace through faith in Christ, and you are reading this, you can probably attest to how easy it is for those who follow Christ to stand strong in times of adversity and struggle. It's a piece of cake, right? Let us all laugh together. Of course not! It's never easy when Christians come under scrutiny because of their decision to follow Christ. This is a given for anyone who has been a Christian for any amount of time. Even those who may have recently given their lives to Him will face difficult times when people find out. This is hard! It's a struggle sometimes to follow God when you know that doing so will result in the loss of friends, family, and maybe even a job. However, the ball is in your court when it comes to making the decision as to who you believe will lead you in the right direction. Will you sacrifice a relationship with Christ for the sake of a nice job, or that relationship, or that paycheck? This is where we as Christians have a choice to make.

In this verse, we find the author encouraging us to stand strong in these times when it seems that the world only wants to pull us down and away from Christ. As was mentioned earlier, this probably sounds easy to many, but in the end, it's not. As we look to our brothers and sisters in Christ overseas, we see these populations of Christians who only want a relationship with Christ, and because of this, everything that they know and love is under constant attack from their own family and government. Their lives, the lives of their families, their assets are all threatened because of their decision to follow Christ. It's probably not the easiest thing in the world for them to read this verse and others like it, which tell them to stand strong and to keep going. However, regardless of where you live, this call goes out to you. Whatever situation you may find yourself in because of your decision to follow Christ, the author of Hebrews calls us to stand strong, remain steadfast in our walk with Him regardless of the consequences.

The interesting thing about the Christian walk is that it seems that, so many come into it with this idea that it's supposed to be easy and comfortable. This is why we see so many walking away from Christ when those hard times hit. They wonder why God would do this. They ask God why He couldn't just give them that job because He knew that they needed it. They ask Him why He couldn't just give them the money that they needed to send their child back to the college of their dreams. Did He want them to be miserable? In so many cases like these, we look to God in times of trouble, and instead of seeking guidance, protection, and love, we ask all these questions and expect an immediate answer. Anything less would be like seeing that someone read your text and didn't reply. We become insulted, confused, and frustrated. We begin to wonder why God would do this at a time like this. All these questions begin to race through our mind, and none of them seem to have answers. In these moments, we begin to wonder if God has left us, but in reality, it's more likely that we wandered from Him while we were searching for our own way to get where we want to go. However, for some reason, we continue to blame God for the things that are going on off-road, so-to-speak. We look to Him when we find ourselves in the woods, and we wonder what we did to deserve this. We wonder why He would do this to us. However, often, it seems that it is usually our own actions that got us to that spot in the first place.

When we face these struggles in our walk, we must resist this urge to turn where we aren't supposed to or ignore that sign that says that the road is closed. We must resist the urge to go our own way in these situations if God is not making His path clear enough for us. However, the problem is that this requires something that seems to be in short supply these days; patience. We must have patience when we make requests of God because sometimes, He makes us wait to assess whether we are truly ready for this opportunity because He knows what we are imagining, and He knows the reality of the situation. Therefore, often, He may use these tense periods in our lives to try and to test us to see if we are truly ready for this opportunity. However, in order for this process to go smoothly, He needs us to follow His lead as He shows us where to go next. This means that we stay in contact with Him as if we have Him on speed dial. This means that we listen when He speaks and call out to Him in those moments of stress and duress. This means that we communicate with Him and listen to His voice, because somewhere in those words, is how you're getting out of this.

Message:

What storm do you find yourself facing today? Maybe it is someone attacking you because of your faith. Maybe you find yourself facing relationship issues. Whatever the situation may be, when you find yourself being worn down and you struggle to see how this is going to help you in any way, turn to God and maybe He will start showing you where the road is so that you can finally get out of the woods.

Share It!

Using these questions, reach out to your friends on social media and get the conversation started!

1. What kind of woods do you find yourself in today? In what are of your own life do you seem to be wandering from the path that God is guiding you down?
2. When was the last time that you found yourself in a place that left you questioning God's plan and path for you?
3. When you find yourself facing times of persecution in your walk with Christ, what do you typically do? Where do you turn?

Pray with Expectation

But without faith *it is* impossible to please *him*: for he that cometh to God must believe that he is, and *that* he is a rewarder of them that diligently seek him.

Hebrews 11:6 KJV

As Christians, just as with any other religion, prayer has always been the center of our universe when it comes to our relationship with Christ. From the time you are little and may not even know Christ as your Savior, if you grew up in a Christian home, your parents probably had you folding your hands and praying before bed and reciting that prayer you learned at daycare before dinner. However, as we grow and mature in our faith, eventually, those kinds of prayers are often not enough to communicate what needs to be said between you and Christ. That's when we begin to really understand how we're supposed to pray. Soon, our songs turn into prayers in which we are actually speaking to God and asking Him for more than to simply bless our food or keep us safe as we sleep. However, while these are a little more advanced, we are often only asking for those immediate things that we have before us.

Now, as we move beyond the bed and the dinner table, we find ourselves in this thing called life and we begin to meet challenges that we cannot effectively conquer on our own and we must come before God and ask for His intervention. However, even at this point when some people have become grown adults and have problems that can often affect the future, so often we find ourselves praying halfheartedly to God to bring us out of this circumstance that we find ourselves in. We look at the situation and we see that we need help and we pray and we ask others to "keep us in their prayers", but when we really investigate our heart and reflect on our motives and those feelings we have deep down, we eventually realize that we are asking God to do something that we don't necessarily think He is capable of. However, we pray to Him and ask Him for His intervention because that's what the pastor tells us to do. We often have this thought that this circumstance is beyond the point of God being able to do anything. We basically poke prayer to make sure it is still available, but we don't actually plan on using it for anything any time soon. The interesting thing about this is that we live in a time when nothing is off limits. We are willing to do practically anything to make something happen. However, it seems that, as crazy as it sounds, beyond that realm of *anything*, we often find prayer. We find prayer on that list of options that got brushed off while we were searching for reasonable solutions because it may take too long to work, or it might not come out right. We find any and every excuse to avoid prayer when things go wrong until it's our last resort. Why is this? Because we come into this dialog with God assuming that He will do nothing. Because there is no faith behind our words, we often fail to see the results we are looking for, so we move on to another method and hope it will work out better. We say that we trust God to help us in our times of trouble, but assume that this job loss or that disease is too big for Him to do anything about.

Okay, now what? If our God is not big enough for what we are going through, what do we do? The answer is simple. We need to reevaluate who we think God is. Is He just a friend that lives in the sky and someone to talk to whenever we want, or is He the creator and sustainer of the universe who has the ability to conquer any situation or circumstance that we may encounter because He knew about it long before we did? This is where we need to start with our reevaluation of who we even think God is. We need to figure out if God is just someone who we use as a last resort in times of distress, or if He is someone we look to first when we are in times of peace and joy as well as when we have those times come when we don't know what to do. Ultimately, it comes down to one question and it is this: Are we using prayer as a last resort? Do we view this direct line of communication with God as if it were a fire alarm or one of those alarm system buttons that call for help to come immediately, or do we see prayer as being a phone call home or to a friend? Do we view this line of communication as a one or two-way conversation? When we are able to answer these questions, we will probably begin to understand why we are getting the results we have been seeing.

Message:

What about you? What kind of attitude do you approach God with when you go before Him in prayer? Do you think he'll actually do anything? Do you believe that He can do anything? Do you think that the God of the universe even cares about you and your problems? If you don't think that He does, then the problem is not Him. It's you. If you approach God's throne and pray for Him to do something while believing that He can't or won't, then why are you praying for this thing or that act to happen in the first place? If you're praying simply because it is customary and are doing so without any expectation of an outcome, there are thousands of religions that are available to try out. However, if you pray with the expectation of an outcome, and have the faith to believe that there will be an outcome, you are in the right place. Ultimately, when you pray, let there be one thing present in your communication with God; expectation. Expect that He will do something. Expect that He will come through for you. If you expect that He will answer your prayers, you will become more willing to be a part of His doing so.

Share It!

Using these questions, reach out to your friends on social media and get the conversation started!

1. Being honest with yourself, take a look at your life and a situation that you are facing right now. What are your expectations of God in that situation?
2. Where does God rank on your list of options in times of trouble? How can you change that?
3. In your mind, what makes God the best option in the situations that we face throughout our lifetime?

Every Man's Race

[1]Wherefore seeing we also are compassed about with so great a cloud of witnesses, let us lay aside every weight and the sin which doth so easily beset *us,* and let us run with patience the race that is set before us, [2]looking unto Jesus the author and finisher of our faith; who for the joy that was set before him endured the cross, despising the shame, and is set down at the right hand of the throne of God.

Hebrews 12:1-2 KJV

Isn't it interesting to think about how life can resemble a race at times? Think about it. We start the race when we get up and face the day in the morning. We look those challenges in the face, whether they be challenges at work or school, or whether they are medical or financial in nature, and we make a conscious decision to face them. Everyone has challenges of some sort that force them to make this decision daily. Nevertheless, we get up and we face them with some sort of attitude. For some people, that may be an attitude of fear. For some people, it may be an attitude of determination to see the task completed, and for some, it may be an attitude of indifference. This last attitude is often how one faces this thing called Monday. Regardless of what the circumstance is that we are staring down at the moment, everyone has something that gives them that feeling of having knots in their stomach when they think of it. However, now that we have acknowledged that there is a situation that we must face, whether we want to or not, what attitude are we going to face it with? If this is a question running through your mind, let this verse become a guide to you in determining where your heart should be when you have those days when you don't even want to get out of bed.

As with most verses, the best place to start is at the beginning. At the beginning of this verse, the first phrase that we find is "Wherefore seeing we also are compassed about with so great a cloud of witnesses". This phrase carries the idea of a mass of people who are there watching us as we go through these times of difficulty. However, included in this cloud of witnesses, we find these people whom we consider friends and family. Today, we may call those accountability partners or something like that, but ultimately, what these people are within this cloud of witnesses, are friends. What kinds of friends do you have around you and how do those friends come through for you in those times when you don't know what to do? This question is an important one for you to ask yourself because often, what the next part of this passage calls "weight" and "sin which doth easily beset us", can come in the form of the company that we keep, because these people whom we let into our lives often have a massive influence on our behavior. Therefore, when we see changes in our behavior that are not pleasing to God, it is our responsibility to address that and to seek God's forgiveness and guidance in those times when we notice the issues being caused by the company we find ourselves keeping.

Beyond human factors that can often set us back in our walk with Christ, however, there are other less significant factors that may creep in without our knowledge. This passage calls for us to set aside those things that may cause us to stumble and fall into sin. This sin that it calls for us to set aside can be anything. This can be an addiction that someone may be struggling with, it could be a relationship that is not being conducted in a godly way, or it can be any number of other things. However, regardless of what the sin is that is causing you to stumble and stray from the path that God has set before you, it is sin that needs to be gotten rid of or set aside. You may be thinking; *this sin isn't bad enough to pull me away from God. I'll notice if that starts to happen.* This is where so many Christians end up finding themselves straying from the path set by God and following a path defined by the sin that they have fallen into rather than the life God had given them.

As we continue with this idea of a race as it relates to life, this passage tells us not only why life is a race, but it tells us how to run it. If you know anything about running, you will know that this is an art that requires a lot of training and a lot of patience. Whether you consider yourself to be a distance runner or one who runs for the purposes of speed, both require a great amount of patience to become proficient. In the same way that this is true for running in 5K's or marathons, this is also true of the race we find ourselves in every day that we run with Christ.

To run this race of life with Christ, we won't be able to simply wake up one day and be flawless in our speed and form. It will take time for us to build up that spiritual stamina and for us to learn how to pace ourselves in these missions that He sets in our path. We won't always feel or look like those families that we see on the church posters who are laughing and smiling with the huge family Bible on the coffee table. The chances are pretty good that we will have times in our lives when we aren't quite sure why God would do this or that. There will be times when we slip and fall into a sin we thought we were done with for good. There will be times when we look at ourselves in the mirror and wonder if we have screwed up too much to be forgiven. However, as we grow and as we experience life one day at a time, we will grow in our walk with Christ and we will begin to see that this race we are running is not necessarily only about the finish line, but also about those people we pass and hang back with along the way. These are the people and the memories and the experiences that will allow us to grow in our walk with Christ. However, before we can experience this race with Him by our side, we must make the decision to get up and take that first step.

Message:

So, what kind of race have you been running? Whose path have you been on lately? God's or yours? When you ask yourself these questions, think about what kind of race you want to run, what kind of life you want to live for Christ and what it will take to get there. Think about what kind of attitude you have been running this race with. Have you been running just to get to the finish line, or have you been running to see the sights and meet the people on a similar path as you? So often, we can get so caught up in trying to reach that next finish line, whether it be Friday or five o'clock that we forget to even pay attention to the people and the opportunities that we have to reach those people for Christ along the way. This is why it is so important for us to run this race with patience and perseverance. Not only will it prevent the infamous burnout that so many people experience at some point in life, but it will allow you to grow and help others to grow in their walk with Him. So, what kind of race are you running? Are you aiming for the finish line, or are you turning your head to see who you can reach on the way there?

Share It!

Using these questions, reach out to your friends on social media and get the conversation started!

1. Running a race requires daily commitment. This means that you are eating, drinking, and sleeping your training regimen. What does this look like for you in your walk, in your race, with Christ?
2. Do you feel that you are chasing after the mission that God has set before you, or are you simply strolling toward it, hoping to catch it eventually?
3. How are you choosing to impact people along the way?

Your Faith is Showing

[17]Even so faith, if it hath not works, is dead, being alone. [18]Yea, a man may say, Thou hast faith, and I have works: shew me thy faith without thy works, and I will shew thee my faith by my works.

James 2:17-18 KJV

Imagine this. You see Jesus walk into a room in His human form, and when He walks in, He immediately lets everyone know that He is, in fact, Jesus. However, after telling everyone who He is, He does something strange. After telling everyone in the room that He is that guy, He walks over to the corner, sits in an armchair, and just basically sits back and watches what's going on, not really doing anything of significance. Now, what's wrong with this picture? Well, first of all, if Jesus were in a room full of people, His chances of being able to sit alone for very long would probably be very slim. However, that's beside the point. The problem with this picture is the fact that, because Jesus is who He says He is, He wouldn't just walk into a room, tell everyone that He was there, and then just hang out, waiting for stuff to happen. If Jesus found Himself in a room full of people, where everyone was hurting in one way or another, He would probably be the first to jump right in and begin ministering to those people through His teaching, as well as His acts of service. If Jesus found Himself in a room with a mass of people, He wouldn't wait for things to happen. He would make things happen, thus giving visibility to His Words.

This concept of making our words visible when it comes to spreading the Gospel is something that can often be confusing for some because we often think that it is enough to simply do those community service projects with our church, or spend the weekend working at that food pantry down the street. However, what does it really look like to put our words, our faith, into action in the lives of those around us and around the world? Hint: It's not a one-time thing. What this means is that we leave the house, or the dorm, or the apartment every day with the intention of showing love to the people that we interact with daily. It is only through doing this that we, the church, will be able to truly reach others with the message of the Gospel. However, while this may sound simple, there will always be barriers that need to be taken down on the part of yourself, as well as the person with whom you are sharing the Gospel, and those are going to be different in every situation. However, the primary barrier that so often gets in our way is ourselves.

All too often, when it comes to witnessing and spreading the Gospel message, we seem to be confused as to how we should go about starting the process. We know which verses to share, we know what we're supposed to say, but when it comes to connecting with the people that we are sharing the Gospel with, we often find ourselves searching the internet for guides on sharing the gift that we may have had for ten or fifteen years. The funny thing about this struggle, however, is that we often end up making it more difficult than it should be. We find ourselves believing that we are supposed to come into this opportunity and lay out this thorough theological argument about salvation and why it is the way to go. However, the biggest tool that you can have at your disposal, in addition to the Gospel, is your life, your walk with Christ, and how He changed you when you gave your life to Him. However, before you continue on this venture of sharing the Gospel with those who need it most, it is important, as I have mentioned before, that you step outside of yourself, look at your life, see what the world is seeing in what you are doing, what you are saying, how you are interacting, and determine if those things are ultimately pointing others toward Christ or if those words that you sing, those words that you say when you are witnessing to someone, are simply that; words. You need to figure out if this guidance that you are giving these lost people is guidance that you yourself have been following in your own life. If this is not the case, then you have a great place to start! Therefore, when you go into the world with the intention of sharing the Gospel with nonbelievers, take the time to stop and take an inventory of everything that you are taking into the discussion so that you can avoid becoming your own stumbling block.

Message:

Take a second to think. What are some things that have gotten in your way in the past when you have tried to share the Gospel with someone? Sure, you can say the words, regardless of the state of your heart, but after the interaction, or maybe even during, what are some of the things that God convicted you about? Over the course of writing this devotional, I have had many moments like this. I've had moments when I was writing a sentence, and as I was writing it, I thought, *it would be really cool if I started doing that.* It has been through these moments that I have been able to make the changes that I need to make to take down just one or two more barriers as I strive to reach more and more people with the message of the Gospel and how it has impacted me and my life. Therefore, when you look at your life, what barriers do you need to take down to make your faith more visible to the lost world around you?

Share It!

Using these questions, reach out to your friends on social media and get the conversation started!

1. If you had to draw a visual image of your life before and after Christ, what would those two pictures look like? Would you be able to tell any difference?
2. If you could point to one area in your life where Christ has had the most significant impact, where would that be? On the flip-side, in what area would you say that Christ has had the least amount of access, and therefore impact?
3. In your life and in your walk with Christ, who has had the greatest impact in helping you to grow? What is it about that person that has helped you in such a significant way?

The "Why" Factor

but sanctify the Lord God in your hearts: and *be* ready always to *give* an answer to every man that asketh you a reason of the hope that is in you with meekness and fear:

1 Peter 3:15 KJV

How often do we encounter questions from people with opposing viewpoints, no matter their relation to us, and we suddenly find ourselves in a spot where we know that we should have an answer for why we feel the way we do, but we just can't come up with one? When it comes to Christianity and the beliefs that we hold, we are the only religion in existence that serves a God, a Savior that isn't dead. We are the only religion that can genuinely say that there is no body in the tomb where Jesus was buried because it has been scientifically confirmed. We are the only religion that does not worship a dead or inanimate god, and yet, it seems that Christianity is one of the most criticized, scrutinized, and in some countries persecuted religions in existence today. However, why is this? The reason that so much opposition is faced by the Christian church, or at least one of the reasons, is the fact that Christ, our redeemer, and Savior, has been proven over and over to have genuinely been crucified in the way that is detailed in the Gospel, and to have risen, with the proof being found in the fact that no scientist has ever been able to uncover a body. Therefore, with all this evidence, we as Christians have nothing to worry about and we can just sit back and relax, right? Wrong.

Today, we live in a world that loves things that can be seen with the eyes with no faith required. Therefore, when we think of that in the context of the Christian faith, this means that we must be able to give evidence, provide an argument for Christ and why He is the ultimate source of forgiveness and salvation for all people around the world. It is up to the Christian church to show the world that the universe was created by a loving, all-merciful, all-knowing God. It is up to us to not only share the news of Christ with all people but to also be able to show those people when they ask, why we believe what we believe. Often, this can be a convicting experience for a lot of Christians. Often, it seems that we are sharing a faith that we eventually figure out we don't actually understand very well. To an even more extreme point, sometimes, Christians will find that, when faced with questions they do not understand, they are soon led away from Christ as a result of their attempt to lead someone to Him. One of the likely reasons why this happens to so many is because, as we grow up in the church, we are told to spread the Gospel and to tell people about Jesus. However, what they do not tell us early on is that many, or even most people we encounter and attempt to reach with the Gospel will either a.) Listen intently to what we have to say, b.) Ask questions that we may or may not have the answer to or c.) Present a counterargument that we are unable to refute and we only end up leading this individual further from believing the truth we are trying to deliver.

What I didn't mention in that list was that, not only could we encounter one of those instances alone, but it is also possible that some combination of those variables could face us at some point as well. Therefore, like a pop quiz, the church has a duty to always be prepared to present some kind of answer for why we believe what we believe. This means that it is not always enough to simply say "because the Bible says so", but rather that we should have some sort of understanding of why we believe what we are taught in Sunday school about how God created the universe in six days and rested on the seventh. This has been scientifically proven, but why? Why is the theory of evolution wrong? Why can we know that there's a God who cares for His creatures? What about the other theories, like Young Earth vs. Old Earth Creationism, theories that present competing views on the age of the earth? What about Day-Age Theory, which calls into question how long the "days" mentioned in Genesis actually are? These are the questions that fill so many minds today, and those minds are longing for an answer. The interesting thing is that many of the people asking these questions may be followers of Christ who have begun to ask questions without a sufficient answer. Many of the people asking these questions may have grown up in a Christian home and never had to face them until the college years or even thereafter. Now they find themselves searching for something that can give them assurance that the God they believe in is still out there and they want to know that what they are learning in Sunday school or in church is true. This is where the church has a responsibility to step in and show non-believers or doubting believers why the Gospel means what it says. It's up to the church to show these people that they can know for certain that the God of the universe that the Bible speaks of is the same God of the universe that cares about the people and the circumstances that are a part of people's lives today. This is where the church can become a vital resource for those in doubt, but another problem that consumes the church today is that, rather than gathering evidence for why we believe what we believe, we simply sit in the pews week after week, assuming that the pastor knows what he is talking about and never asking questions. The church, in doing this, risks falling into following an "I guess" faith rather than a faith that says, not only do I believe that God created the universe and everything in it but here's why. Today, we live in a time when the most important part of that phrase is that last word. Why? Do we believe simply because someone tells us to, or do we believe because we have reasons for believing that what He is saying and what the Bible says is true and reliable? This is a question that so many have failed to answer, but need to answer because that answer may uncover some doubts, some questions that need to be addressed. Therefore, not only does the church have a duty to know the Why of what we believe for the sake of the nonbelievers, but also for the sake of themselves, as we continue to strive to understand the Why to what we believe, as well as the Who.

Message:

So why do you believe in the God of the Bible? Why do you believe that Jesus died on the cross for your sins? Because a preacher or a Sunday school teacher said so? This question is one that is not addressed nearly enough in the church and within other Christian circles. However, there is also a reason why these questions have entire fields of science dedicated to answering them. With this in mind, it should become relatively clear to us as to the importance of establishing an answer in our mind, should someone ask an answer of us. So, someone asks you why you believe in Creation. Someone asks you why being a Christian is the only way to Heaven when the world says that there are many. One of your classmates asks you why you believe that Jesus died on the cross for your sins. What will your answer be? Will you have one?

Share It!

Using these questions, reach out to your friends on social media and get the conversation started!

1. Name one non-Sunday school answer as to why you believe in the God of the Bible. Now think about how someone could go against that. How will you respond?
2. Think of one way in which you could use an apologetic conversation to share the Gospel with someone. How would that conversation unfold?
3. What was it that made you recognize that this God, the God of the Bible, was the God that you wanted in your life, in your heart? Is that still your reason today?

Looking for Approval in All the Right Places

[5]Likewise, ye younger, submit yourselves unto the elder. Yea, all *you* be subject one to another, and be clothed with humility: for God resisteth the proud, and giveth grace to the humble. [6]Humble yourselves therefore, under the mighty hand of God, that he may exalt you in due time: [7]casting all your care upon him; for he careth for you.

1 Peter 5:5-7 KJV

In the world that we live in today, humility can often be difficult to come by. This is because the world has begun to place such great value on this idea of class, sophistication, this idea of "Look what I have/can do". In reality, this is how most people get jobs. Today, being confident in our abilities and our wealth has almost become somewhat of a pastime. When we have guests over to our home right after Christmas, we cannot wait to show them the new TV or the new car or whatever new and improved item we may have gotten that year. It has almost become a part of the culture today. We share these things, as I mentioned earlier in the book, because we are proud of them and we want people to know how well-off we are. That's totally respectable because, when you work for and earn the things that you own, you have a right to be proud of those things. However, in this passage, we find a call from Peter to abandon this pride, because this pride ultimately stems from a desire to have more praise from man, rather than God. We desire the praise that comes in the form of "I need that right now", rather than the praise from God that says, "Well done, my good and faithful servant". Now why is this? Why is it that we desire to hear people's praise over the praise that comes from God? Well, what if I told you that the answer was at the back of this book on the very last page? (Spoiler: It's not). However, if it were, I'm sure you would totally read the rest of this front to back to find out the answer, right? Of course not! You would stop right now and flip to the very back to find out the answer, which would be extremely ironic, because the answer is immediate gratification.

Immediate gratification fuels so much of what we do and how we live today. This need for knowing, having, getting this thing right now is the reason for online shopping and the drive-thru. It's why restaurants offer super-speedy delivery service. Today, we want what we want, and we want it now. This is why we place so much value in gaining the approval of others, fleeting as it may be, over the approval that comes from God over time. It seems that we get so tired of waiting to find out if we did this or that right, that we ask man to tell us that we were right, that we hit the nail on the head. However, the problem with this is that it can often result in an ego as big as the night is long. This approval that we get from man is so fulfilling, but it only lasts for a short time. This approval gives us that pat on the back, whatever that may look like, and then we move on. However, eventually, the gratification that comes with this will be a distant memory.

Think about the reactions that your posts get on social media. Think about how long it takes for you to say "Cool", click the little heart, and keep scrolling. Can you honestly say that you remember every single post that you ever reacted to? Unless you have exceptional memory, the chances are pretty good that your mind is blank on that subject. This is the nature of gratification that comes from man. It lasts long enough to give you some kind of warm feeling, and then it's over. No eternal significance, no eternal reward, but simply the tap of a screen. This is why it is so critical to understand the importance of ensuring that we are directing our attention not to the concerns, the thoughts, the perceptions that others may have about us, but that we direct our attention, keep our focus on the will and direction of God. When we do this, will we always be able to refresh the GodWill app and see how we are progressing in His will for our lives? No. However, will we always have Him by our side to guide and direct our steps as we go? Yes. Will this take time to fully understand? Absolutely. Therefore, if there's anything that needs to be understood and taken from this passage it is that, to be able to incorporate humility into a believer's walk with Christ, they must first be able to figure out where it is that they are getting their appreciation, their love, their encouragement from. If they rely on the world, people, and media for this encouragement and support, it will only last as long as their most loyal friend's phone battery. However, if they find their encouragement, their support in their relationship with Christ and make a conscious decision to follow Him and to surround themselves with people who will encourage them in that walk, they will always have someone to raise them up when their low, but also bring them down when they get a little too full of themselves.

Message:

Who is that person for you? Is it a friend, a parent, a classmate? Whoever it may be, we all need that person in our lives who will stop us dead in our tracks and put things into perspective. However, on that same token, it is also critical that we remain aware of ourselves, so that we can take a step back and put things into perspective on our own as well. This is important because, in the end, humility can be very difficult to hold onto in the world that we live in today. It can become very difficult to keep things in perspective when the world only wants things to be bigger and better all the time. The problem is that sometimes, people fail to realize the need for humility before God decides to take care of it on His own. Therefore, let us always remain aware of who we are in Christ and who He has made us to be, and let us remain determined in our venture to never allow the world to change this image.

Share It!

Using these questions, reach out to your friends on social media and get the conversation started!

1. If you were to give up your electronic devices, your social media for an entire week, as you (hopefully) did some time ago for the social media hiatus, who would be there to motivate you, to encourage you in your walk with Christ, or even when you are just having a bad day?

2. What does it mean for you to find fulfillment in Christ? How does this fulfillment show itself in your life and in your walk with Christ?

3. If you were to line up God, your three closest friends, and (in a group) all the friends on social media, how would you rank those in order of the impact that they have on your life and your walk with Christ?

Facing the Lion

Be sober, be vigilant; because your adversary the devil, as a roaring lion, walketh about, seeking whom he may devour:

1 Peter 5:8 KJV

Throughout the Gospel, Satan manifests himself to society in many different ways. However, one thing that all these manifestations have in common is that they all prey on the innocent and the weak. However, one thing that the prey has in common is the fact that they are often distracted by the outside and not paying enough attention to what is happening around them. In this same way, Satan tends to attack not only those who may be too spiritually weak to defend themselves at that moment, but He also will be more likely to go after those who have taken their guard down because they have not been nurturing and growing the relationship, they have with Christ, if they have one at all. This swiftness with which Satan often attacks is the reason followers of Christ should pay particularly close attention to the commands issued at the beginning of this verse. The commands, *be sober, be vigilant* should tell us a lot about how Satan attacks and the impact He can have on someone's life and relationship with Christ. Think about a lion. It doesn't go after that boa constrictor that is on the prowl for dinner. He goes after that mouse that is scurrying away to try to get to its hole in time. It targets the prey that it knows has no chance of defending itself. It is in this way that Satan resembles a lion.

Because of the way Satan chooses to attack, believers must always remain aware, or as the verse says, vigilant, of the surroundings of their heart and mind. This is where Satan will likely begin his attack. This is the area where a lot of damage can be done, and it is also one of the areas where it can often be most difficult to recover. However, sometimes it seems that Christians go about life feeling as if they are somehow immune to the battles that so often plague the heart. Unfortunately, the truth is exactly the opposite. Often, it seems that Christians face an increased amount of struggle and conflict from the world because they choose to follow Christ. Whether it comes in the form of persecution, temptation, or any other number of obstacles that face the world, no Christian will ever be immune to these worldly struggles. However, what believers do have is Christ as a resource to run to both in those times when things are tough, as well as in those times when it seems that everything is smooth sailing. Sadly, it often seems that it is in those smooth sailing periods when Satan has the potential to hit the hardest.

Something else that has always been interesting to me about this verse in the King James Version is the use of the phrase "seeking whom he may devour". I find this phrase interesting because it really starts to capture the power of Satan. In the church, it seems that we often try to downplay the power of Satan and therefore, we are always surprised when people who were once so intimate in their relationship with Christ eventually find themselves in deep water with nowhere to turn for direction. This enemy of God is actually rather powerful, and therefore, he is someone that Christians should genuinely build up a strong defense against. If we choose not to and simply label him as being a threat that will go away if we just simply ignore him, we will find ourselves in a state of utter shock when he shows up one day in a place where we least expect him and all the sudden, we find ourselves engaged in a battle that we haven't trained for. This is so often the case for so many Christians today. While God will protect us from the threats presented by the world, there is also a responsibility on our part to take those threats, the temptation, the sin that so often plagues the world and society seriously. This means that we must employ every asset as if we were about to go into battle. If we choose to do this, we will become better prepared for the moments when Satan tries to strike. We will be able to face him head on and remain aware of how he may try to tempt us or pull us away from Christ. However, the greatest asset that we can have in our arsenal aside from Christ, is our preparation to face whatever Satan may try to throw at us. Will you be ready?

Message:

When we look at the Christian walk, so much of what we need to do what God has called us to do comes down to one thing, and that is preparation. We must always be prepared, because whether it be Satan himself or some worldly entity, there will always be challenges that we must face in our walk with Christ, and so many of these challenges are so much easier to face when we know how we can best face them and who we have on our side. However, that takes time and initiative on the part of the church and each Christian in their own life. It takes the initiative of the church to arm themselves with the knowledge and intimacy with God that will allow them to know what the right thing is to do when the time comes that Satan places a battle in front of us that we cannot necessarily handle on our own. Therefore, as you continue to face your classes, your social life, and any other pieces that come with being who you are, how are you preparing yourself to go to battle and to defend yourself from whatever threats may come your way?

Share It!

Using these questions, reach out to your friends on social media and get the conversation started!

1. Having a secure and reliable defense on standby is a critical part of battle. Therefore, what kind of defenses are in your arsenal as you head out to face the world every day?
2. What is one battle in your life right now that has caused you to become worn out and fatigued in your life and in your relationship with Christ?
3. What types of defenses have you chosen to employ during those downtimes when you are not necessarily completely aware of what may lie around the corner?

Sharing Our Undeserved Love

My little children, let us not love in word, neither in tongue; but in deed and in truth;

1 John 3:18 KJV

"I Love You". These three words can mean so much when spoken by someone we care about and who cares about us. The question is, what is love? How do we define it? Today, it seems that we toss this word around a lot. Whether that be in the context of a marriage or a dating relationship or in the context of a family, or even in the context of a friendship, simply knowing that we are loved by someone means the world to most, if not all people. As human beings, God created us to be relational. He created us to experience and to give love. He created us to share His love with the world. However, the chances are pretty good that when He made us to be relational, He did not intend for the extent to which we show love to stop at three words. He intended for those words to be proven through our actions. He intended for us to act on that love beyond sweet cards on birthdays and holidays. He intended for this love to be something we live out on a daily basis through our interactions with friends and strangers alike. This is one reason why this verse in the KJV Bible is somewhat interesting. In this version of the Bible, practically the only time we ever see this word love is when it is used as a verb. One of the obvious exceptions would be in the case of the Fruits of the Spirit in Galatians. All other uses that would be found in other versions of the Gospel are replaced with the word, charity. While this word works into love, it seems that almost every writer in the Gospel intended the idea of love to be considered a verb to be lived out rather than a noun that simply exists in the world. These writers seemed to realize that just as faith without works is dead, love without action is also dead.

When we love someone, how do we show them? Do we simply walk up to them when we see them on holidays and other family gatherings and say, "I love you" and walk away? Most likely not. When we love someone, we are going to call them. We are going to learn more about them. What makes them happy? What disappoints them? What makes them tick? These are all things that we find out as we love someone for a long time. We begin to understand who they are and what they're like and what makes them special. When we love someone, we spend time with them and make ourselves available to them. When we love someone, this love is meant to be for life. This commitment doesn't only apply to a marriage relationship. This commitment applies to that friend that you've had for twenty years. This commitment applies to the relationship we have with our parents. This commitment applies to the people we work with and those people we walk by every day on our way back and forth during our daily routine.

The funny thing about love is that, even though we have been focusing on close friends up until this point, we as followers of Christ have a responsibility, a duty to love everyone, whether they be family, friends, or that random stranger you just met on the way home. While I understand that this is an idea that has been tossed around a lot in the recent days, it also seems that this definition of love is somewhat skewed in the minds of those asking for more of it. While the world today definitely needs more love, what it seems so many people are asking for is not love, but acceptance of all lifestyles and no confrontation about the sinful behaviors taking place today. However, true love means loving the people engaged in those behaviors while leading them away from the sin and closer to Christ. This love that we should be showing those around us is extremely important in the life of the Christ follower. This love is purposeful and intentional, in that it helps to lead these people to a better life, a better future and to the point of beginning to understand what it means to have a relationship with Christ, should they be interested in pursuing one. Therefore, the love that we show to people through our actions has the power to change lives. It has the power, when combined with the power of the Gospel, to bring people what may be their very first glimpse of a life with Christ. Ultimately, the love that we as followers of Christ show to the world around us can be incredibly impactful, because, while scripture verses are incredible in certain situations and the Gospel is definitely a valuable and necessary asset when it comes to bringing people to Christ, so often, what people are looking for is a visual image of what it means to live out that Gospel message. The question is, are we living what we have been preaching? This is something that should be seriously considered by all who are part of the church, because when we ask ourselves this question, we may begin to understand why so many people are being turned away by the church and choosing to follow alternate paths.

Message:

How do you love? Think about this question for a second. How do you show love to the world you live in? How do your actions match up with the words you have been speaking and the scripture that you have been quoting? So often it seems that we quote these verses because they sound good and get a lot of positive reactions on social media, but we often forget to truly understand what is being said and we forget to examine our lives in an attempt to identify how we are living that verse out in every area of our lives. Therefore, it is critical that the church takes time to stop before we go into the world telling them what they're doing wrong, and identify how well we are living up to these principles on our own. If we take time to perform this diagnosis, we may be able to make huge progress in creating more love simply by making the decision to love people ourselves. How will you choose to love?

Share It!

Using these questions, reach out to your friends on social media and get the conversation started!

1. Christ calls us repeatedly in His Word to love those around us in a very visible way, but what kind of deeds show someone, whether it be a complete stranger or our closest friend, that we love them?
2. Take a moment and reflect on the life of Christ. Think about those fish and bread and feet-washing moments. They were somewhat simple on their own, but the impact was beyond anything anyone could've imagined. What would a moment like this look like in your own life? How are you choosing to wash people's feet, to feed those people around you with truth?
3. How do the people in your own life show their love for you? How could you go about replicating that?

The Ultimate Decision

Behold, I stand at the door, and knock: if any man hear my voice, and open the door, I will come in to him, and will sup with him, and he with me.

Revelations 3:20 KJV

Imagine that you are sitting at home in your family room watching television, and you hear a knock at the door. What is your response? Well, depending on the time and who's home, you may respond in a variety of ways. If it's daytime and you are home alone because you are on break from school and your parents are at work, you may peek secretly out the window to see who it may be and if you know them or not. If you know them, you will probably go to the door and see what the reason is for their visit. If you peek out the window and see someone standing there who doesn't look familiar, you probably go hide in your room until they assume that no one is home. Now assume that it's a Friday at 2:00 in the morning. You and your family hear a knock at the door. The chances are pretty good that someone jumps out of bed, grabs a gun, and goes to the door to see what might be going on. Here we have two different sets of circumstances, and therefore, two very different reactions. Our reactions differ based on where we are at the moment and who we have around us.

How do we greet God when He stands at our door and knocks? When God comes into our plans for the future and wakes us up in the middle of a spiritual sleep, how do we react? Do we tell Him to get out of here and that we will take care of it later? Do we shove our plans for the future in His face and hope that that will be enough for Him to leave us alone, or do we let the door stand wide open and maybe even step outside to communicate with Him? What about when He comes to us in the middle of those good times when the sun is shining, and the future is looking good, and we see Him standing there with what looks like a box of plans with a packet labeled "Missions" sticking out? Will we go to the door and accept what He is offering us, acknowledging that the plans He is offering are going to be so much greater than anything we could ever create for ourselves? Or will we turn Him away, telling Him that what He is trying to give us is too much right now, and He should come back later? Too often, the majority of believers probably fall into the last category. When it seems like everything is going smooth and we are having a good time, the last thing that we want to happen is to be pulled away from that and into something completely unfamiliar. The last thing we want to do is to travel halfway across the world and virtually start over from scratch. Why can't we simply just live like this or keep these friends or this job for the rest of our lives? After all, it's making us happy, so why change anything? "Why fix it if it ain't broke?" some would say in the south. However, what we often fail to realize is that, sometimes, God has to pull us away from something in our lives that is becoming toxic to us and to our relationship with Christ in order for us to fully realize the extent to which it was causing us harm. Often it is through this that we begin to understand why certain things occurred in the way that they did and at the time they did. Often it is through His doing this that we begin to see for ourselves the toxicity of the relationship or the practice for ourselves.

Something else that so often comes from experiences like this that have been pulling us away from Christ, is a stronger-than-ever thirst for a renewed, stronger, more devoted relationship with Him. We find ourselves coming back to Him, and we realize that the guidance and direction we once resisted with so much stubbornness, we now long for. We find ourselves longing for Him to intervene in these situations that leave us in the dark if we try to face them on our own. We find that we must be somewhat retrained in how to walk with Christ in this relationship that we kind of forgot to feed during those days when we found ourselves preoccupied with whatever it may have been that we considered more important. Ultimately, while God never moved from being beside us, when we reach the point of needing to kind of start from scratch on our end of the relationship, it takes time to figure out how we are supposed to approach Him. It takes time to see Him in a new way that makes the relationship better than it has ever been. Basically, we all backslide at some point in our walk with Christ, but what makes the difference is how quickly we stand back up and start doing what needs to be done to make our way back to where we once were. Will it be easy? Probably not. Will it take work? Definitely. Will you ever regret coming back to Him? Most definitely not. Ultimately, the point being made here is this. There will be times in your walk with Christ when you find yourself slipping away or unable to hear His voice as clearly as you once did. However, we must ensure that we live our lives in such a way that will allow us to hear Him when He knocks and allow us to open the door without fear of what He may see or hear. Will you answer?

Message:

Is there anything in your life that is tuning out the knock of Christ at your heart's door? Is there something blocking the door and keeping Him from getting in? What is it that is keeping God from having unlimited, universal key access to every part of your life? When He knocks, do you let Him in without limitations, or do you tell Him, "Don't go back there. It's a mess"? All these questions boil down to one thing and that is, what is keeping you from letting Christ in, regardless of what period of life you may be in? Is it fear that he'll get rid of that activity you haven't quite grown tired of yet? Is it anxiety that He may mess up your plans for the future that you have been working on for several years? What is it? Once you determine what it is that is blocking the door or even keeping you from getting up to open the door, you may begin to understand why you may not be seeing the results you wish to see in your life and in your walk with Him.

Share It!

Using these questions, reach out to your friends on social media and get the conversation started!

1. Do you hear Christ knocking at the door? How are you going to react? Will the door stand wide open, or will you peek out the window to see if he'll go away?
2. What is an opportunity that you see Christ presenting to you right now that you are hesitant to commit to?
3. When you think about your Christian walk, would you say that it is all-in, or one foot in, one foot out?

God Wants That

for thou shalt worship no other god: for the LORD whose name is *jealous,* is *a jealous God:*

Exodus 24:14 KJV

Jealousy is a powerful thing, isn't it? This is something that everyone in the history of human existence is familiar with in some way. How does it work? When we are jealous of a person or an item, what are we thinking? The chances are, we are probably thinking that we want what they have; whether that be the person they're dating or the car they drive, or where they attend school, the things that make us jealous can come in many forms. However, when we get jealous of someone or something, how much of that thing do we want? We want all it. We don't want only what the store or that person is willing to give us. We don't settle for close to perfect. We want that thing, and we want all it. No exceptions or substitutions accepted. Now, if this is what we expect of those things and those people we are jealous of, why would we give God anything different?

When we enter into the relationship that we have with Christ, we are supposed to be making an agreement that, in exchange for God's forgiveness of our sins, we will enter into an eternal relationship with Him. While we may bring others along for the ride and allow others to become an encourager and a guide in this relationship, the relationship that we have is between ourselves and God. Often, this relationship that we have with Him is considered a marriage. Not only is it for life, but it is a commitment to love Him and to honor Him for the rest of our lives and to never turn anywhere else to seek a substitution for the love that He gives us. We make this commitment to Him when we make the decision to accept His forgiveness and invite Him into our lives. However, so often, it seems that those who make the initial decision to follow Christ forget the commitment that they made, and they begin to turn away and seek love, comfort, and forgiveness from those places, people and things in the world that can only bring temporary, quickly fleeting satisfaction. They forget that God wants all us, not only what we are willing to give. They forget that it hurts Him when we turn to people or money or possessions, just because the relationship that we have with Him doesn't turn out to be as great and exciting as we expected it to be. The crazy thing is, the God of the universe wants a relationship with us and sent His Son to die on the cross to make it possible, and yet, so often we are not willing to give up the things in our lives that are keeping us from that relationship, to make it possible.

Maybe you find yourself in the boat of people who have given themselves to Christ and seem to be doing their part in nourishing the relationship. However, you still have that one pesky piece of your life that you haven't quite turned over to God. Regardless of what it is or how small it may seem compared to all the other pieces of your life, God is looking at that spiritual closet that you are shoving the door closed on, and He is thinking, "I want that". Imagine that you go to buy a car, but you open the door, and there's no mechanism to open the windows. Are you going to tell yourself that that's just one tiny detail and that this car is great otherwise? No. You're going to look that salesman in the eyes and ask him how you're supposed to roll the windows down. He replies that he hoped you wouldn't notice, but he'll fix that once you make the first down payment.

So often, this is how we treat our relationship with Christ. We agree to give our lives over to Him and allow Him to take control, but we hold back that tiny piece of our lives, our language, what we do in our free time, our friends, and we hope that He won't notice it as we stuffed it over there in the closet where we hide all the stuff we don't want the world to see. We hope that He'll glance right past it without a second thought, but when we do this, we are not tricking God. We are only hurting Him by thinking that He doesn't see every part of our lives, whether we want Him to see it or not. We are causing Him pain by holding back those things in our lives that make us fall into sin and further away from Him. In reality, He sees the things you are holding back from Him, and He wants those things too. However, until we give Him control of those things, all He can do is see it and think "I want that".

Message:

What is it that you are holding back from God? What are you denying Him access to for fear that He will mess it up or take it away? What part of that thing makes it hard to give up and why can you not find that property in a relationship with Christ? These are all questions that we should be ready to answer when we realize that we have been holding something back from Christ. We must look at this thing that we are holding back and identify why we are continuing to hold onto it. Once we perform this analysis, we may come to realize that what is making us hold onto this thing is the exact reason why we should hand it over to Him. What is this in your life? Whatever it may be, without a doubt, God wants it.

Share It!

Using these questions, reach out to your friends on social media and get the conversation started!

1. When you think about your life, your walk with Christ, and all the pieces that it's composed of, what are some pieces, some habits, some thoughts, that you find hard to put out in the open when it comes to being transparent with God?
2. Why do you think you hold one certain area of your life back from God? What could you do to change that?
3. In your mind, who is God?

Forgetting God

And the children of Israel remembered not the LORD their God, who had delivered them out of the hands of all their enemies on every side:

Judges 8:34 KJV

How often do we find ourselves in these situations that life throws at us, and all we want is to get out of them, and move on? You know what I'm talking about. Whether it's a stressful period in the semester when it seems that there's never time to breathe or whether it be issues in a relationship or difficult economic times, we find ourselves looking to God in these times, desperate for rescue, and sometimes, we make promises during these periods of stress. This is similar to what happened with the children of Israel. This group of people found themselves in this situation where it seemed that there was no course of action that would eventually lead to a rescue. They looked everywhere for an escape and found none. Once they had established that this pickle would be pretty difficult to get out of, they decided to get to work. From this point on, God provided them with the instructions and the resources that they needed to make it out of this alive. He stayed with them the whole time, and they did the best that they could to listen for His guidance and direction. They became attentive to His voice during this time when they needed to hear it most. Soon, after God had led them to the point where they could now escape this terrible situation, they were on their way. However, there was a problem. When God brought them out of the situation that was threatening their lives and was causing them to suffer, suddenly, they somehow forgot about Him and all that He had done for them in that time of desperate need. Suddenly, they forgot about the promises, the praises, that they had made to God in that time of desperation when there seemed to be nowhere to go. Now that they were out of trouble, they basically decided that they didn't really need God anymore, or at least until the next tragedy came about.

How often do we, as Christians adopt this same attitude in our relationship with God? When we get that diagnosis at the doctor's office or find out that our company doesn't need us anymore, you can bet that we will be on our knees every chance that we get, but when we find that new job or find out that we received a clean bill of health from the doctor, life, like a light switch, goes back to normal. Once all that stuff that made our lives a struggle is gone, we seem to lose that hunger for a closer, more intimate relationship with Christ. This is interesting to consider because this doesn't only apply to our relationship with God, but this also applies to relationships with other people. Specifically, when we face times of stress or conflict, we want that closeness to someone that we consider to be a source of comfort. However, once the stressor is gone, we go back to our normal routine. This is basic psychology, so it should not come as a surprise that this is how we often treat our relationship with Christ. When we face those times of hardship, conflict, temptation, we crave that closeness, that intimacy with God, but when the issue is no longer perceived as a threat, we have this feeling of relief that allows us to go back to what we were doing. However, just as your parents don't just want hugs and closeness when there's something that may be stressing you out, God wants to be intimate with you, not just when you are stressed out, but when you want to understand Him better and in a deeper way. He wants that intimacy to be ongoing and not just as needed for pain. This is why this approach to our relationship with God can sometimes become dangerous. It's dangerous because, what this attitude says about our relationship with Christ is that we are only in it for the stuff, for what He can give us. Besides that, it doesn't really play that big of a part in our lives. We would miss it if we didn't have it, but only because that would mean losing the benefits that come with it. No relationship can function with this attitude being at the core of it, including our relationship with God.

If we are going to see our relationship with God begin to grow and become fruitful, we absolutely have to rely on Him every second of the day, rather than just on holidays and following disasters. We must begin to view Him and treat Him, as not just a tool, but as a father, as a friend. Until we do this, we will find ourselves in a place where we are constantly in this cycle of disaster, prayer, recovery, forget; and this cycle will continue to flow until we decide to do something that will stop it. At what point will we look at the world around us and realize that, regardless of everything that may be going on, God has been working in incredible ways and continues to do so? This is where we have to start if we want to see change happen in this world today. Therefore, regardless of the phase of life that you may find yourself in today, don't let God become a button that you push, a number that you call in the case of emergencies. Strive to make Him the core, the foundation of your life, so that you may never turn around and forget the God that, time after time, brings you out on the other side.

Message:

Think back to the most insane week you have ever had in terms of coursework. How often did you talk to God that week? Probably quite a bit. Now, look at the past twenty-four hours. How much have you communicated with God in that time period? If you had to think about the last time you prayed about anything, the chances are pretty good that it's been too long. See, it seems that when we look at the people of Israel in this situation, somewhere deep inside of ourselves, we see the world today. Sure, not everyone is guilty of adopting this attitude all the time, but it definitely reflects a majority of the world today a majority of the time. We basically treat this relationship that we have with Christ as if it were some kind of convenience store on the corner. We get in, get what we need, and get out. Let us strive to change our attitude toward our relationship with Christ, and treat God as more than just a place of comfort in times of trouble.

Share It!

Using these questions, reach out to your friends on social media and get the conversation started!

1. Do you think you would notice if there were a wall between yourself and God?
2. When was the last time you had an intimate conversation with God about your walk, your life, all those things that can be uncomfortable to talk about at times?
3. How are you able to best hear God, not during a tragedy, not during a bad time in your life, but just on those average days?

In the Eyes of a Savior

…for the *LORD seeth* not as man seeth; for man looketh on the outward appearance, but the LORD looketh on the heart.

1 Samuel 16:7(c) KJV

Think back to the last person that you saw but didn't know. What was your first thought when you looked at them? The chances are that it was somewhere on the scale of "Have they looked in the mirror today" to "Wow". This is basically the scale of how we judge people when we first see them with no knowledge of who they are, where they come from, or what circumstances are in their life. This is how we usually decide who *we* want that person to be in our mind. We do all this based on that person's looks at one moment in time as we pass by on the street or in the mall, or in practically any other public gathering place. Before we even know the person's name, we have decided as to whether we want to learn it or not. As if this needs to be said, this is a problem.

Appearances are something that society places very high value on today. This is why there is an entire industry dedicated to changing them. Therefore, when it comes to appearances, it can be tempting to place all our time and effort into making our outward appearance better and more attractive, while our inward appearance, our relationship with Christ, our love of people, slowly begins to deteriorate. We so often spend so much time focusing on what the world sees, that we can sometimes forget to consider what God sees.

See, God doesn't make judgments based on what the world sees. God doesn't look at you at 8 a.m. and think, "What's wrong with her today?" He doesn't judge us based on the clothes we wear, the house we live in, the job we work every day. He looks at us, and He sees not just a person with a name, an education, a past, and stuff. God looks at us and He sees a person made in His own image. He sees a man, a woman, a child that belongs to Him. He sees a mother, a father, a student, a faithful servant, a loving heart, the list goes on. When God looks at us, He sees, not the shell that we walk around in and put fancy, expensive clothes on, but rather, His own child. He sees His child that He is proud of and that He loved enough to sacrifice His own Son for. He doesn't see our mistakes, or shortcomings, the flaws that we spend hours in the mirror trying to fix. He sees a child who is perfect, regardless of their sin. He sees a child who is forgiven because of His Son's blood that was shed on the cross. When God looks at us, He sees a child who, simply put, is forgiven and made new. Everything else that the world sees in us, our shortcomings, the labels that have been placed on us, the things we have done, is irrelevant to how God sees us because He has already forgotten all that if we are saved by His grace. If we have called on Him and accepted His forgiveness for the things that the world tries to use as a means of defining us, then those things are no longer a piece of who we are. If we are saved by His grace, we are genuinely a new creature and we are no longer the person that the world sees, but rather the person that is seen by God.

You've probably heard some variation of this before. There's very little doubt about that. Today, we also live in a world that values comebacks and recovery. This idea is often spread within secular circles as well. However, what is often left out of those public announcements that come across the television during the day is this idea of forgiveness that can only come through Christ. All this is also dependent on our asking for and accepting forgiveness for the things that we have in our past. If we don't ask for forgiveness, these things don't simply go away. However, they do go away with the blood of Christ, because regardless of what you've done, regardless of who you were, regardless of what happened in your past, you can be made new. When you make the decision to be made new, regardless of how long the world chooses to hold onto the things you've done, the person you were, the way you lived, you can rest assured that the God of the universe who sees and knows everything, has forgiven and forgotten through the blood of His Son, the sins of your past, thus allowing you to become the person God wants you to be and not who the world thinks you are. However, it is up to you to take that first step of making the decision to ask for forgiveness and to want to be that new person that lives their life for Christ rather than for the world.

Message:

What image have you spent most of your life trying to improve? The one the world sees, or the one that the all-knowing, all-seeing creator of the universe sees? Oddly enough, it's probably a safe bet that most would answer, whether with pride or humility, that they are more focused on the visible appearance than the invisible one. The interesting thing about the world's opinion is that a) it changes so fast that it is almost impossible to keep up with, b) there's so much that the world doesn't know when it creates these opinions, and c) we can never know with any certainty that we are actually making any headway in fulfilling the image that they want us to live up to. The world has standards that are different for practically every single person. Therefore, any attempt to try to create the perfect image and perfect person that has no flaws in the minds of any person in existence would simply be in vain, as it would be impossible. Let us begin to move back toward fulfilling the image that God wants us to fit and let us move away from spending our lives trying to fit an image set by the world that can never truly be fulfilled. Let us simply strive to please God and allow all other standards to take a backseat to the one that truly matters.

Share It!

Using these questions, reach out to your friends on social media and get the conversation going!

1. Go to the mirror. When you see that reflection looking back at you, what story does it tell? What is one thing that makes that person who they are today?
2. What is it about the words of people that can so often overpower the words of Christ that we find in the Gospel and through prayer?
3. In what ways have you allowed God to use you in the last week?

Why God?
And the LORD said unto Satan, Hast thou considered my servant Job, that *there is* none like him in the earth, a perfect and an upright man, one that feareth God and escheweth evil?

Job 1:8 KJV

We all know about Job. He was basically the epitome of a godly man in the Bible, and yet, he also endured some of the worst trials and suffering ever recorded in that same book. If there was ever a man who deserved a peaceful, relatively pain-free existence, it was Job. However, when Satan came looking for a target of temptation and trials, the first person that God referred him to was Job. God's first choice for Satan to tempt and try was this man whom He called perfect and upright. When Satan was looking for someone to tempt, someone to test to the highest degree, God said, "I've got your man". Was this because God wanted to see Job suffer and struggle? No. Was this because God felt like Job deserved what was coming to him? Not at all. However, God did know that Job was a man whom He could place in these trials and temptations that had the potential to kill some, and know with all certainty that Job wouldn't turn his back on God.

It can often be difficult to resist the urge to turn our backs on God when we find ourselves in these situations that seem to have no way out. So often, it can seem like an easier decision to turn away from God and try to do life on our own than it would be to praise God and glorify Him in the midst of these trials. We all have trials at one point or another in our lifetime. There is no doubt about this. Without trials, we would simply drift away from God, maybe without even realizing it. Without these trials, we would never know what it means to find rest, peace, and restoration in God. While trials are not necessarily something that anyone desires in their life and something that people make a conscious effort to avoid, they can often become a critical factor in the restoration or enhancement of the relationship that we have with Christ. When we face trials, we can find strength in the fact that God is giving this trial to us in this specific season of our lives because He believes, and He knows that we have the faith and the strength in Him to draw closer to Him because of these trials rather than pulling away from Him and blaming Him for putting us through that. This is something important for God's people to remember when we, both individually, as well as within the church as a whole, face trials that seem exceptionally large. These trials may become so large that people begin asking questions that they never thought that they would be asking about God. However, there will also be those Jobs in the church who refuse to question or curse God through these trials. These are the people that God knows He will be able to use in incredible ways when the time comes.

How do we face the trials we encounter throughout our lifetime? Maybe you're at a liberal college and you have professors who question the legitimacy of your faith in Christ. How do you handle this? What about those people in these war-torn countries where people are being killed by the thousands for their belief in Christ and their refusal to believe otherwise? There is obviously a wide-ranging scale for the types of trials people will face every day. However, when it comes to how we manage these situations, do our actions reflect God and give glory to Him, or do they show people that we are not necessarily trusting God to the extent we may be encouraging them to? Often these trials that we face, regardless of the severity, can be a very good indication to both ourselves and to God as to how much we truly trust Him and how we really see Him. These trials can often be an eye-opening experience to the Christ-follower. Often these trials can diagnose shortcomings and areas of needed improvement in our walk with Christ. Therefore, when you face a trial in your life, instead of looking to God and asking why He would give you this, ask Him how He wants to use this. At this point, you will have turned your suffering, your trial into a mission to love others and to glorify God, no matter the circumstances.

Message:

Have you ever had any of these trials that made you question God? Have you ever wondered, "Why God"? If you said no, think again. While some people have had worse trials than others, every person who makes the decision to get up in the morning will face trials of some sort that will make them wonder why it had to happen to them. Job had every right after all that happened to him, to ask, "Why me?" He didn't have to praise God in the midst of all this. As a matter of fact, most people thought he was crazy for doing so. However, Job knew that God was not inflicting this suffering upon him for no reason. He knew that joy would come in the morning[1], even if that morning took forever to get there. It is because of his determination to glorify and honor God that we must remember Job when we face those times of trial and uncertainty. While we may find a list of reasons that we shouldn't give God glory through these trials, God will give us one huge reason why we should give Him glory. The cross. Through His Son's death on the cross, we were freed from suffering that would result in death for our sins. However, just because Christ died for the sins of the world, doesn't necessarily mean that pain and suffering will depart from us forever. Therefore, when we encounter it, we must resolve to hold to Christ and to honor Him in the process.

Share It!

Using these questions, reach out to your friends on social media and get the conversation started!

1. Would you say that you have suffered in your lifetime? If so, what was the situation?
2. When you look at Job, what qualities do you think made him able to endure these trials that God placed in front of him? How can you integrate those qualities into your own life?
3. When was the last time that you turned away from something because it got too difficult to handle?

The Power of Fear

The LORD is my light and my salvation; whom shall I fear? The LORD is the strength of my life; of whom shall I be afraid?

Psalm 27:1 KJV

Fear. It's a powerful feeling that everyone feels practically every day in some shape or form. We fear what the future may hold. We fear that we may lose our job tomorrow. We fear that we will lose those closest to us. We fear so much in our lives today. This fear so often comes from our thinking that things could possibly go terribly wrong and suddenly, we're left in the dark without a plan. We fear that some piece of our lives is going to fall apart one day, and we won't know what to do. There's not a single person out there who hasn't felt this at one point or another. However, the problem with fear and the way it can so often paralyze us is that so often we find ourselves in so much fear, so much anxiety over a situation, or a person or a possibility, that we often forget to trust God with the outcome.

The problem with fear is that it's easy. Fear is easy because we don't even have to think about it. It just kind of happens. Fear can do so much damage in so little time. It can ruin days, weeks, months, and even entire lifetimes. Some people find that they are living their lives in fear day in and day out, but so often, they fail to realize this before it's too late. One day, they look back and realize that they have spent more time in fear of a situation or circumstance in their life than they spent doing anything about it. So often, because fear is easier than boldness that can only be found in God, we kind of take our time conquering that fear, but it also holds us back from the plans that God has for us. Fear can so often be a tool that Satan uses to make us second-guess the path that God has set before us, and if we are not fully committed to the relationship that we have with Christ, we often do a lot of Satan's work for him because we are not really driven to do what God is calling us to do in the first place. We like the label of being a Christian, and we are willing to stand up for it to an extent, but ultimately, we don't really want to do anything that would require too much initiative on our part to make anything come of it.

In this passage, David looks at the fear that can so often hold us back from what God has planned for us. He specifically looks at the area of people, but he also looks at the impact of our circumstances, and how having God as an asset can help us to overpower and conquer those fears. He begins the verse by calling God our "light" and "salvation". When God gives us a mission and tells us where He wants us to go and what He wants us to do, He doesn't give us those instructions and send us off with a pat on the back and a wave good-bye. When God sends us somewhere to do something, He makes Himself a light unto our path. He guides our steps the entire time. However, He is also there when those times come that we take our eyes off Him and trip or wander into unfamiliar territory. He doesn't keep staring straight ahead and continue without us. He is our salvation. This means that He tells us where to go, but he's there when we aren't willing to listen and begin to stray from the path.

David continues in this verse by asking a question. He asks, "Whom shall I fear?" Recently, this phrase has become very popular in modern church culture. It kind of has a unique ring to it, but it also presents a question that is supposed to make us think. It's perfect for t-shirts, bumper stickers, or any other variety of Christian advertising media. However, even though we stick it on our cars, our shirts, our binders, and our computers, do we ever stop to really think about this question? Imagine that the verse says, "Without God, whom shall I fear?" This would change things. The things that we have to fear without God in the picture are innumerable, but a few things on the list are: sin, death, enemies of ourselves and our country, financial problems, the list goes on. Without Christ in the picture, the fear of things that the world so often places in front of us is all too real. Quite simply, without God in one's life, without God's guiding of our steps in those dark times when we aren't quite sure what lies ahead, the list of things that we have to fear is rather extensive. However, with God, all the fear that can cripple us concerning these things disappears because we can know that God has it taken care of. This doesn't mean that we won't have to put work into it or that it will turn out exactly as we thought it would, but it does mean that we won't be in those dark times alone. It means that even when we don't know where we are going, we can know that we are being led by someone who does.

Message:

What is it in your life that you have to fear? Financial problems? The future? Some sort of disease or diagnosis? Whatever it may be, while it may be difficult and trying to yourself and your family, God will not lead you into this without guiding you through it. He will not put you in unfamiliar territory with no intention of seeing that you make it to the other side of this piece of His plan. While this is something that should bring us peace and rest, so often, we tend to forget that God is right there with us through it all. This is when we usually start freaking out and trying to figure out a back-up plan. When we look at this passage, David asks us "Whom shall I fear?" However, the funny thing about this question is that it answers itself, as he intended for it to. With God, we have absolutely nothing to fear *if* we commit to trusting Him with all the pieces and parts of the situation and don't hold anything back. What is it today that you find yourself in fear of? How much of it have you handed over to God?

Share It!

Using these questions, reach out to your friends on social media and get the conversation started!

1. What are you afraid of? What is it about this thing that makes you doubt, makes you nervous, makes you unsure, or simply scares you to death?
2. How has God used your fears and uncertainties in the past to help you fulfill parts and pieces of His plan?
3. How has your fear gotten in the way as you pursue the mission that God has set before you?

Still God
Be still, and know that I am God…

Psalm 46:10a KJV

What does it mean to be still? To be still means that we stop our mind from racing. We force ourselves to slow down in a world that considers that a sin. To be still means that we turn ourselves, our mind, our racing thoughts off for a little bit, and we simply allow ourselves to rest peacefully and quietly in the blessings, the life, the "right now", if you will that God has given us. In today's world, this almost seems to be frowned upon, because we feel this need to get on to the next thing. We forget to take the time to thank God for what He has given us up until this point. So often, because we forget to thank God for where He has brought us and what He has given us, we fail to see and understand the greatness, the incredible nature of what He is showing us and where He is taking us right now and where He wants to take us later. If we fail to stop and realize the incredible things that He has done and is doing, it will be impossible for us to see the greatness, the power of the things that He will do in us and through us in the future.

What does it look like for us to slow down, or to stop and thank God for what He has done for us and given us? This verse uses the phrase "Be still". The chances are that if you were raised in the south like this North Carolina boy, you were probably told more than once to "be still", but what does this mean? This means we stop moving, making noise, thinking about everything we need to be doing right now, and we place ourselves at the feet of the God we are so blessed and fortunate to be able to serve, and we don't tell Him how impossible it will be to survive this chapter we are in. We don't sit there and tell Him everything that's wrong with our lives. We come before His throne, and just for a moment, for a little bit of time, we simply thank Him and allow ourselves to rest in Him.

This all seems like it should be relatively easy. After all, it's not like college students have a billion and a half hours of work to do in half as much time, right? As someone who has experienced first-hand the joys and struggles associated with the college lifestyle, I can sympathize with the lack of "Be still" time in the average student's schedule. However, it is due to this lack of time for stillness that it becomes even more critical for those who have a schedule similar to that of a college student to find or make time to simply be still. When you make the decision to make this time in your daily schedule, regardless of what it may look like, to simply rest, to turn everything off around you in your mind and your environment and simply rest in God's love and what He has given you, you will begin to experience a new level of intimacy in your relationship with Him. You will begin to hear things and understand things in a brand-new way, if you simply choose to be still.

In the second part of this verse, it says, "and know that I am God". The keyword here is "know". Too often it seems that we, as followers of Christ, spend our lives simply acknowledging that God is real without ever making Him real in our lives. We acknowledge that He exists and that He has all this power to do all this stuff, but when we encounter the situations in life that need this power and intervention, suddenly it becomes insufficient on its own. Suddenly, this power that we claim is so great, becomes not so great in this case. Suddenly, we need a back-up to give God's power a boost. This phrase "…know that I am God" is an all-encompassing phrase that basically tells us that a boost is not necessary. God's power doesn't need our backup. God doesn't need us to help Him out. He can most definitely take care of whatever we are asking of Him. Does He like to have our cooperation? Absolutely. Is there anything we can do to stop Him from doing what He needs to do? Nope. See, when we face these times in our lives when everything seems to be spinning around us and we have all these questions and no answers, we want to be able to pray for God's intervention, click our heels together, and suddenly we find ourselves rescued from the situation and all is well with the world. Anything less makes us believe that God is somehow absent from the situation. However, regardless of how fast or slow He may work in the situation we are in, He is still God. He is still powerful. He is still in control. So, when this verse comes together, what we find that, when we take time to turn the world around us off, and we focus on what God has done, we realize that even in those moments when God seemed so far away, so silent, He was, and is still there and He was and is still God.

Message:

Stillness is so often something that we find ourselves afraid of today because it doesn't always tell us what we want to hear. So often, stillness can open our eyes and our heart in ways we have never experienced. However, when we make this decision to be still, to stop and simply listen to what God needs us to hear, we will begin to understand just a little more clearly why, even in His silence, even in the moments of fear and uncertainty that we face, even in those moments when we wonder what's coming down the road, God is still God and He alone is still enough, regardless of where you may find yourself today.

Share It!

Using these questions, reach out to your friends on social media and get the conversation started!

1. When do you choose to *be still* during the day? What does that time consist of?
2. What are some reasons that this concept of being still can be difficult or even scary for you?
3. How does God reveal Himself to you during these moments of stillness?

Accepting the Call

Also, I heard the voice of the Lord, saying, Whom shall I send, and who will go for us?

Then said I, Here *am* I; send me.

Isaiah 6:8 KJV

Often, we come into this stage of life, whether that means college or a job, or maybe even both, and we have these plans. We have plans to live in this place, to do this job, to have a certain number of kids, and to make this level of income. We come into this stage of life knowing what we want and how we're going to get it, and we are determined not to allow anyone or anything to stop us from achieving that plan. This is an admirable approach to life in some respects. Ben Franklin once said, "If you fail to plan, you plan to fail". Therefore, this approach to life is one that is understandably respected by most in the world today. However, where these plans become a problem is at the point that they are not moldable to God's plans, which will never fail.

In this verse, the author is answering a call from God that likely changed every plan he had ever made for his life. Answering this call would have an impact on his family, his finances. Basically, everything he had ever known would be impacted and changed by his answering of this call. However, the author knew this and knew that they would have some uncertain times ahead of him, but he also knew that whatever God was training and equipping him for would be worth the sacrifice that would need to be made to allow him to fulfill this call from God.

One thing that is somewhat interesting about this situation is the fact that, so many people spend years of their life unsure of what God wants them to do, where He wants them to go, and when God makes it clear to them, it's almost as if they find themselves thinking, Oh, that's not exactly what I was expecting. This is the interesting thing about the ways in which, so many people choose to follow Christ and the plan that He has for them. Maybe a high school senior is praying for guidance as to where they should go after they graduate. Sure, they've only applied to their dream school and anything less is beyond unacceptable, but they are totally open to God's plan for their life. Maybe this hypothetical senior goes to the mailbox one day and gets a piece of mail addressed to them from that mission organization that is always on TV asking for donations. But surely

God wouldn't call them to missions because God knows that they don't like dirt or flying. Maybe they keep getting calls from that college that's two hours away from home, but surely God wouldn't pull them away from their family and friends that they have known for their entire life. Ultimately, whatever the situation may be, regardless of how God may show His will to His people, there will always be a minority, or maybe a majority that will doubt that this is actually from God and maybe it's just a coincidence.

When we look at this verse from Isaiah, there's one thing that is missing from this commitment. One thing seems to always precede any commitment that is made in this day in time. One thing that is missing from this commitment? Questions. Conditions. A contract. When the author received this call from God asking for a willing volunteer, he didn't ask what would be demanded of him. He didn't ask what would be in it for him. He didn't tell God that he would go if he got this type of reward in the end. He didn't ask for family leave time. He heard the call from God and he simply said, "Here am I; send me". These five words are so simple and yet they commit his family and himself to a lifetime of pursuing a mission that God set before him. While this sounds great in writing, most people would be terrified by this. Most people would tell God to slow down and clear some things up so that they knew what they were getting themselves into. The writer had no clue what he was getting into, but he knew that this was a mission from God and he was prepared to accept that.

What does this mean for us? What does it look like for us to receive a call from God on our lives and for us to say, "Here am I; send me"? For some, this means accepting a mission in your hometown, but for others, it will mean accepting a mission like the one that this individual was accepting that doesn't provide any sense of understanding as to what may lie ahead. In the case that you find yourself in a situation where it seems that God is asking this question and you feel that He is speaking directly to you, understand that this is not an easy decision. When the author accepted this mission, he probably had some sweaty palms and a faster-than-normal heart rate. However, he knew that God was not throwing him out into the world with this mission and no intention of walking with him through it. The same is true for any mission that God may send you on. Regardless of what God calls you to, and regardless of what it may require you to give up, you can pursue this calling, this mission that God has placed on your life wholeheartedly, knowing that He chose you for a reason. Somewhere within this calling, there is a purpose, there is an outcome that God made to fit His plan for your life. Therefore, if you fail to accept this plan and you choose to go your own way, it may be easier, and it may be more predictable, but it will never flourish or become as fruitful as the plans that God has put in place for you to follow. Therefore, while it may be easier or more convenient for you to say, "Somebody else will do it. I don't have time", or "I don't have the resources" or "I don't have the money right now" or "Let me finish college first", all these things will only make it easier and easier for us to step further and further away from what God is calling us to.

Here's something else to think about. What if you don't like what God is calling you to? What if it makes you feel weird or uncomfortable? Should you just step away and say, "I'll wait for His next call"? Often it seems like we treat God's plan like a bus. Sometimes, it takes a long time to see it coming, but if it gets there and there aren't many people or there aren't any friendly-looking people on the "bus", we turn and run and say that we'll wait for the next one. However, unlike buses, God's plan won't keep coming around with different people, different options, different shapes and forms, until we feel comfortable about hopping on, so to speak. If we continue to ignore God's plan for our lives long enough, eventually we will begin to forget about it altogether. Does that mean that it will disappear and never become available to us again? No. However, if we continue to run from God's plan because we are afraid of where it will take us or who it will put us in contact with, that fear will never go away regardless of how many times we wait for it to come back around. See, God isn't here to make us comfortable or make us happy. God is here to build a relationship with us and to challenge us to follow Him instead of the world. This isn't done through telling us that we can do [insert mission here] any way we want, as long as we get to the desired end-goal. When God places a call on our lives, He also places instructions with that call, but before you are able to receive the instructions, you must be willing to simply say without question, "Here am I; send me".

Message:

How are you accepting the call that God is placing before you? Maybe you haven't received it yet and you are still waiting. When it comes, will you accept it and begin pursuing it, or will you toss it aside and say, "That'll never happen" and wait for the next attempt. Too often we tend to lean toward the second approach because it makes sense most of the time. If we don't have the resources, the education, the income to do something, we simply say it won't happen and we move forward with our lives until God brings another idea to us. However, the problem is that we often treat these calls that God places on our lives as proposals for us to accept or reject. This where we are often wrong. God brings us a mission, a plan that He wants us to follow and He wants us to accept it. It's not a job offer or a price negotiation on a car or a house. It's a plan that God has crafted for your life specifically, and for you to do anything beyond accepting that plan, is to diminish and insult the sovereignty, the all-knowing nature of God. Therefore, challenge yourself, when the day comes, to set aside all questions, all concerns, all possible alternatives, and simply reply, "Here am I; send me".

Share It!

Using these questions, reach out to your friends on social media and get the conversation started!

1. If you're in college, you are probably pursuing some kind of degree, and that degree is probably based on a call that you feel God has placed on your life. What was it about this particular call that made you abandon all questions, concerns, and apprehensions? If this is not the case, what questions did/do you have about this call?
2. For you, what is the most difficult or scary part about accepting a call from God regarding your future?
3. How are you preparing yourself for the call that God has placed or will place on your life? Are you ready for a sudden change if that were to happen?

The God Box

[8]For my thoughts are not your thoughts, neither are your ways my ways, saith the LORD. [9]For as the heavens are higher than the earth, so are my ways higher than your ways, and my thoughts higher than your thoughts.

Isaiah 55:8-9 KJV

How big is your God Box? What is in your God Box? Is there anything that you have taken out of the box? These are all questions that affect everyone who has given their lives to Christ, but in the college years, this question becomes even more critical and relevant for us to understand. Now, before we begin discussing these questions, what is a God Box? A God Box is the box that each follower of Christ subconsciously creates at some point during their Christian walk that contains everything that they believe God is capable of and everything that they have given Him access to. For some, this box is the size of their entire life, because that is exactly what they have given God control over. For some, this box is the size of their weekly tithe and their church attendance. However, regardless of the size and content of each person's God Box, it is important that we, as believers strive to understand our box and what needs to be in it. Now, this sounds easy because, as followers of Christ, we recognize that our God Box should contain all parts of our lives, thus giving the control over to Him and allowing Him to do what He wants with all areas of our lives. We recognize that this is what we are supposed to do, and often we want to do that, but somewhere deep inside, when we begin building this box, we find ourselves setting things aside that we couldn't imagine Him being able to handle. We set aside that diagnosis, that addiction, that struggle that we find ourselves facing at the moment. We take these things, and in the process of compiling our God Box, as if we were cleaning out a closet, we toss these things aside for us to hold onto, as we begin to decide what God is capable of and what we should probably keep to ourselves to handle later when we have the time. At the point that we begin doing this, we begin placing boundaries, limitations on God that ultimately only hinder us in what we are able to give to Him. It is at this point that we begin to understand how this passage plays into the concept of the God Box and how the passage can help us to break open that box and allow all parts of our lives to spill out onto the floor and allow God to have access to all it.

In the first part of this passage, we find that the author begins to look at this concept of putting man's boundaries and limitations on God's potential, as well as His will for each person's life. When he opens with this concept of thought, he immediately dives into the deepest part of a person to look at how we often can place limits on God without even realizing it. An individual's thoughts are something that often paints a very real picture of who that person is, what they feel, and often, these very same thoughts can be the ones that are forming these ideas about what God is and isn't capable of doing in one's life. Therefore, when the author writes this characterization of God, he is trying to tell us that, regardless of the boundaries and limits that we place on God in our mind, regardless of what we decide that He is capable of, those thoughts and feelings will never be enough to deter Him from doing what He wants to do, and we should be rejoicing at that fact.

When we look at God and look at this financial situation in our family, we look at it and we think that there's no possible way that He could do anything with this. We look at the situation and we look at God and we begin compiling this list of reasons why that could never happen. We see the substantial amount of debt that has already piled up. How could God possibly handle that? We look at the damage that this disease or this addiction has already done to us or someone we love. How could God possibly reverse that? We look at all the compromises that we have already made in that toxic relationship. How could God ever bring us back from that? These are the things that are sitting on the floor outside of our God Box because we have left them out. We left them out because we knew that it wasn't possible for Him to do anything beyond what had already been done. It is at this point that we move to the next piece of the passage.

In the next portion of this passage, he tells us that, not only do His thoughts go beyond anything that we could ever imagine, but he also talks about His ways, His methods for doing what He does. See, it is here that He begins to knock down those barriers, those boundaries that we had set up, because those barriers were based on the capabilities of a god with human capabilities, and it's probably safe to say that our God's efforts are most definitely not human, and we are thankful for that. However, when we look at God and His ways of doing things, this passage tells us that we may not always understand how he did this or that. When we look at that tuition bill that was more than the entire family made in a year, and we see that it is paid, we may not be able to understand that, because God's ways, as the author echoes in this passage, are far beyond anything that we are capable of even beginning to comprehend. Just as a CEO of a company has more power to take care of things and make things happen, God has the ability to make things happen that we never thought possible. He will take these things that we left outside of that God Box and He will pull them in and begin making things happen using those resources that we tried to deny Him. Therefore, if you just cut open your God Box and allow everything to fall in front of Him in the first place, then you won't have to worry about what you may have put in or what may have been left out. Therefore, before you put anything past God, remember that His ways are much greater and go much further than anything that we could ever do, so give Him that situation, that disease, that addiction, and let Him do what He needs to do to show you that nothing is impossible when He is in the picture.

Message:

Now that you know what a God Box is, what's in yours? What kind of boundaries, what kind of limits have you been placing on God? What have you been holding back for fear that He wouldn't be able to handle it the way you wanted Him to? Well, spoiler alert: whether you want God to have something or not, whatever that thing may be, He will eventually get to it and begin working. Therefore, instead of trying to contain God within a box the size of what you're willing to surrender, just take down those boundaries that you have set for Him and allow all the contents of your God Box to spill out onto the floor so that He can begin His work.

Share It!

Using these questions, reach out to your friends on social media and get the conversation started!

1. When you look at your God Box, does it look like it belongs to someone who is fully committed to God's will?
2. In addition to us putting things in or taking things out of our God Box, there's also the factor of God Himself doing the same thing. What are some things that you find yourself pulling back out or hiding at the bottom, hoping He won't find it?
3. What condition is your box in today? That is, is it barely held together by duct tape or is protected and maintained as if it contained your entire life, because it does?

Made in the USA
Monee, IL
23 March 2023

30414321R00157